The Posthuman Pandemic

Also Available from Bloomsbury

Political Philosophy in a Pandemic: Routes to a More Just Future, ed. Fay Niker and Aveek Bhattacharya
Philosophical Posthumanism, Francesca Ferrando
Being Posthuman: Ontologies of the Future, Zahi Zalloua
From Deleuze and Guattari to Posthumanism, ed. Christine Daigle and Terrance H. McDonald

The Posthuman Pandemic

Edited by
Saul Newman and Tihomir Topuzovski

BLOOMSBURY ACADEMIC
LONDON • NEW YORK • OXFORD • NEW DELHI • SYDNEY

BLOOMSBURY ACADEMIC
Bloomsbury Publishing Plc
50 Bedford Square, London, WC1B 3DP, UK
1385 Broadway, New York, NY 10018, USA
29 Earlsfort Terrace, Dublin 2, Ireland

BLOOMSBURY, BLOOMSBURY ACADEMIC and the Diana logo are trademarks
of Bloomsbury Publishing Plc

First published in Great Britain 2022
This paperback edition published 2023

Cover design by Charlotte Daniels
Cover image: Blank frames hanging on art gallery wall (© Grant Faint / Getty Images)

A catalogue record for this book is available from the British Library.

Library of Congress Cataloging-in-Publication Data
Names: Newman, Saul, editor. | Topuzovski, Tihomir, editor.
Title: The posthuman pandemic / edited by Saul Newman and Tihomir Topuzovski.
Description: London, UK; New York, NY, USA: Bloomsbury Academic, 2022. |
Includes bibliographical references and index.
Identifiers: LCCN 2021025533 (print) | LCCN 2021025534 (ebook) |
ISBN 9781350239067 (hb) | ISBN 9781350239074 (epdf) |
ISBN 9781350239081 (ebook)
Subjects: LCSH: Humanism.–Forecasting.
Classification: LCC B821.P5922 2022 (print) | LCC B821 (ebook) | DDC 144–dc23
LC record available at https://lccn.loc.gov/2021025533
LC ebook record available at https://lccn.loc.gov/2021025534

ISBN: HB: 978-1-3502-3906-7
PB: 978-1-3502-3910-4
ePDF: 978-1-3502-3907-4
eBook: 978-1-3502-3908-1

Typeset by Deanta Global Publishing Services, Chennai, India

To find out more about our authors and books visit www.bloomsbury.com and
sign up for our newsletters.

Contents

10 Thinking and/over/in the pandemic: From *contact points* towards *contact zones* potentially reconciling us with the ultramicroscopic sub-layers of life *Martin Grünfeld*

11 Viral agencies and curating worldly life differently in museum spaces *Fiona Cameron*

Figures

Contributors

Editors

Saul Newman is Professor of Politics, Goldsmiths University of London.

Tihomir Topuzovski is Interdisciplinary Programme Director, Museum of Contemporary Arts, Skopje, Macedonia.

Contributors (in order of appearance)

Christine Daigle is Professor of Philosophy, Chancellor's Chair for Research Excellence, and Director of the Posthumanism Research Institute at Brock University.

Iris van der Tuin is Professor in Theory of Cultural Inquiry in the Department of Philosophy and Religious Studies at Utrecht University.

Stefan Herbrechter is *Privatdozent* at Heidelberg University.

Saul Newman is Professor of Politics, Goldsmiths University of London.

Josephine Berry is Lab Lecturer, Culture Industry MA, Goldsmiths, University of London.

Amanda Boetzkes is Professor of Contemporary Art History and Theory, University of Guelph.

Anna McWebb is a PhD candidate in the Department of Art History and Communication Studies, McGill University.

Rick Dolphijn is Associate Professor of Media and Cultural Studies, Utrecht University.

Amanda du Preez is Associate Professor, Department of Visual Arts, University of Pretoria.

Ada Smailbegović is Assistant Professor of English, Brown University.

Martin Grünfeld is Associate Professor at Medical Museion, Novo Nordisk Foundation, Center for Basic Metabolic Research, University of Copenhagen.

Fiona Cameron is Senior Research Fellow, Institute for Culture and Society, Western Sydney University.

Introduction

The posthuman pandemic

Saul Newman and Tihomir Topuzovski

The Covid-19 pandemic has had dramatic effects on our world and has radically disrupted our daily lives. It has not only killed millions of people (over 3 million at the time of writing) but has devastated economies, destabilized institutions, interrupted normal social behaviour and changed our understanding of ourselves and our relations with others, forcing us to confront our own mortality and vulnerability – as individuals and as a species – in a radically new way. It has made us aware of the permeability of our bodies to viral contagion and of the fragility of all social bonds. The effect of social restrictions and lockdowns creates a profound sense of alienation and of the virtualization of our lives, as we become ever more dependent on internet communication technologies to replace the physical interactions that we once considered normal. Even after the vaccines are rolled out and this version, at least, of the pandemic is over (there will no doubt be further mutations and new viruses to contend with) we will continue to experience its effects for years to come; indeed, it is unlikely that life will ever return in the form we once knew it.

The absence of human agency, which has become a characteristic of urban landscapes during the lockdowns, is exemplified in the following quote: 'Pictures were taken of a newly ubiquitous nothing: of no people on city streets, no people in major plazas of the world, no people in classrooms, no one in abandoned markets, no one in churches without mourners where closed coffins conveyed the ever-silenced dead into the afterlife.'[1] One historical example is provided by Michael Foucault, who describes these places as the 'plague towns', seeing street-level administrative procedures for quarantine in the Middle Ages in terms of strict spatial partitioning,[2] illustrating spatial politics during the pandemic period. Nothing much has changed, it seems. During the lockdowns, this strategy has been implemented and urban landscapes become 'segmented, immobile, frozen space. Each individual is fixed in his place. And, if he moves, he does so at the risk of his life, contagion or punishment.'[3] A new, empty urban landscape is opening up.

The pandemic has served to remind us of longer-term trends that will only accelerate – namely the effects of human-induced climate-change and ecological destruction. The fact that the virus resulted from an accidental contagion between man and animal, apparently emerging from wildlife meat markets in Wuhan, China, brings into sharp relief the dangerous and unpredictable consequences of our commercial exploitation of nature and of non-human species. From industrial farming, to genetic manipulation of seeds, mining, and the continued burning of fossil fuels, we have dramatically altered, destabilized and depleted the earth's ecosystems, leading to global warming and climate instability, widespread deforestation, rising sea levels and temperatures, air pollution, the poisoning of land, oceans and waterways, species extinction, loss of biodiversity – and, of course, viral mutations. We inhabit the age of the Anthropocene (Paul Crutzen), in which human activity comes to have a profound and irreversible impact on the Earth. Yet, the Anthropocene – born of anthropocentric illusions of our ontological separation from nature – is also an experience of vulnerability and impotence, as we become aware of our dependence on increasingly unstable ecosystems and unpredictable natural forces, and we reap the consequences of our destructive activities. The pandemic is exemplary of this condition, appearing as nature's retribution for our hubris.

Covid-19 is not only a biological virus but also a political virus. Not only does it destroy the body's immune system, but it also throws our political systems into crisis. The fact that governments around the world, both liberal and authoritarian – a distinction that appears increasingly blurred now – can subject their entire populations to a form of house arrest and impose far-reaching restrictions on free movement, economic activity and social life highlights the state of exception we are living through today, where unprecedented state powers are invoked in the name of a public health emergency. Borders are closing, and governments are responding to the pandemic with nationalist gestures and policies. This no doubt sets a dangerous precedent. It also unleashes new viral political forces of both the Right and Left – from right-wing populism and the proliferation of conspiracy movements to Black Lives Matter and mobilizations for racial and environmental justice – that have spread like a contagion around the world. The pandemic has delegitimized the neoliberal economic order and the whole doctrine of fiscal austerity, as we rediscover the importance of the public sector and governments are forced to spend vast amounts of money on public health and propping up the economy. We do not quite know what sort of world will replace the one that is rapidly disintegrating before our eyes. The pandemic introduces a strange *interregnum* between worlds, full of dangers and uncertainties, as well as radical, emancipatory possibilities. This gives much greater complexity and dynamism to a life which includes the creation of new arrangements or assemblages. Therefore, according to James Baumlin, such new assemblages exist where 'the COVID-19 viral presence, though invasive in our world, changes our self-perception: no longer a single macro-organism, we are in fact an "assemblage" of microorganisms, upon which life depends absolutely'.[4] This allows us to produce new and different worlds. In a discussion of the pandemic crisis, it is crucial to recognize these new relations, focusing on the edges between them, or the lines of flux, where it is difficult to distinguish between 'the compound of nonhuman forces of the cosmos, of man's nonhuman becomings'.[5] Like any major global crisis, the pandemic forces a renewed reflection on the limits of the human experience. It undermines our faith in human progress and disturbs our conceptions of human agency and autonomy. It can therefore be seen as an aspect of the posthuman condition.

The coronavirus pandemic has prompted philosophical debates mainly around the notion of emergency. Giorgio Agamben, in his initial reflections on the pandemic in early 2020, understood the emergency measures and restrictions imposed by state authorities as the unfolding of the Schmittian sovereign state of exception, and complained about 'the frenetic, irrational and entirely unfounded emergency measures by the state authorities'.[6] The response on the part of governments – democratic and authoritarian alike – showed, according to Agamben, that the sovereign state of exception was becoming the normal paradigm of governing. One year on, at the time of writing, many of Agamben's dark predictions seem to be proving correct: seemingly endless lockdowns, the use of emergency powers by the state with very little parliamentary scrutiny, restrictions on protests, to say nothing of the deployment of new surveillance techniques and technologies – from contact tracing apps, biometrics to digital vaccine passports, which are likely to become a permanent feature of everyday life. However, in response to Agamben's intervention, other thinkers like Sergio Benvenuto emphasized that 'everything that's being done in Italy (closing schools, stadiums, museums, theatres and so on) has a purely preventive function, it only slows down the spread of the virus. It plays on large numbers, but appeals to each particular being.'[7] Panagiotis Sotiris argued that the virus would show that a democratic – rather than purely authoritarian – biopolitics was possible.[8] And Jean-Luc Nancy claimed that the epidemic was indeed real and was evidently capable of causing far higher levels of mortality,[9] suggesting that state intervention was necessary. Philosophical debates on the current crisis continue, with a consideration of what possibilities might lie ahead on the social horizon after the pandemic. For example, Bruno Latour believes that 'the virus could serve as a dress rehearsal for the next, ecological crisis, the one in which the reorientation of living conditions is going to be posed as a challenge to all of us'.[10] Slavoj Žižek speculates that the virus will see the possibility for a new social organization in favour of community.[11] These contemporary debates trace the new posthuman contexts and horizons opened up by the pandemic.

Posthumanism and philosophy

Posthumanism – which forms the philosophical framework and orientation of this book – refers to a condition in which the universal figure of Man, derived from the discourse of humanism, Enlightenment rationalism, Cartesian dualism and, ultimately, from monotheistic religions has become decentred, more opaque and diffuse; its conceptual boundaries and discursive limits are less clear, its identity has become more pluralized and differentiated and its autonomy and sovereignty are less certain. The posthuman experience is one of growing awareness of our situatedness within, and dependence upon, complex ecosystems and networks that include other non-human actors and forces, whether natural or technological. When Foucault famously predicted some time ago that Man would disappear 'like a face drawn in sand at the edge of the sea', he was pointing to the discursive and epistemological limits of humanism, and to the recognition that the figure of Man was a relatively recent and contingent historical artefact whose future could be not guaranteed: 'It is comforting, however, and a source of profound relief to think that man is only a recent invention, a figure not yet two centuries old, a new wrinkle in our knowledge, and that he will disappear again as soon as that knowledge has discovered a new form.'[12] It is this point that marks the end of the humanist and modernist traditions that have dominated European thought for centuries. Genealogical analysis reveals that the figure of Man – central to the discourse of humanism – has not always been universal, and that its dominance has in fact been based on unstable discursive binaries and arbitrary and violent exclusions, of women, non-Europeans, children, slaves, the mad, the abnormal and the otherwise socially marginalized, and, of course, of non-human animals. If we understand the concept of the human as historically mutable and discursively constructed, rather than a fixed, essential and transcendental identity, then its limits become less distinct.

There are of course a variety of definitions of posthumanism, a diversity of approaches, which are reflected in this book. Like the virus itself, the term has mutated and shifted with time. It is impossible to date its origins as a philosophical concept – did it emerge with Stirner and Nietzsche and their radical assault on the discourses of humanism, or with Heidegger's pronouncement of the 'closure of metaphysics', or with later poststructuralist thinkers like Foucault, Derrida, Deleuze and Guattari, and Lacan, whose analyses displaced the human subject within networks of power, language, desire or the unconscious? The term 'posthumanism' was originally announced by Ihab Hassan in 1977, who referred to the possibility of a new posthumanist culture that reflected transformations in the idea of the human as a result of new technologies like AI.[13] Such technologies have indeed changed our conception of what it means to be human. Here, though, we would be inclined to draw a distinction between posthumanism and *transhumanism*, two terms that are often conflated. Transhumanism is the triumphalist project of human enhancement through technological means – such as prosthetic and robotic implants, surgical procedures, genetic manipulation and cloning, digital augmentation, the use of artificial intelligence and so on. But surely this technocentric ideology, concerned as it is with surpassing current human limitations of health, performance, intelligence, even mortality, is simply an extension of humanism in all its hubris and Promethean ambition; it remains tied to the fantasy of Man's control and mastery of the world, now enabled through technology. It is a fetishistic disavowal of humanity's limits. We believe that such a triumphalist and technocentric narrative is simply unsustainable in the era of the Anthropocene and, indeed, of pandemics.

By contrast, posthumanism is much more modest and tempered; it is a *deconstruction* of the category of the human through the recognition of its finitude, not an attempt to exceed or escape it. As Derrida taught us, to attempt to transcend the Subject, to replace it with a new Signifier, as structuralism sought to do in relation to humanism, is to simply re-establish its centricity.[14] In the same way, transhumanism is another form of substitution that replaces one central identity, one figure of authority, with another – technology in place of humanity – but, in doing so, it restores Man's position at the centre of the universe. Not only does posthumanism question the ethical implications of human technological enhancement – and here it is even compatible with a certain techno- and bio-'conservatism', especially when it comes to genetic engineering[15] – but it also reveals the visage of humanism behind its latest transhuman guise.

Posthumanism is the realization that the human is an unstable category. Here the *post-* in posthumanism does not necessarily signify a coming after in the sense of historical time – for what would that be other than another kind of humanism? – but, rather, an invitation to reflect upon the limits of the human and to think beyond them. It is to acknowledge that if the human is understood in terms of sovereignty, autonomy and rational agency, of the separation of mind from body, of ideas from materiality, of man from animal, then we have never been human and never will be. Our existence as human beings has always been dependent on complex relations and interactions with other agents and forces, whether natural or technological, such that we can never claim self-sufficiency or autonomy. This not only radically 'democratizes' and 'pluralizes' the human experience, but also imposes upon us certain ethical obligations – to others who have been historically excluded, and to the non-human organisms with whom we share this precarious planet, whose survival depends on us, and upon whose survival we also depend.

Francesca Ferrando identifies three associated understandings here of this philosophical approach: *posthumanism*, which refers to the irreducible plurality of the human experience, the way that it cannot be assimilated within one universal category or metanarrative; *post-anthropocentrism*, the de-centring of the human in relation to the non-human; and *post-dualism*, referring to the breaking down of the rigid binaries (black/white, male/female, human/ animal and so on) upon which the identity of the human has historically been established.[16] As Cary Wolfe explains, posthumanism is the acknowledgement of the embeddedness of the human within broader social systems – natural, communicative, cultural, technological – which blurs the binary division between the human and non-human, while at the same time giving greater meaning and specificity to the human condition: 'the decentering of the human by its imbrication in technical, medical, informatic, and economic networks is increasingly impossible to ignore.'[17]

Of course, there are a number of ways in which we can understand posthumanism, and it draws on a diverse range of philosophical and theoretical perspectives and approaches, whether deconstruction and poststructuralism, Spinozist and Deleuzian ontologies of immanence and becoming,[18] feminist theory,[19] cybernetics,[20] science and technology studies,[21] critical animal studies,[22] the 'new materialisms',[23] or process philosophy and new forms of eco-theology.[24] All these approaches, as different as they are, converge around a certain condition defined by an experience of the limits of present. Where philosophy, politics, culture, art, scientific enquiry and indeed every other register of knowledge and activity was hitherto dominated by the discourse of humanism, we now have to take stock of our finitude and come to terms with our interconnectedness and entanglement with other non-human actors, forces and objects that disturb this centricity. The posthuman condition is therefore a radical decentring of our understanding of ourselves and our place within the world. It produces, in the words of Rosie Braidotti, 'on the one hand the sharp awareness of *what we are ceasing to* be (the end of the actual) and on the other the perception – in different degrees of clarity – of *what we are in the process of becoming* (the actualization of the virtual).'[25] The posthuman condition is one of both sadness and joy; a sense of mourning for what we once were, and a feeling of exuberance (coupled with trepidation) at the possibilities that now open before us.

The posthuman condition may be best understood through the notion of *ontological anarchy*. The drawing to a close of the metanarrative of humanism and its related ideas of progress and rationalism introduces and induces a profound sense of uncertainty about our world, a feeling that the ground has been removed from beneath our feet, that the foundations of our reality are disintegrating. The Heideggerian thinker Reiner Schürmann defines anarchy as the withering away of the epochal first principles, the *arché* that defined metaphysical thinking:

> The anarchy that will be at issue here is the name of a history affecting the ground or foundation of action, a history where the bedrock yields and where it becomes obvious that the principle of cohesion, be it authoritarian or 'rational', is no longer anything more than a blank space deprived of legislative, normative, power.[26]

For Schürmann, this is an experience of freedom: it frees action from its *telos*, from fixed normative frameworks, from the rule of ends that hitherto sought to determine it. Action becomes 'anarchic' – that is to say, groundless and without a predetermined end.

Posthumanism and politics

What new forms of politics emerge with the posthuman condition? Is there a posthuman politics? We have seen new political mobilizations from both the Left and Right, both of which reject the (neo)liberal consensus that has dominated the political scene for decades. The global surge in right-wing populism – coupled with outlandish conspiracy theories which are like a new form of religious belief – is deeply reactionary in the way that it seeks to preserve the illusion of a traditional ethnic, national or cultural identity. It is also deeply nihilistic in the way it seeks to destabilize governing institutions, violate democratic norms and accelerate capitalism's destruction of the natural environment. It is an extreme politics of the Capitalocene. By contrast, environmental activist movements such as Extinction Rebellion (XR) invoke a deliberately apocalyptic and millenarian discourse to prompt governments to declare a climate emergency in order to protect what little is left of our depleted natural environment. Yet, both forms of politics, as radically different and opposed as they are, may be seen as symptomatic of the posthuman condition: the former, as a paranoid reaction to, and the disavowal of, the experience of human finitude; the latter, as a recognition of it. The pandemic opens up new forms for political action, no longer tied to the ideological horizons of the past, but with unpredictable consequences for the present. While there may be a temptation to engage in more abstract philosophical speculations on the pandemic, we should not forget that the current crisis brings up real and urgent political questions, not least of which are the effectiveness and proportionality of governments' responses, and the social inequalities that have been revealed and accelerated by the pandemic. Finding new ways of responding to these questions is the challenge of posthuman politics. Posthuman politics is a politics of the *rhizome*, with multiple and unpredictable connections, strange ideological promiscuities and crossovers, as well as new forms of expression and mobilization.

One way to think about the politics of posthumanism is through the category of 'postanarchism' (Newman) – a poststructuralist, and one could also say *posthumanist*, articulation of anarchist politics and theory.[27] Postanarchism is a way of understanding new radical political struggles which we have seen emerging in recent times around ecology, economic justice, migrant rights and racial equality. Like posthumanism, postanarchism is a deconstruction of the humanist and rationalist metanarratives that characterized the anarchism of the nineteenth century. Without abandoning the radical emancipatory potential of classical anarchism – particularly its rejection of domination, hierarchy and state sovereignty, and its politics of egalitarianism and solidarity – postanarchism at the same time questions its positivist claims about human nature and the immanent rationality underlying its vision of social relations. It calls into question the modernist idea of revolution as a universal event aimed at the destruction of power and the transformation of the whole of society. Power relations in late modernity are far too complex to sustain this sort of narrative, which pits society against the state, humanity against power, freedom against servitude and rationality against obscurantism. Instead, postanarchism embraces the idea of *entanglement*, with power relations, laws and institutions, that activists at the same time are contesting, as well as with the non-human natural world with whose fate we are, in a broader sense, inevitably bound up. Postanarchism might therefore be seen as a non-anthropocentric form of anarchism that promotes new solidarities and alliances with the natural world, expanding political networks to include non-human species. It is an anarchism that refuses the binary oppositions between revolution and reformism, between total transformation and gradual change, between class struggle and localized resistance, between political representation and direct democracy. To revolutionize today is also to conserve and protect existing life forms and the natural commons against rapine capitalist exploitation. It is to defend certain traditional cultural and social forms, practices and communities, centred on ecologically sustainable living, against the ruthless logic of modernization, development and economic growth. In this sense, anarchism, even in its more 'classical' form, has always been more sensitive to ecological concerns than Marxism, for instance, which sought to harness and accelerate the industrial processes of capitalism in the name of human emancipation and progress.

To think about our planetary entanglements is to establish a new political relationship with nature, one that recognizes that nature and politics can no longer be separated, indeed, never could be. Bruno Latour has recently called for a new political ecology, even a new 'political theology', of Gaia based on the complex networks of relations we share with other natural organisms, objects and forces. Latour argues that we can no longer think of nature as a separate, stable, unified identity outside of culture and politics, just as we can no longer think of culture and politics as distinctly human spheres of activity that transcend or operate outside of nature. The Anthropocene has irretrievably broken down this distinction. We now have to come to terms with the fact that politics and nature shape and influence one another, and that we therefore have an ethical and political responsibility for its protection. This is a realization that can inspire new practices of interspecies cooperation, and indeed new forms of political community. Latour even talks about a new kind of social contract, no longer of the Hobbesian or Lockeian kind, but a compact that somehow incorporates nature, rather than regarding it as an externality: 'The desire to build the Republic, the veritable *res publica*, is always *before* us. Thanks to the emergence of Gaia, we are becoming aware that we had not even *begun* to outline a realistic contract, at least a contract that might hold up on this sublunary Earth of ours.'[28]

Posthumanism and art

The pandemic not only creates a political emergency – forcing renewed reflection on the shape of our political institutions and practices – but an artistic state of emergency as well. At the most immediate level, we think of the closure of art galleries and museums, or of the restrictions placed on artistic performances and the consequent loss of employment and financial support for artists. How will the crisis, with all its untold implications, be represented in aesthetics? As paradigmatic of the posthuman experience, the pandemic will no doubt provoke further questioning of our accepted notions of human autonomy, sovereignty, agency and centricity, which will find expression in new cultural and artistic forms. We believe that art offers a unique way of interrogating and understanding the posthuman condition.

We believe that new cultural forms and artistic practices will emerge, and indeed are already co-evolving, with the pandemic, as are other social forms – they are in a process of what Deleuze calls becoming.[29] The pandemic has changed the institutional dynamic within what is signified as the art world, 'as the historically ordered world of artworks, enfranchised by theories which themselves are historically ordered'[30] and the entire network of institutional components that enable the work of art. By analysing these conditions, we can look at how artists' responses are relevant in debating and visualizing the pandemic. In particular, the pandemic crisis challenges our accepted understanding of the relationship 'between life and death, between nature and culture, and between humans and other living beings'[31] and how these complexities are expressed in many artworks. The essential relevance of contemporary artistic practices is discussed in Arthur Danto's work, where he claims that 'artists have become what philosophers used to be, guiding us to think about what their works express. With this, art is really about those who experience it. It is about who we are and how we live'.[32]

On a more thematic level, various aspects of posthumanism are deeply involved in artistic practices, particularly those pursuing ethical and political concerns raised by the 'interactions between socioeconomic and environmental conditions and biological and physiological or physical processes'.[33] This results in the proliferation of a variety of artistic forms and practices, such as bioart, or art that is created with technologies and processes taken from the natural sciences: from molecular biology, cell biology, neurobiology, nanotechnology, robotic art, biotelematic art and transmedial science fiction.[34] This thematic focus consists of a compilation of approaches and a synthesis of visual materials regarding various contexts within the contemporary posthumanist art, which includes environmental ecology, the conceptualization of the earth, heliotropism and surroundings that take many diverse forms,[35] exploring and expressing 'the ways we currently produce, reproduce, and consume our material environment'.[36] Examples include the works of Dewey-Hagborg, who is working with research scientists and a biotechnology company to create a custom retrovirus that infects its human host with a gene; Guy Ben-Ary, who works on a completely autonomous instrument that consists of a neural network that is bioengineered from his own cells; and Joey Holder's work, which consists of multimedia installations that explore human limits and how we experience non-human, natural and technological forms. When examining the field of posthumanism and art that engages with the question of global warming and climate change, Olafur Eliasson's 'The Weather Project' is noteworthy: here the artist recreates conditions of being close to the sun, thus conveying the fragility of our planetary system. Shezad Dawood, through his work 'Leviathan', considers a wide range of aspects that affect climate change, while reflecting on the neat boundaries between different living worlds in our ecosystem. Oliver Kellhammer focuses on processes of environmental regeneration, by engaging the botanical and socio-political aspects of the landscape; and Levi van Veluw transposes landscape contours onto his own face.

In addition, posthumanist art includes works that consider the significance of machines and technologies, which are close to Heidegger's conceptualization of technology as a mode of revealing (its *Gestell*), where technological objects are seen to have their own novel kind of presence.[37] For example, Stelarc's works relate to what can be conceived as posthuman corporeality, pointing to a radical transformation of the perceptual capabilities and cognitive orientation of bodies, visualizing their various demarcations between human and non-human by combining the human body with technological prostheses. Alongside their theoretical reflections and conceptual claims, these works of art represent new configurations of bodies and strategies of resistance towards the binary logic of human/non-human. Thus, the 'increasing agreement here that all bodies, including those of animals (and perhaps certain machines, too), evince certain capacities for agency'.[38] Technology is not separate from humanity today, but *within* humanity, pointing to Heidegger's idea that things are not detached from us, but are connected to us. Furthermore, in the contemporary context, this implies 'a broader digital logic and discourses of posthuman embodiment, action bodies must now be comfortable with seamlessly merging not only into digital environments but also with digital "prosthetics" and "make-up"',[39] and 'also includes a complex assemblage of human and non-human, planetary and cosmic, given and manufactured, which requires major re-adjustments in our ways of thinking'.[40]

Now, the crucial question is how the pandemic crisis, through an encounter with non-human agency, is reordering or re-semiotizing culture. The pandemic affects collective culture, rescheduling or cancelling the main cultural manifestations, rearranging museum spaces, changing attendance patterns through physical distancing and replacing tactile activities with digital engagement, such as online exhibitions and virtual tours. This means that the digital realm and technological platforms offer common spaces for interactions and disseminations of cultural and artistic works. According to this model, artists in quarantine conditions 'are also making their own culture – music, journals, stories, paintings and poems – and sharing them with others and they are proving increasingly vital to preserving the sense of life being lived and for considering what culture itself might be or become.'[41] However, this also generates the potential for new forms of artistic dissent expressed, for example, by graffiti street artists who 'have found their way to bring urgent messages of hope, resilience, and dissent'[42] through to digital arts activism, which provides avenues to help people channel suffering, trauma or their outrage into persuasive messages[43] and visual expressions.

Structure of the book

This book is an exploration of the posthuman condition across the three registers of philosophy, politics and art (while we have grouped the contributions under these categories, the themes reflected therein inevitably overlap and cross-pollinate with one another in an entirely deconstructive manner). The book brings together thinkers and writers working within and across these fields into a productive and cross-disciplinary exchange. We believe this is the only adequate way of tackling the problems and questions opened up by the pandemic. The guiding theme that all contributions explore is the posthuman condition, and the different ways this is revealed and illuminated by the pandemic.

Philosophy

Christine Daigle argues in Chapter 1, 'The (post)human and the (post)pandemic: Rediscovering our selves', that the crisis brought about by the Covid-19 pandemic has disruptive and generative potentials, allowing us to grasp ourselves as the posthumans we always were. She shows how the sudden and fearful confrontation generated by the pandemic with our own bodily entanglements is potentially a generative moment. Invoking posthumanist materialist feminist thinkers such as Stacy Alaimo, Karen Barad, Rosi Braidotti and Samantha Frost, Daigle explores the manifold entanglements that compose us and that we participate in. She proposes that we are transjective beings, namely beings that are concomitantly transsubjective and transobjective. We are dynamic assemblages of unfolding relations, experiences, beings and agentic capacities, not the autonomous agents posited by the humanist view. This deflation of the notion of human agency, and the emphasis on agentic capacity, is helpful in understanding the disruptions generated by pandemic and the agentic capacity of the virus. Confronted by the powerful agency of this tiny being we learn a lesson in humility as we fully realize how deeply entangled our beings are and thereby how vulnerable we are. Daigle also considers the break in trust that the pandemic has caused. We tend to believe that individuals are autonomous wilful subjects whose actions are guided by their good intentions. In the case of Covid-19, trust has been shaken and needs to be rebuilt. The pandemic has shown us that we cannot trust others and even ourselves even if we are all fully well intentioned. Taking mask-wearing as an example of agentic capacity, she discusses how it impacts our relations of trust with others. Those who resist or ignore pandemic mitigating measures are not ill intentioned, but simply fail to recognize the extent of our entanglement. They have not learned what the pandemic has taught us: the body we are is an unknown, a permeable and thereby vulnerable being. Realizing this about ourselves and others necessitates a reassessment of our relations with others. We have come to fear the other – the virus, our body as potential carrier, the other human who might be a carrier – and yet we have also come to long for the other as we have been forced to isolate. Our conception of ourselves and of others has been shattered, according to Daigle, and we need to rebuild a trustful relation that rests upon the acceptance and active embrace of our vulnerability.

Pursuing the theme of borders and boundaries and their permeability, in relation to the virus, Iris van der Tuin, in her chapter (2), "'Life is obviously not easy to define'': Viral politics and dynamic patterning in Susanne K. Langer's philosophies of art and life', reflects on the work of philosopher Susanne K. Langer, particularly her three-volume series *Mind*. The first volume (*Mind I*), published in 1967, is important in this context as it deals with biology, physiology, genetics and the theory of evolution. Here van der Tuin focuses on Langer's interest in the virus as a 'borderline case,' or, in the words of Donna Haraway, as a 'boundary object.' Viruses, as with all other borderline cases, are characterized by an interplay of 'individuation' and 'involvement.' The former is a concept that we nowadays ascribe to Gilbert Simondon. The latter captures a process that we, today, describe in terms of 'entanglement' (Karen Barad) or, alternatively, 'assemblage' (Deleuze and Guattari). Engaging in a close reading of sections of *Mind I*, as well as other material from Langer's corpus, van der Tuin's seeks to grasp the idea of the virus as a 'borderline' concept.

The uncanny life of the virus is further explored by Stefan Herbrechter in his chapter (3), 'Dead, alive: Deconstruction, biopolitics and life death'. Herbrechter applies a Derridean analysis to investigate the virus' ambiguous biopolitical status as an entity that is, strictly speaking, neither alive nor dead but inhabits the 'zone of indistinction' between these states. Viruses, he suggests, are in fact *more* alive than life itself, they are the 'differ*antial* trace', or the 'supplement' that makes life possible in the first place. They are that which produces life's autoaffective impulse – its survival instinct and its (auto)immunitarian logic. In this 'originary' scenario, however, the virus, life and death become virtually indistinguishable – similar to Derrida's formula 'lavielamort', in the seminar from 1975–6, bearing this title. This seminar, Herbrechter argues, allows us to understand Derridean deconstruction as a 'philosophy of life', or as 'biodeconstruction'. Herbrechter's chapter tracks the beginning of this development in Derrida's work and its reception, and connects it with two problematics relevant for a thinking 'in the age of pandemics' and for an understanding of deconstruction as a philosophy *for* life: What is deconstruction's 'biopolitics'? And what is the relation between the 'originary vitality' of the virus referred to earlier and the 'originary technicity' of the trace? In engaging with these questions, bioart has an important role to play, namely as a critical mediator in the time of pandemics. Tagny Duff's work on 'viral tattoos', in which she uses Lentivirus (a synthetic retrovirus) 'as an artistic medium and subject . . . to explore how perceptions and tensions around infection and contagion might be re-imagined and rearticulated by engaging with viral vectors' is exemplary here. As a specific discourse and practice engaged in mediating the question of life death, bioart can have an 'ecological' function in the context of contemporary biopolitics, and can thus become a locus of critique and resistance to the totalization and technicization of Life (itself).

Politics

Saul Newman, in Chapter 4, 'Contagious politics: Posthuman anarchism', sees the virus as a political contagion, one that reveals a crisis of legitimacy in governing institutions and political (and economic) rationalities, and which releases and accelerates new viral political forces and antagonisms, from the Far Left to the Far Right. In attempting to make sense of this new political horizon, he proposes the category of 'postanarchism', which he formulates here as an anarchist philosophy reconstructed through a poststructuralist and posthumanist lens. Building on, and yet departing from, the revolutionary anarchist political theory of the nineteenth century, exemplified by the likes of Pierre-Joseph Proudhon, Mikhail Bakunin and Peter Kropotkin, Newman argues that, today, by contrast, the structures of power are too diffuse and the category of the subject too obscure and differentiated to sustain the totalizing metanarrative of the revolution of society against the state. He engages in a deconstruction of some of the humanist and rationalist categories that underpin this idea of emancipation, emphasizing instead posthumanist themes of ecological entanglement and our interconnectedness with networks of power and discourse that we seek, at the same time, to gain some autonomy from. In outlining the ethical and political coordinates of postanarchism, Newman develops the idea of 'ontological anarchy', a concept he derives from thinkers like Michel Foucault and Reiner Schürmann: ontological anarchy is a post-foundational way of thinking about politics and ethics, without the certainties of guiding principles or a rational *telos*. However, while ontological anarchy opens up the potential for new understandings of radical politics, its consequences are fundamentally ambiguous, he argues, because power itself has also become dangerously anarchic and, as a consequence, unleashes new forms of reactionary politics that try to *re*territorialize the ontological.

Radical and emancipatory politics, in the form of contemporary movements for economic, racial and ecological justice, must therefore navigate the opaque, unstable and uncertain terrain characteristic of the posthuman condition.

The political contours of the pandemic are further elucidated by Josephine Berry, in her chapter (5), 'Spectatorial splitting and transcultural seeing in the age of pandemics'. She explores the emerging 'spectatorial regime' that the Covid-19 pandemic has brought to light within the institutions and practices of Western art. She investigates the art museum, during the pandemic, as a unique space in which (bio)political questions of capitalist exploitation and colonial domination are dramatically brought into focus. Berry shows the way that the art viewer is increasingly addressed, both as paradigmatic Life – the still transcendent I/eye of Western reason – and as less than fully human, namely as the bare life that has hitherto been reserved for the West's colonial Others. This conflation of ontological and biopolitical orders of the human within the pandemic museum is triggered by, but also mimics, the behaviour of the virus itself, which treats humans and objects interchangeably – while also exploiting the systems and behaviours that uphold these differences. Given how deeply invested Western ontology is in such a separation between Life and Nonlife, *bios/*zoë and *Thanatos/geos,* and the associated universe of semantic, ethical, political and economic values produced on this basis, such a lack of recognition is profoundly destabilizing to the social order which presupposes it. Such a separation of (qualified) Life and (Non)life, *bios* and *zoë/Thanatos,* is also sustained by a way of seeing that Western art and its exhibition in public space have helped to produce; a way of seeing exchangeable with the transcendently universal I/eye which is premised on a non-seeing of Others. It is this non-seeing of Others whose devalued labour has created the very production conditions of the universal, Berry argues, that the pandemic has rendered impossible. She considers the role played by Western art in co-constructing the racial regime, a political-symbolic order whose ethical justification of the unsustainable extraction of value from all other (Non)life has itself helped to create the destabilized conditions in which the zoonotic transmission of disease occurs. The virus compels art institutions, and by extension art itself, to address the spectator as the split subject of universal reason *and* bare life, thereby creating a rhizomatic link between different ontological states of humanness. While the virus has in so many ways retraced the differentials of race and class, its yoking together of post-Enlightenment and decolonial ways of seeing and being seen is shaking up the Western liberal regime of universality which produces such differentials in the first place.

In a further exploration of the political issues and questions thrown up by the pandemic, Amanda Boetzkes and Anna McWebb, in Chapter 6, 'Posthuman vectors and the production of a common flesh', investigate the global economy of 'virus dumping' and practices of factory farming that result in the production of a common flesh between human and non-human animals. As vectors of viral contagion, these two examples bring into sharp relief the fragile and unstable political ecology of the Anthropocene. Here they consider the insights of Marxist evolutionary biologist Rob Wallace, who argues that every viral outbreak is preceded by an influx of capital. Wallace comes to this conclusion through an understanding of viruses not as discrete microorganisms, but rather as integral parts of forest ecologies that, when perturbed by farming monopolies, reproduce at an accelerated pace, unmitigated by the stochastic noise of the forest that normally controls its replication. In drawing, further, from Achille Mbembe's concept of necropolitics, and Syl Ko's history of black veganism, Boetzkes and McWebb see the factory farm in terms of its yielding of human and non-human bodies as vectors of viral transmission and evolution. Posthumanism, they argue, must be reconsidered in terms of the management of bodily death and not merely the management of life. While early theorizations of posthumanism have been beholden to a Foucaultian paradigm of biopolitics, and an associated biomediatic perspective of ontology, Boetzkes and McWebb propose that the coronavirus pandemic identifies the limitations of the biopolitical account of posthumanism precisely by transgressing the abstract division between human and non-human animal, life and death. The Covid-19 pandemic might be better understood in the context of necropolitical sites in which labour, bodily suffering and death become the means by which privileged humans historically distinguished their lives *as* human. Pandemic conditions destabilize such divisions and the bodily substructure that upholds them. The coronavirus is therefore a crucial fulcrum for rethinking the political pretence by which humanism and posthumanism are defined. Here Boetzkes and McWebb consider the politics of posthumanism at stake in the representational practices of British graphic artist Sue Coe. For decades, Coe has documented scenes of animal cruelty and slaughter, as well as the corporate, pharmacological and political regimes that produce factory farms, viral outbreaks and social misery. They suggest that Coe's work shows how the coronavirus pandemic reveals an underlying necropolitical situation in which human and non-human animals are united in a common planetary flesh.

Chapter 7, 'While you were at home, confined: Control and technology after the city', looks at how the pandemic impacts on cities as public – and therefore political – spaces. Here Rick Dolphijn describes Rotterdam in early April 2020, during the lockdown, witnessing how the cityscape and its social dynamics changed overnight, and perhaps permanently. He shows how the posters for cultural events now seem to evoke something completely alien, like an obscure historical event that no longer resonates with the present moment. Furthermore, he argues that the idea of the city as a kind laboratory for a biopolitical surveillance and control has now been given further impetus by the pandemic and measures introduced to combat it. As we learn from Foucault and his study of epidemics and regimes of discipline and security, forms of disease and technologies of power are always interrelated. However, Dolphijn emphasizes the transformation, charted by Deleuze, from disciplinary to control societies. Thus, a whole new system is being realized today, a system which is capable of turning the whole of society, not just discreet institutions, into a panopticon. This is a panopticon inverted, at which one finds oneself at the centre, surrounded by an infinity of potential eyes, a digital panopticon that uses sophisticated algorithms to flow from object to object. Of course, this inverted panopticon still depends on capitalism, and it will continue long into future, as a means of control 'After the City'.

Art

Amanda du Preez aims to develop (Chapter 8) (9) a framework relevant to understanding how Covid-19 creates a new imagining of the earth. According to du Preez, to be human is to have a particular form versus becoming posthuman, which aspires to a state of formlessness. In other words, to become posthuman is to no longer submit to the constraints of taking a particular form: posthumans can hypothetically appear in *any* form and shape. In her chapter, 'Is human to posthuman as Earth is to post-earth? Notes on terraforming and (trans) forming', she draws parallels between Earth and Mars, human and posthuman, or what can be exemplified with certain forms or characterized as formless. On the one hand, Earth prescribes certain laws (forms); on the other hand, Mars is considered as formless, and can therefore undergo limitless acts of terraforming, so that it can be formed to become habitable or suitable for Earth's life forms. As a result of the coronavirus pandemic, the act of 'terraforming' will enter a new episode. The world beyond Earth as we know it is open to our imaginations, to create a habitat of our wildest dreams, post-earth. Thus, terraforming necessarily calls for the (trans)formation of humans to survive in the new context, or for re-programming humans to relate to their environment in more ethical and ecologically sustainable ways. This also raises questions about the formation of the image of the new planet and what form it will take in a new reality. Finally, du Preez discusses how the aesthetics of posthumanism corresponds with the aesthetic category of the *sublime* (formless), while the notion of being human refers to the containable and limiting category of *beauty* (form). Here she uses comparative images from the arts, cinema and social media to expand on the intersection between human and posthuman, Earth and post-earth, form and formlessness.

Ada Smailbegović, in her chapter (9), 'Quarantine in Waiting: Plant Clocks and the Asynchronies of Viral Time', sees the Covid-19 pandemic as a moment in which humans have been forced to recognize their insertion within the contours of non-human time and to perform a series of translations or transpositions between these divergent temporal rhythms. It has been, alternately, a time of finitude and of waiting, with each period of quarantine delineated as a window within which human temporal attunement occurs in relation to the rhythms of activity imposed by the virus; as well as a time of deferral or lag, with a sense that human interactions in the present shape the contours of a future that will not be sensible to human perception until two or three weeks later. Smailbegović considers ethologist Jakob von Uexküll's observation that what constitutes a moment for different species is 'the shortest segment of time in which the world exhibits no changes'. This differs for different organisms, so that 'a human moment lasts one-eighteenth of a second', for instance, while 'in the snail's environment, a stick that moves back and forth four or more times a second' is perceived by the snail as being at rest. Smailbegović draws on Uexküll's snail to articulate a methodology that she calls 'snail cinema' as a way of becoming attuned to differences in temporal rhythms that permeate material worlds and often occur below thresholds perceptible to the human sensorium. As such, 'snail cinema' becomes an injunction to see the Covid-19 pandemic not as an isolated event, but as embedded within other processes of ecological change, many of which, such as climate change, are caused or accelerated by anthropogenic activity and lead to a proliferation of asynchronies between organisms that had hitherto had more synced up rhythms taking place over long periods of evolutionary time. Such instances of 'snail cinema' are explored, both conceptually and through a series of poetic interludes, in which the quarantine temporality of the past year has created opportunities for observing the processes of change in the non-human world, and, in particular, plants. This consideration of plants, in turn, becomes the basis of the second focus of the chapter, which is the HIV/AIDS epidemic of the 1980s and 1990s. Here Smailbegović reflects on the experiences of director, writer and artist Derek Jarman, who was diagnosed with HIV in the late 1980s. Jarman turns to creating a garden at Dungeness and keeps a detailed journal, much of which revolves around the seasonal growth of plants in his garden. At the same time, the garden in this case is not a site of idealized or essentialized nature; rather, it is in close proximity to the Dungeness nuclear power station, and, as ideas around global warming are gaining greater publicity, Jarman is often reflecting on the temporalities of these broader ecological processes. Such 'plant clocks', with their heterogeneous and composite rhythms of time, resist both the incremental regularity of more mechanized forms of timekeeping and the pull of teleological time, which forecloses the vectors of potentiality in the present, by setting a deterministic course towards human finitude and death and, in the larger context, beyond the temporalities created by the virus, towards ecological catastrophe.

Martin Grünfeld in his chapter (10), 'Thinking and/over/in the pandemic: From *contact points* towards *contact zones*', focuses on how the invisible ultramicroscopic virus becomes entangled with our everyday practices and experiences. In a pandemic, even the seemingly simple everyday act of opening a door becomes a potential *contact zone* with the more-than-human. Yet, this potential encounter also marks an opportunity for us to think and act beyond the habitual. Here he turns to the debate, referred to earlier, among major philosophers in the early days of the contagion in 2020, considering the widely different responses of Giorgio Agamben and Slavoj Žižek: while the former tended to downplay the seriousness of the viruses, bemoaning instead the exaggerated response of the state in declaring a state of emergency, the latter saw it as an event that would change everything, that would have the potential to usher in a radically different world. As an alternative to these two opposed and ultimately inadequate responses, Grünfeld instead considers how we can reconcile ourselves with the virus as a more-than-human sub-layer of life. He does this, first, by discussing artist Tagny Duff's daring proposition to perceive viruses as evolutionary companions. Duff shows two different paths, one in the form of a speculative dialogue, the other as material encounters of companionship. Second, Grünfeld considers the space of the museum as a potential *contact zone* with the more-than-human. While the spread of Covid-19 has led to closed museums and galleries across the globe, he argues that perhaps such places can become sites for reconciliation providing orderly and safe, yet utterly strange, material encounters.

The ways in which museum spaces are being transformed by the pandemic, and how they might operate as alternative sites of viral experience, is also the focus of the final chapter (11). In 'Viral agencies and curating worldly life differently in museum spaces', Fiona Cameron examines the ways in which the pandemic reorganizes the space of the museum, changing attendance patterns and disrupting existing structures and relations between people, buildings, staff and audiences, and creating the possibility of new ways of perceiving the world and our relations with non-human species, objects and forces. The pandemic starkly illustrates the permeability of nature and culture, undermining anthropocentric ideas of human autonomy and sovereignty, and reminding us of our embeddedness within broader networks and ecosystems. We are not singular organisms; indeed, we host multiple entities, including billions of viruses, and are part of integrated biological systems and processes. This realization also challenges the traditional functioning of museums where the world is ordered in a certain way, reinforcing the ideologies of capitalism and anthropocentrism and accentuating gender and class inequalities. Instead, Cameron argues, we must adapt to the new reordering of the world created by the pandemic. Here, earthly life is curated by all manner of entities through a process of sympoiesis, understood by Cameron in terms of ecological compositional design or eco-curating processes of *becoming*, in which one action begets another, and another, in a complex mesh of begetting. The power of viral 'eco-curating' lies in the ability to disrupt and rearrange social and conceptual spaces. Here Cameron puts forward the notion of the 'rhizomic liquid museum', referring, by way of example, to movements such as 'Free the Museum' that seek to radically rethink the role of the museum today, beyond mere practices of digital engagement.

Notes

1 Hannah B Higgins, 'Sonic Images of the Coronavirus', 2020 (https://critinq.wordpress. com/2020/06/17/sonic-images-of-the-coronavirus/ accessed 14 January 2021).

2 Michael A. Peters, 'Philosophy and Pandemic in the Postdigital Era: Foucault, Agamben, Žižek', 2020 (https://link.springer.com/article/10.1007/s42438-020-00117-4 accessed 18 January 2021).

3 Ibid.

4 James S. Baumlin, 'From Postmodernism to Posthumanism: Theorizing Ethos in an Age of Pandemic', *Humanities* 9, no. 2 (2020): 46.

5 Gilles Deleuze and Félix Guattari, *What Is Philosophy?* trans. Hugh Tomlinson and Graham Burchell (New York: Columbia University Press, 1994), 183.

6 Giorgio Agamben, 'The invention of an epidemic', *The European Journal of Psychoanalysis,* (2020). https://www.journal-psychoanalysis.eu/coronavirus-and-philosophers/. Accessed 30 March 2020.

7 Sergio Benvenuto, 'Welcome to Seclusion', 2020 (https://www.journal-psychoanalysis.eu/coronavirus-and-philosophers/ accessed 4 January 2021).

8 Sotiris Panagiotis, 'Against Agamben: Is a Democratic Biopolitics Possible?' 2020 (https://criticallegalthinking.com/2020/03/14/against-agamben-is-a-democratic-biopolitics-possible/ accessed 5 January 2020).

9 Jean-LucNancy, 'Viral Exception', 2020 (http://www.journal-psychoanalysis.eu/on-pandemics-nancy-esposito-nancy/)

10 Bruno Latour, 'Is This a Dress Rehearsal?' 2020 (https://critinq.wordpress. com/2020/03/26/is-this-a-dress-rehearsal/ accessed 17 December 2020).

11 See Slavoj Žižek, *PANDEMIC! COVID-19 Shakes the World* (Cambridge: Polity, 2020).

12 Michel Foucault, *The Order of Things: an Archaeology of the Human Sciences* (London and New York: Routledge, 2005), xxv.

13 Ihab Hassan, 'Prometheus as Performer: Towards a Posthumanist Culture?' *The Georgia Review* 31, no. 4 (Winter 1977), 830–50.

14 Jacques Derrida, 'Structure, Sign and Play in the Discourse of the Human Sciences', *Writing and Difference,* trans. Alan Bass (London and New York: Routledge, 2001), 351–70.

15 See Francesca Ferrando, *Philosophical Posthumanism* (London: Bloomsbury, 2019), 128–40.

16 Ferrando, *Philosophical Posthumanism*.

17 Cary Wolfe, *What Is Posthumanism?* (Minneapolis: University of Minnesota Press, 2010), xxv.

18 See Rosie Braidotti, 'A Theoretical Framework for the Critical Posthumanities', *Theory, Culture & Society* 36, no. 6 (2019): 31–61. See also Braidotti, *The Posthuman* (Cambridge: Polity Press, 2013).

19 Donna Haraway, 'A Cyborg Manifesto', *The Socialist Review,* 1985 (http://users.uoa. gr/~cdokou/HarawayCyborgManifesto.pdf accessed 9 January 2021).

20 N. Katherine Hayles, *How We Became Posthuman: Virtual Bodies in Cybernetics, Literature and Informatic* (Chicago: University of Chicago Press, 1999).

21 See Bruno Latour, *We Have Never Been Modern,* trans., Catherine Porter (Cambridge, MA: Harvard University Press, 1993).

22 See Donna Haraway, *When Species Meet* (Minneapolis: University of Minnesota Press, 2007).

23 See Karen Barad, *Meeting the Universe Halfway: Quantum Physics and the Entanglement of Matter and Meaning* (Durham, NC: Duke University Press, 2007). See also Jane Bennett, *Vibrant Matter: A Political Ecology of Things* (Durham, NC: Duke University Press, 2010).

24 See Catherine Keller, *Cloud of the Impossible: Negative Theology and the Planetary Entanglemen* (New York: Columbia University Press, 2015).

25 Braidotti, 'A Theoretical Framework for the Critical Posthumanities', 36–7.

26 Reiner Schürmann, *Heidegger on Being and Acting: From Principles to Anarchy,* trans. C.-M. Gros (Bloomington: Indiana University Press, 1987), 6.

27 See Saul Newman, *Postanarchism* (Cambridge: Polity Press, 2016).

28 Bruno Latour, *Facing Gaia: Eight Lectures on the New Climatic Regime,* trans., C. Porter (Cambridge: Polity Press, 2017), 228.

29 See Topuzovski Tihomir, 'Introduction: Visibilities of Becoming', *The Large Glass* 27/28 (Museum of Contemporary Art Skopje, 2019), 4–5.

30 Arthur Danto, *Beyond the Brillo Box: The Visual Arts in Post-Historical Perspective* (University of California Press, 1992), 38.

31 Pernille Leth-Espensen, 'Posthuman Temporalities in Science and Bioart', in *The Bloomsbury Handbook of Posthumanism,* ed. Mads Rosendahl Thomsen and Jacob (Wamberg: Bloomsbury, 2020).

32 Arthur Danto, *Unnatural Wonders: Essays from the Gap Between Art and Life* (New York: Columbia University Press, 2006), xvi.

33 Diana H. Coole and Samantha Frost (eds), *New Materialisms: Ontology, Agency, and Politics* (Durham, NC and London: Duke University Press Books, 2010), 19.

34 See Mads Rosendahl Thomsen, Jacob Wamberg eds., *The Bloomsbury Handbook of Posthumanism*.

35 See Topuzovski Tihomir, 'Introduction: Visibilities of Becoming', 4–5.

36 Coole and Frost (eds), New Materialisms, 3.

37 See Topuzovski Tihomir, 'Introduction: Visibilities of Becoming', 4–5.

38 Coole and Frost (eds), New Materialisms, 20.

39 Drew Ayers, *Spectacular Posthumanism: The Digital Vernacular of Visual Effects* (London: Bloomsbury, 2019), 105.

40 Rosi Braidotti, *The Posthuman* (Cambridge: Polity Press, 2013), 159.

41 Mark Banks, 'The Work of Culture and C-19', *European Journal of Cultural Studies* 23, no. 4 (2020), 648–54, 648–9.

42 Benedetta Ricci 'Coronavirus Street Art: How The Pandemic Is Changing Our Cities', https://magazine.artland.com/coronavirus-street-art-how-the-pandemic-is-changing-our-cities/. Accessed 21 January 2021.

43 Art and online activism amid the pandemic: lessons from around the world (https://theconversation.com/art-and-online-activism-amid-the-pandemic-lessons-from-around-the-world-140161 accessed 22 January 2021).

Part I

Philosophy

1

The (post)human and the (post)pandemic

Rediscovering our selves

Christine Daigle

The Covid-19 pandemic is being experienced individually and collectively as a crisis. Referred to as the 'disease of stoppage'[1] that brings about a 'rupture' of the 'everyday'[2] and heightened defamiliarization;[3] the pandemic is causing massive social and economic disruption, physical and mental suffering and deaths. And yet, it also has the potential of being generative: the first evidence of a potential silver lining to it being the radical diminution of pollution caused by significantly reduced human traffic leading non-human animals to thrive and venture into urban settings. Images and reports of wild goats and boars roaming urban settings and dolphins enjoying the Bosphorus and getting closer than ever to the city of Istanbul have elicited smiles and wonder at the power of nature to reclaim the world once humans cease to be so active, giving us glimpses of what would follow our species' extinction. However, for the humans relegated to their private spaces and forced into different variations of quarantine and lockdowns, the pandemic has reduced, rather than expanded, horizons. Examining the meaning of 'crisis', 'emergency' and 'catastrophe' in the context of the pandemic, Rebecca Solnit argues that the pandemic is an instance of sudden large-scale disruption, a point after which we need to reorient ourselves. Solnit explains that disasters teach humans lessons, the first of which being 'that everything is connected . . . [Disasters are] crash courses in those connections'. She further argues that 'Our sense of self generally comes from the world around us, and right now, we are finding another version of who we are'.[4] I contend that the being we are discovering – this other 'version of who we are' – is actually the being we have always been but forgotten we were: a radically materially entangled being. The pandemic is allowing us to grasp ourselves as the posthumans we always were, namely the materially entangled beings that we are rediscovering.

In this chapter, I explore the disruptive and generative potentials of the pandemic as experienced by a being that has lived under the humanist delusion of existing as an autonomous exceptional subject: the human being. This is a delusion we have lived under until Covid-19 hit us with its powerful agentic capacity. The biothreat we face, hidden yet deadly – the 'invisible enemy' as it has been called by some – has confronted us with the fissure at the heart of the concept 'human': we were never human and always were posthuman. I examine how the sudden and fearful confrontation generated by the pandemic with our own bodily entanglements is potentially a generative moment. However, this moment in which we recognize that our embodied and subjective existence is deeply entangled with that of all human and non-human others is first lived in anxiety as we discover our ontological vulnerability. Our relations with others have deeply shifted in the crisis: we fear the Other as invisible – the virus – or the once familiar and non-threatening Other – the potential carrier we cross paths with while out – or even our own body either as healthy but asymptomatic, therefore still a carrier and a threat to others, or as disrupted and incapacitated by a potentially deadly host – our body as sick patient. Yet, as much as we fear the Other, we still long for that Other as our quarantined selves are forced into physical distancing. I argue that the pandemic experience, which is rewriting our imaginations[5] and bringing us back to the body,[6] is an opportunity to be seized: it has the generative power to allow us, rather than 'returning to normal', to reinvent 'normal' as we embrace our vulnerability and become the posthumans we always were, existing as such in a post-pandemic world.

My view of the posthuman is formed along the lines of posthumanist material feminist theory, which explores the manifold entanglements that compose us and that we participate in. I propose that we are transjective beings, namely beings that are concomitantly transsubjective and transobjective. We exist and unfold through a web of material and subjective relations that both shape us and undo us. We are dynamic assemblages of unfolding relations, experiences, beings and agentic capacities. This assemblage, which materializes as an embodied being, is itself a porous and permeable being, constantly changing materially and subjectively. I use the term 'transjective', which blends the material (objective) and the subjective, as I do not see those as separate. We refer to them as if they were of a different nature but, in fact, the material inflects the subjective just as much as the subjective inflects the material. It is impossible to disentangle those relations and webs of affect. Nor is it possible to conceive of beings as autarkic. This is true of all beings, and not merely the human.[7] All beings, humans included, are porous and permeable beings. As Samantha Frost puts it, if there is no traffic of molecules through our various membranes, there is no life.[8] This is also true of the traffic of ideas, affects, images, etc. While porosity sustains life, it also renders it vulnerable. This is the double-sided coin of porosity: the condition for a being's thriving is its vulnerability. The very openness of beings, which is at the foundation of their thriving, also renders them vulnerable and thereby potentially toxic – as discussed by Stacy Alaimo in the context of environmental exposure to pesticides and pollutants – and potentially infected when encountering a virus such as SARS-CoV-2, whether one develops symptoms and perhaps dies from it or not. One is toxic in two ways: as having various toxins in their assemblage but also toxic to others, in the case of the pandemic, as a carrier of the virus.

It is important to emphasize that our entanglements are manifold. Rosi Braidotti recently captured this by suggesting we are zoe/geo/techno framed subjects.[9] Material feminists have offered various terms to capture the entangled and dynamic being of both the human and non-human such as 'mangle', 'transcorporeal being', 'biocultural creature', 'cyborg' and, most recently, the 'zoe/geo/techno framed subject' discussed by Braidotti.[10] I add to this list the transjective. Importantly, each view not only rejects the humanist notion of subject but, with it, the notion of autonomous agency. Karen Barad, Jane Bennett and Samantha Frost are important resources in reconceptualizing the notion of agency as distributive agency or agentic capacity.[11] Barad explains that agency is 'not an attribute but the ongoing reconfigurings of the world'.[12] These unfold through intra-active relations in which the human is entangled. One cannot single out human agency. Likewise, Bennett argues for what she coins 'distributive agency'. Grounding her proposals in Spinoza's views on affect and bodies and Deleuze and Guattari's notion of assemblage, Bennett claims that agency is distributed in a continuum: the assemblage has agency just as its different members each have agency. The result is an 'effervescence of agency'[13] and 'a swarm of the vitalities at play'.[14] Human intention is one among many forces with which it always congregates, which is why she also speaks of 'congregational assemblages'.[15] In addition to this, I find it useful to consider Frost's distinction between intentionality, as may be found within human agency/consciousness, and the intentless direction she identifies in relation to the biochemical processes that constantly unfold within bodies and necessarily also inflect agency. Thus, we are always dealing with assemblages of agency and intentless direction, and using the phrase 'agentic capacity' allows us to capture either form of impetus that drives dynamic unfolding.

Deflating the notion of human agency and emphasizing that of agentic capacity is key to the posthumanist material feminist enterprise, and is helpful in understanding the disruptions brought about by the Covid-19 pandemic and the agentic capacity of the virus. Living through this as individual humans, we are suddenly faced with the power of the agentic capacity of a tiny being, the virus. We are also faced with the power of the agentic capacity of its cumulated effect via its myriad entanglements. The repeated admission, on the part of multiple scientists trying to understand the mechanics of the virus and its spread, that we do not understand exactly how transmission occurs or what kind of havoc the virus can cause in a human body has caused major anxiety and forced us to adopt the humility not characteristic of the subject of humanism. We must be humble about our capacity to understand a novel virus that does not behave like the ones we know. We must be humble about the power of our human agency to defeat the virus.[16] We must be humble about the power of our own human agency in the face of the fantastic power this tiny being's agentic capacity holds. Humility is the name of the game when one realizes fully how deeply entangled one's being is and thereby how vulnerable one is.

There is something reassuring in clinging to a humanist notion of self. The autonomous rational subject that can orient its action through a simple operation of its will and sometimes in utter disregard of one's body, circumstances, others and world is one that we can either trust or not. Moral education trains that autonomous humanist subject to make the right decisions, among which not harming others is primary. The notion of the posthuman as radically entangled does not do away with moral responsibility entirely. But this notion makes room for the agentic capacity of a myriad of beings and factors that make the posthumanist subject through its multiple entanglements, porosity and seepage. Political theorists have provided various origin stories for human societies. Social contract theories often rest on pessimistic views of human nature whereby a contract needs to be put in place to control natural human violence or the propensity of humans to do wrongful things. I do not want to debate whether these views are right or wrong. The fact of the matter is, however, that the socialized humans we now are operate on trust. When I board a bus, I trust the driver will not drive us off a cliff. When I use my new appliance, I trust the installer did their job right. When I consult a health-care professional, I trust they take my well-being seriously. When I meet someone new, I expect they are well intentioned. It is precisely because trust is at the foundation of our interactions with others that we are so surprised, shocked and hurt when others fail to meet our expectations, which they, unfortunately, sometimes do. This all rides on the humanist delusion of an autonomous wilful subject whose action is guided by their good intentions. In the case of Covid-19, trust has been shaken and needs to be rebuilt. The pandemic has shown us that we cannot trust others and even ourselves even if we are all fully well intentioned. This is because we are abruptly discovering the myriad entanglements of beings all exercising their agentic capacity.

At all times we are confronted with various others. But this new Other, the virus, is particularly threatening. Not only does it affect human bodies in ways that other viruses have not – and in ways we are still far from fully understanding – but it is also having a long-term impact on survivors that we are only beginning to glimpse. This virus is novel not only in the way in which it affects bodies but also in the way it does not. The asymptomatism noted in many carriers has made the management of the pandemic particularly difficult. It has also heightened our sense of threat and distrust of other individuals we meet who look healthy but might be a threat to us. The common cold or flu, or even recent more severe viruses like SARS, are much easier to handle since carriers display symptoms. This also allows us to identify who may be a threat and who may not be. But with Covid-19, there is a long list of very different symptoms and, if one is a carrier, one can suffer from one or many, or even none at all. Some are the same as for other illnesses including seasonal allergies, indigestion or the common cold. How does one trust one's own body's signals or even lack thereof? How does one trust another human body we encounter or interact with given they may pass as healthy and non-threatening but in fact may render us sick? Is it indeed safe to enter into a social circle, which was encouraged by some authorities to palliate the mental health effects quarantines were having on individuals?

The Canadian province of Ontario's guidelines put forward at the beginning of June 2020 encouraged individuals to form social circles, allowing them to eliminate physical distancing for a limited number of persons. Each individual was to belong to one circle only, the members of the circle had to always be the same and, within it, physical contact such as hugs were permitted. At the same time, any member of a social circle could engage in social gatherings provided those were limited to ten people and a physical distance of two metres was maintained between members of the group. One could navigate and participate in many different gatherings but not in more than one circle.[17] If this reads a little confusing it is because it was, and most of the population had a hard time interpreting the guidelines or simply did not trust that these measures would suffice in containing the spread. In addition to those, recommendations for mask wearing were put forward to be followed by mandatory indoor mask-wearing measures adopted by municipalities and regional governments.

I do not want to discuss in detail the frenzy that erupted around recommendations or implementations of mandatory mask wearing. Pretty disgraceful incidents of various individuals protesting against this measure or simply refusing to obey mandatory mask-wearing policies have flooded traditional and social media. The issue has become polarized and politicized to an unimaginable degree in the United States where any kind of social behaviour tends to be interpreted as an expression of political partisanship of one brand or another. Canada has seen its own instances of resistance and the formulation of various conspiracy theories equating mask wearing to sheepishness and willingness to be controlled by the dark forces trying to enslave individuals, whatever those might be.[18] That a protective device – be it a homemade simple fabric mask, a surgical mask, or even an N-95 mask – would trigger such passions is quite surprising especially because the main purpose of mask wearing is the protection of self and of others. It is a gesture of care.[19] Resisting it in the way we have witnessed in North America certainly appears unreasonable to the many Asian societies in which mask wearing is very common.

I am more interested in mask wearing insofar as it inflects our relations to others through the message this measure conveys. If I wear a mask when in public, I am not only well intentioned, but I am also communicating that I can be trusted. Wearing a mask flags that I have understood that I may be a threat to others without knowing it. I am doing my best to curb that threat and indicate that to others. Likewise, when I encounter others who wear masks, I perceive a sense of awareness of the risks they might pose to me and others. Those others can be trusted again just like I can be when I wear a mask. Now, the mask does not eliminate the threat, and, if one is a carrier, one may still transmit the virus if one does not also practice proper hygiene such as hand washing and sanitizing and wearing the mask in the appropriate manner without touching it or pulling it under one's nose or chin. Wearing a mask is also a protective gesture for oneself. One understands that being in the presence of others for such mundane activities like grocery shopping can expose oneself to that invisible threat. Wearing a mask is a measure one can take to curb the entanglement of which one is a part and limit the possibility of being infected.[20] Mask wearing is an acknowledgement of one's being as entangled in these relations and the recognition of our individual and collective vulnerabilities as materially entangled beings.[21]

From this, it would be easy or tempting to think that anti-maskers are just ill-intentioned people who refuse to protect others or themselves or that they just don't care. I want to venture that they are, most of them, well-intentioned individuals, but that they have failed to understand themselves as entangled beings. In most cases, this is due to a misunderstanding or even mistrust in science and data that points to the contrary. They see themselves as the autonomous subject of humanism whose action is the outcome of their intentional decision-making. They do not recognize that they are parts of material entanglements that make them potential transmitters against their will. Likewise, and in a much less extreme form, those neighbours, friends or family members who make us shake our heads in disbelief because they are engaging in risky behaviour – having friends over, fetching the newspaper every morning at the corner store as usual or standing too close to you if you see them on the street and stop to chat – these are all well-intentioned folks who sincerely believe they are taking all due precautions and doing the right thing. Theirs is a failure to recognize the extent of our entanglement and not an expression of ill will.

The pandemic has taught us that the body we are is an unknown. The body we thought we knew shows itself to be quite other than what we conceived. We have suddenly and forcefully learned about the permeability of our bodies and how we always exist as an assemblage of beings. My body hosts millions of organisms. It is itself a bundle of atoms, molecules and membranes that function together and exist in an environment which does not merely surround it but also penetrates it. Very efficient marketers have convinced us for years that foreign bodies such as probiotics are good for our guts and that we should support our microbiome by ingesting products that contain those healthy bodies. This idea has been embraced even if individuals continued to have a somewhat fuzzy understanding of their body's innerworkings. Over the years, we have also understood that viruses and some bacteria can be bad for us as well as some allergens but typically our body alerts us when such damaging bodies enter our own. The alert can be rather benign, such as sniffles, headache, mild coughing or an itchy throat or mouth, but it can also be sudden and violent such as vomiting, intense fever and anaphylactic reaction. Our understanding of the fact that our body can host healthy or damaging bodies has come along with an understanding that our body will somehow let us know what is going on: we will feel healthy or sick, depending on the bodies hosted. Covid-19 threw this off completely. Add to that the fact that many people have experienced all kinds of psychosomatic symptoms from chest pains to extreme fatigue caused by the anxiety generated by the disruption brought about by the pandemic and the general sense of threat and uncertainty that came with it. Thus, the body signals could be very misleading.

I had the following experience over the summer. I had an itchy throat. My skin temperature was high, but I had no fever. I had a headache (a rare occurrence for me). I had some chills and muscle aches. I thought: 'Must be Covid-19!' Or was it seasonal allergies and the intense yard cleaning session from the previous day? I felt great and ready to run 10 km. I thought: 'I must be virus free if this is the case.' But I could have been asymptomatic. I threw myself into the run. The thought was: 'If I make it, I must be OK.' I did make it and, no, I was not sick. Going out for a run to prove to myself that I was OK is a strategy I reverted to too many times to count, although that one time when I had these 'symptoms', I did go and get tested the next day to ensure I was clear.

I run in a residential area to avoid the crowded path and multiple close encounters with other humans. The streets are not busy, and I can run on them by the sidewalk, keeping a distance from those others that may be out for a walk. If I am out for a walk, I use the sidewalk and can step on the street to avoid another walker coming my way. This has been my strategy to keep active with walks and runs while respecting physical distancing, but the experience is uncanny. Prior to the pandemic, I did not have to think about my moving in the world in this way. Encountering an Other did not involve strategizing to avoid being close to them. The inner narrative goes: 'The other human coming toward me looks well-intentioned enough but are they an unaware carrier? I went grocery shopping yesterday. Might I have been infected despite taking all precautions? I have to protect the Other just as much as I have to protect myself.' Trust is broken. The Other and I are two well-intentioned bodies moving about and no longer trusting that the Other is not a threat. This lack of trust is perceptible in the body language, furtive eye contact and hesitations as to who will step off the sidewalk so we can avoid each other. A behaviour unimaginable not too long ago. My first few outings, I would half-jokingly refer to potential other humans to be encountered as zombies. It was and still is not funny.

Existential and phenomenological philosophies have explored the problem of the Other and how the subject relates to the Other it encounters. I relate to the Other in my encounters with them in the world. I encounter self-contained conscious bodies and enter an intersubjective relation in which I am acknowledged as an Other consciousness while acknowledging the other as an embodied consciousness. That relation can be positive and enhance one's existential and phenomenological experiences or it can be fraught with ambiguity. Worst, it can also be hellish, as famously theorized by Jean-Paul Sartre in his early philosophy. In his view, rather than acknowledging me as a free consciousness, the Other objectifies me in their own appropriation of the world and this experience is lived as conflictual. 'Hell is other people!' is a claim Garcin makes in the play *No Exit*. They are such because they make him into a coward; they determine that the essence of his being is to have been a coward. As a free subjectivity, Garcin experiences this objectification and essentialization of his being in a negative way. As interesting as they might be, the existentialist/phenomenological analyses of the relation to the Other tend to focus on the intersubjective realm and how one subjectively experiences being in the presence of others. While thinkers like Beauvoir and Merleau-Ponty provided key insights on embodiment and how the body one is matters in shaping one's subjective experiences, the focus still remained on the latter.[22] As such, they fail to capture the extent to which our material entanglements matter just as much, if not more, than our subjective ones. Heirs of humanist thinking, they still think in dualist terms and privilege the mind over the body. For posthumanist material feminist thinking, hell is Other people – or rather Other beings are – and for rather different reasons. Our materially entangled beings are fundamentally vulnerable, and our relations may enhance our thriving or radically impede it.

In *The Ecological Thought*, Timothy Morton puts forward the notion of the 'strange stranger'. He explains: 'The strange stranger is not just the "other" – the "self" is this other. Since there is no (solid, lasting, independent, single) self, we are the strange stranger: "I is another".'[23] Morton speaks of all creatures as monsters, 'they are chimeras, made from pieces of other creatures. The strange stranger is strange to herself, or himself, or itself'.[24] To experience oneself as strange is what the pandemic has afforded us. It has shed light on our material entanglements, on ourselves as porous assemblages, on our limited and entangled agentic capacity. Philippopoulos-Mihalopoulos's description, grounded in a Spinozist stance, focuses on the collective in an evocative manner. He says, 'We are all collective bodies, with histories and futures, bacteria and mites, mobile phones and prostheses, moving along like clouds of affects, emanating presence and attachments, fears and desires. . . . We are all collective bodies leading collective lives with other collective bodies.'[25] This means, for him, that in pandemic times, we must embrace an ethics of withdrawal. 'Covid demands an ethics of self-positioning (physically and at the same time ethically) in relation to other bodies, of removing ourselves from the collectivity that we might harm despite our best intentions, of thinking beyond the edge of our skin.' Or, I would add, through our skin as porous membrane. This amounts to the realization of the manifold entanglements I have been speaking about and the gestures we can make to communicate that we understand our entangled nature and seek to engage with others in a way that acknowledges the threat we or they may pose. As Philippopoulos-Mihalopoulos further claims, 'The Virocene, a taste of which we have been having with the various viruses of the past few years, throws into relief the ultimate continuum amongst the various bodies, whether this continuum is desired or undesired.'[26]

As materially entangled beings, we are also entangled with various spatio-temporal affects. This leads me to question: Is there a season better than another to elicit a pandemic response in the mode of an ethics of withdrawal? Are there times – and locations – better suited for retreating to ourselves, in our private indoor spaces? Over the summer, we have complained that people were taking fewer and fewer precautions. The pandemic hit North America at the tail end of winter. Spring was cool and slow to onset. Three months into physical distancing and various orders of isolation, quarantine-fatigue set in. At the same time, spring bloomed, followed by a hot jump into summer. Nature was lush and life was bursting. How could the world be ending when flowers grow, bushes hustle and birds and critters multiply? This was our affective experience of the world; one we are familiar with and long for after cold winters. Spring is usually the time we drop multilayered clothing and expose our skins to the elements. Spring fever is an embrace of the possibility of exposing oneself. I – along with many others, I presume – experienced this spring/summer with a major cognitive dissonance. Nature was giving us every visible signal that things are good, and life continues. Moreover, with humans isolating and working from home, nature has been even more prolific thanks to reduced pollution levels and empty streets. Non-human animals have ventured into urban spaces, making themselves more visible. All of these signals were going against the message we were receiving via our news feeds that we were faced with a biothreat. The bios we were encountering – or more properly zoe, life itself[27] – gave every indication of thriving. It was difficult to reconcile this affect with the need to continue to withdraw. The affective charge was such that it was difficult to maintain the heightened level of caution practised until then and tempting to revert to our comforting humanist delusion.

There are great disparities in the ways in which the pandemic is experienced across the world. I acknowledge that I am writing and thinking about it from a position of privilege as a homeowner who had the space and resources to follow recommendations and guidelines. With that said, the affective experience as it relates to the pandemic is worth pondering. Moving from one country to another, as I had to while working on this paper, made me experience yet another dissonance in how to relate to the threat posed by the virus. Moving from Canada to Finland was the equivalent of time travelling, and not just because of time zones (Finland is 'ahead' of Southern Ontario by seven hours). But for a Canadian who was slowly moving through the phases of reopening after a few months of physical/social distancing and experiencing public debates at home over mask wearing and its efficacy – debates triggered by a proliferation of mandatory mask-wearing measures put in place by local and regional governments and the resistance put forward by various anti-maskers and conspiracists[28] – arriving in Finland generated a dissonance. This was magnified by the clash of two experiences. Travelling from Toronto to Helsinki via Paris meant a total of twenty hours of travel with a mask on and in the company of others who were all wearing masks, with some airport and flight staff also wearing gloves. This was the longest I wore a mask ever; my previous experiences having been limited to contexts such as grocery shopping or medical appointments. The masked travel experience reinforced the sense of risk and the sense of the virulence of the pandemic and the threat posed by the virus which any of these others I was travelling with could be carrying (I knew I was not a carrier since I tested negative right before travelling). However, the minute I was riding the taxi from the Helsinki airport to my apartment, masks disappeared. The driver was not wearing one (nor were any of his colleagues at the taxi station at the airport). I only spotted one cyclist with a mask even though there were many pedestrians and other cyclists, as well as motorists. Very few people wear masks and even on public transportation not everyone does. Some measures are still in place. One can see traces such as the plexiglass panes at cash registers in stores and the now ubiquitous hand sanitizer dispensers. The University of Helsinki has pushed back resuming normal operations due to a resurgence of cases in the country (and mostly in the region of Helsinki), which might be the sign of the looming second wave, but otherwise everything looks very normal. For a Canadian, propelled within twenty-four hours from a context in which measures are still very strict because Canada is still dealing with a strong first wave, to a context in which the first wave is behind, was grounds for yet another sudden shift in the affective fabric of my being. One thing this virus has taught us is that things can change very quickly, and so it is quite possible that by the time this chapter is in print another set of experiences will have taken place.[29] But what I want to reflect on here is how the affective fabric of existence is altered for any single individual experiencing the pandemic as a posthuman subject done and undone by its affective relations. To exist in a world where masks are worn, restrictions are in place and visible and the news is saturated with numbers of cases and deaths is completely different from moving about in a world where those seem to have disappeared. Granted my lack of exposure to Finnish news contributes to that. My news feeds are mostly populated by news from Canada and North America, with the odd item about Europe and the world, with regards to Covid-19. Relocating, and its affective fabric, can quickly give the false sense that one has either moved back in time to a pre-pandemic world or forward in time to a post-pandemic world. In either case, one need not worry. This, as mentioned, is a false sense of safety, of a return to 'normal' in which one ignores one's multiple entanglements and the vulnerability and risks that come with them. These are shifts that beings come to negotiate as they go about through the world as the materially entangled beings they are.

There is no doubt that the Covid-19 pandemic has caused massive manifold disruption likely to continue to unfold for a long while. We have come to fear the Other – the virus, our body as potential carrier, the Other human who might be a carrier – and yet we have also come to long for the Other as we have been forced to isolate. A recurring theme in discussions about the experience of the pandemic was the longing for a return to normal, all the while acknowledging that this may be impossible or even undesirable. Indeed, many have pointed out that the 'normal' was problematic in many ways and the pandemic provided us with a magnifying lens to recognize those problems as underprivileged individuals suffering much greater hardship than others. This being the case, a return to normal would mean a return to a world in which class, race, geographical location, etc. determine one's thriving. This is not acceptable. This is yet another way in which the pandemic experience has taught us to recognize our entanglements. What happens at the other end of the world is happening to me. Having to interiorize the idea that we too are vulnerable beings, that a story of deadly disease is not only about others[30] – which is how North Americans and Europeans typically think about epidemics such as Ebola, zika or dengue – comes as a shock.

As Molly Andrews argues, we are now faced with the challenge of reconstructing the Other and the added challenge of seeing them and ourselves as vulnerable.[31] This involves reimagining who we are, as argued by Solnit.[32] The shock of the pandemic has brought about a high degree of defamiliarization, one to which we have responded in various ways. But, as Alberto Godioli argues, this provides us with an occasion to critically reflect on 'normality', on those things we took for granted and no longer can.[33] While this opens up a vast array of questions and potential answers, I would offer, as a means to conclude my reflections on the pandemic and how we have discovered ourselves, that 'normal' is what we make it. We have now understood that the autonomous exceptional subject of humanism was a delusion and that we in fact are and always were posthuman, namely radically materially entangled, open to all the Other beings and the world upon whom we depend for our thriving but through whom we are also vulnerable. This recognition shatters how we have conceived of ourselves and of others, and we need to rebuild a trustful relation that rests upon the acceptance and active embrace of our vulnerability. This is no easy task, but one that can open up brighter future

Notes

1 Andreas Philippopoulos-Mihalopoulos, 'Covid: The Ethical Disease', *Critical Legal Thinking*, 13 March 2020 (https://criticallegalthinking.com/2020/03/13/covid-the-ethical-disease/ accessed 11 May 2020).

2 Molly Andrews, 'The COVID-19 Pandemic and the Failure of Narrative Imagination', *European NetIAS Lecture*, 24 June 2020 (https://www.youtube.com/watch?v=GW7J9VjXAe0 accessed 22 August 2020).

3 Alberto Godioli, 'Stranger Things: Defamiliarization in the Time of COVID-19' Cultures of the Crisis series, 8 May 2020 (https://www.youtube.com/watch?v=wTQmKJcKnpo accessed 22 August 2020).

4 Rebecca Solnit, '"The impossible has already happened": what coronavirus can teach us about hope', *The Guardian*, 7 April 2020.

5 Kim Stanley Robinson, 'The Coronavirus is Rewriting our Imaginations', *The New Yorker*, 1 May 2020 (https://www.newyorker.com/culture/annals-of-inquiry/the-coronavirus-and-our-future accessed 5 May 2020).

6 Achille Mbembe, 'The Universal Right to Breathe', *In the Moment*, 13 April 2020 (https://critinq.wordpress.com/2020/04/13/the-universal-right-to-breathe/ accessed 5 May 2020).

7 This also allows me to retain a space for the experience of consciousness and subjectivity while displacing it from the center of human existence and radically entangling it in its manifold relations. Thereby, a space, albeit minimal, is provided for human agency and responsibility. This has been a problem faced by material feminists: the common critique leveled against their position is that their emphasis on materiality evacuates a notion of the subject to whom we could ascribe ethical and political responsibility. My claim, instead, is that it is still possible – and necessary – to ascribe such responsibility to the human all the while recognizing that human agency is always and ever entangled materially and subjectively and thus much less potent than the history of philosophy has wanted it to be.

8 Samantha Frost, *Biocultural Creatures. Toward a New Theory of the Human* (Durham and London: Duke University Press, 2016), 54–5.

9 See Rosi Braidotti, *Posthuman Knowledge* (Cambridge: Polity, 2019). I have started to delineate the contours of posthuman vulnerability in a previous piece (See Christine Daigle 'Vulner – abilité posthumaine', *Con Texte. Notes and Inquiries. An Interdisciplinary Journal About Text*, Special Issue on 'Posthumanism: Current State

and Future Research', 2, no. 2 (2018): 9–13). In an article co-authored with Ilaria Santoemma, I explore the different aspects of posthuman vulnerability, working with the frame proposed by Braidotti. See in preparation.

10 For the concept of 'mangle', see Susan Hekman, *The Feminine Subject* (Cambridge: Polity Press, 2014); the concept of 'transcorporeal being', see Stacy Alaimo, *Exposed. Environmental Politics and Pleasures in Posthuman Times* (Minneapolis and London: University of Minnesota Press, 2016); the concept of 'biocultural creature', see Samantha Frost, *Biocultural Creatures. Toward a New Theory of the Human* (Durham and London: Duke University Press, 2016); and the concept of the 'cyborg', see Donna Haraway, 'A Cyborg Manifesto: Science Technology, and Socialist-Feminism in the Late Twentieth Century', in *Simians, Cyborgs and Women: The Reinvention of Nature* (New York: Routledge, 1991): 149–81.

11 See Jane Bennett, *Vibrant Matter. A Political Ecology of Things* (Durham: Duke University Press, 2010); Karen Barad, *Meeting the Universe Halfway: Quantum Physics and the Entanglement of Matter and Meaning* (Durham: Duke University Press, 2007); and Samantha Frost, *Biocultural Creatures. Toward a New Theory of the Human* (Durham and London: Duke University Press, 2016).

12 Barad, *Meeting the Universe Halfway*, 141.

13 Bennett, *Vibrant Matter*, 29.

14 Ibid., 32.

15 Ibid., 33.

16 The war language adopted to speak of the virus in the pandemic is problematic and using phrases such as 'defeating the virus' or 'the invisible enemy' which I used earlier is common but posits the human as way more powerful than it actually is.

17 One can consult the guidelines here: https://www.ontario.ca/page/create-social-circle-during-covid-19. These have been updated since then but the population continues to complain about the lack of clarity.

18 The rise to prominence that conspiracy theories of all kinds have gained, and the speed at which they are spreading, is quite alarming. I do not claim to know the psychology behind it and what attracts certain individuals to them. But I would claim that faced with the sudden realization that one is not the powerful agent one thought oneself to be, this might be a way to try and reclaim that agency rather than recognize one's own vulnerability. But it would require a whole study to ground my claim.

19 This gesture of care is part of an ethics of withdrawal as proposed by Philippopoulos-Mihalopoulos (see his 'Covid: The Ethical Disease', *Critical Legal Thinking*, March 13, 2020 (https://criticallegalthinking.com/2020/03/13/covid-the-ethical-disease/ accessed May 11, 2020). More on this later.

20 It has been interesting to see that rates of infection to other viruses such as the flu have diminished significantly in those countries where mask wearing has been

widely adopted. See https://www.wsj.com/articles/covid-19-measures-have-all-but-wiped-out-the-flu-in-the-southern-hemisphere-11595440682.

21 It should be noted that frontline workers such as hospital personnel, grocery store clerks and public transit operators were very keenly made aware of their own vulnerability when their livelihood was tied to exposing themselves to threat. They did not have the luxury of quarantining and working from home. That many did not have access to the protective gear they needed to carry on their tasks pointed to a fundamental flaw in our social fabric: their work is deemed essential, but their lives are not.

22 In an article on Beauvoir as precursor of posthumanism, I have argued that her unprecedented attention to biology, the body, sex and gender, and situation opens the way for the development of posthumanist material feminist views and a rejection of the humanist subject. See Daigle 2020.

23 Timothy Morton, *The Ecological Thought* (Cambridge, MA, and London: Harvard University Press, 2010), 87. The latter is taken from Arthur Rimbaud's letter to Georges Izambard from 13 May 1871 in which he says: 'C'est faux de dire: Je pense: On devrait dire: On me pense. – Pardon du jeu de mots. – Je est un autre' (Arthur Rimbaud, *Complete Works, Selected Letters. A Bilingual Edition*, Trans. Wallace Fowlie (Chicago and London: The University of Chicago Press, 2005), 370). The last sentence is translated as 'I is someone else' (Ibid., 371), but it would be more precise to translate as 'I is an other', to which Morton comes close here.

24 Morton, *The Ecological Thought*, 66.

25 Andreas Philippopoulos-Mihalopoulos, 'Covid: the ethical disease', *Critical Legal Thinking*, 13 March 2020 (https://criticallegalthinking.com/2020/03/13/covid-the-ethical-disease/ accessed 11 May 2020).

26 Andreas Philippopoulos-Mihalopoulos, 'Covid: the ethical disease', *Critical Legal Thinking*, 13 March 2020 (https://criticallegalthinking.com/2020/03/13/covid-the-ethical-disease/ accessed May 11, 2020). In the midst of all the discussions occurring around the term 'Anthropocene' which has been chosen to refer to our new geological epoch and is meant to be evocative of the hubristic and damaging agentic capacity exercised by humans over centuries, the proposed 'virocene' shifts things around in a provocative way. What if indeed the agentic capacity of a virus such as SARS-CoV-2 far exceeded that of humans, individually and collectively, and contributed to shape our existence and force us to be more humble in our approach to other beings?

27 For a discussion of zoe and a distinction with bios see Rosi Braidotti, *The Posthuman* (Cambridge: Polity, 2013) and *Posthuman Knowledge* (Cambridge: Polity, 2019).

28 At the time of writing this piece, the provincial government was still only recommending that individuals wear masks.

29 Indeed, the recent surge in cases in Finland, albeit very small compared to other countries, is leading authorities to reinstate border restrictions with some countries with whom they had reopened earlier in the summer as well as issue strong recommendations for mask wearing supported by distribution of free masks to those in need and tax deduction for the purchase of masks for others. To support this recommendation, the national railway company adorned the famous stonemason sculptures of the Helsinki train station with masks (https://www. helsinkitimes.fi/finland/news-in-brief/17968-in-pictures-helsinki-railway-station-gets-a-mask-friendly-makeover.html).

30 Molly Andrews, 'The COVID-19 pandemic and the failure of narrative imagination' European NetIAS Lecture, 24 June 2020. (https://www.youtube.com/watch?v=GW7J9VjXAe0 accessed 22 August 2020).

31 Molly Andrews, 'The COVID-19 pandemic and the failure of narrative imagination' European NetIAS Lecture, 24 June 2020. (https://www.youtube.com/watch?v=GW7J9VjXAe0 accessed 22 August 2020).

32 Rebecca Solnit, '"The Impossible Has Already Happened": What Coronavirus Can Teach Us About Hope', *The Guardian*, 7 April 2020.

33 Alberto Godioli, 'Stranger Things: Defamiliarization in the Time of COVID-19' Cultures of the Crisis series, 8 May 2020 (https://www.youtube.com/watch?v=wTQmKJcKnpo accessed 22 August 2020).

2

'Life is obviously not easy to define'

Viral politics and dynamic patterning in Susanne K. Langer's philosophies of art and life

Iris van der Tuin

In this chapter I work with Volume One of the interdisciplinary trilogy *Mind: An Essay on Human Feeling* written by the American philosopher Susanne K. Langer (1895–1985).[1] Langer's earlier monograph *Philosophy in a New Key: A Study in the Symbolism of Reason, Rite and Art* was a Harvard University Press bestseller from its publication in 1942 onward,[2] and her work was widely read by college students in the 1960s.[3] In 1953, Langer's monograph *Feeling and Form: A Theory of Art* was published,[4] a monograph that was developed from *Philosophy in a New Key*. The work gradually fell off the canon though, with Langer's readership growing into a small number of dedicated and committed readers in the years after Langer's death. Langer is back to getting a larger following today.[5] I would argue that the three *Mind* volumes – first published in 1967, 1972 and 1982 respectively – are the pinnacle of Langer's philosophical career. They use 'human feeling' as the common ground from which to integrate knowledge and insights from a great many disciplines and fields of study covering the full academic spectrum.[6] According to the logic of integrative interdisciplinarity, the three hefty volumes, when taken together, form a more comprehensive understanding of 'mind'. *Mind*'s first volume engages primarily with biology, physiology, genetics and the theory of evolution. In this chapter, I zoom in on Langer's work on the virus as a 'borderline case', in her language, or as a 'boundary object', in the language of American feminist, theorist and historian of science and technology, Donna Haraway,[7] as a launch pad to expose how, as per the project of this twenty-first-century post-pandemic book, art has a prefigurative capacity for exposing and understanding forms of sociability and of life. After all, engagement with the biological sciences and with psychology is taken on in *Mind I* from the sole vantage point of the theory of art as it was expressed in *Feeling and Form*.

In the chapter, I do not argue that Langer's philosophy is posthumanist. I will, however, hint at how her unique and innovative work, the starting point of which are the expressions of *human* feeling as *living* forms, can only be fully appreciated with the benefit of hindsight. About viruses and all other borderline cases, Langer ends up saying that they are characterized by an interplay of 'individuation' and 'involvement'. The former is a concept that we nowadays ascribe to the French philosophers Gilbert Simondon (1924–89) and Gilles Deleuze (1925–95). The latter captures a process that we, today, describe with a word such as 'entanglement', from American theoretical particle physicist and feminist theorist Karen Barad or, alternatively, with the word 'assemblage' – in French '*agencement*' – from Deleuze and his co-author, the French psychiatrist, philosopher and activist Félix Guattari.[8] The following quotation from *Mind I* provides a first introduction to both Langer's use of art as steppingstone and the intricate dynamics of individuating-in-involvement:

> Though we have no physical model of [the] endless rhythm of individuation and involvement, we do have its image in the world of art, most purely in the dance; for this dialectic of vital continuity is the very essence of the classical ballet. Think only of that perfect example, *Les Sylphides*: individual figures emerge and submerge, *pas de deux* develop and melt back into the web of choric movement, divisions for only to close over what was, for a moment, the path of an advancing stream. And not only in dance but in all choric works of wide range this largest rhythm appears: the 'tide in the affairs of men, that, taken at the full, leads on to fortune'; or, in the highest musical form that has yet been developed, the sonata, which is choric in structure whether scored for the keyboard or the full symphonic orchestra: a scarcely discernible new theme may begin a history, but even if it rises to apotheosis it can never transcend the stream, which may finally integrate with another individual form or even simply engulf it.[9]

It is my goal in this chapter to unpack the 'politics' of the virus as well as dynamic patterning per se in a series of close readings of relevant sections from Langer's *Mind I* as well as of auxiliary material that gives insight into the development of the trilogy and its philosophical propositions.

Susanne Langer started out as a logician studying for her BA (1916–20), her master's degree (1922–4) and her PhD (1924–6) first under Ukrainian-American logician Henry M. Sheffer (1882–1964) and later under English mathematician and philosopher Alfred North Whitehead (1861–1947). She received her degrees at Radcliffe College, then the women's annex of Harvard University in Cambridge, Massachusetts. In spite of her start as a logician,[10] Langer became established for her philosophy of art, particularly as the result of the publication of *Feeling and Form*. Following a career of teaching philosophy at various colleges and universities in the United States, Langer received a grant from the Edgar J. Kaufmann Charitable Trust of Pittsburgh, Pennsylvania, in 1956 in order to do the full-time research for what eventually became the *Mind* trilogy.[11] This trilogy was developed from *Feeling and Form*, but it is a masterpiece in the philosophy of life.

Langer wrote the three volumes of *Mind* in Old Lyme, Connecticut, where she had bought a cottage halfway through the 1950s. Prior to that, Langer lived in Cambridge for her education at Radcliffe and the first years of married life (1916–21, 1922–3); in Vienna, Austria, for an exchange (1921–2); in Worcester, MA, for her husband's first job at Clark University (1923–7); and again in Cambridge when William Langer (1896–1977), a Harvard alumnus, returned to Harvard after his time at Clark for a tenured position in the Department of History. Susanne returned to the city of her birth – New York – after their divorce in 1942, a painful event that coincided with the publication of *Philosophy in a New Key*.[12] Before the divorce and while raising two sons with the help of a nanny, Langer worked as a tutor at Radcliffe for fifteen years; after the divorce, she took on the teaching positions at different academic institutions both in New York City and elsewhere in order to finally land a full professorship at Connecticut College in New London, CT, in 1954: that is, by the time she was fifty-nine years old. By 1962, and as a result of the long-term Kaufmann grant getting more generous over time, she was able to step down from all administrative duties and from teaching in order to devote herself fully to reading and writing for *Mind* in both Old Lyme and in the woods of Ulster County, NY, where Langer owned a cabin around the town of Hurley.

Mind I is a volume with two interconnected goals. The first goal is to read biological knowledge and insights rigorously; the second is to establish the study of psychology on its own terms, not on terms of either biology or of the well-established disciplines of physics and chemistry. It is the project of *Mind I* to demonstrate how 'the artistic semblance of life' opens up to a 'holistic symbol' or a 'synoptic view' that biology studies parts of already, which psychology has not yet gotten around to, and for which physics and chemistry do not offer the overarching model.[13] In later volumes of the trilogy, Langer takes the more comprehensive understanding of 'mind' gradually as the starting point for organizing disciplinary materials ranging from anthropology and archaeology to computer science and mathematics. This is how Langer formulates the genesis and gist of her philosophical undertaking in the introduction to *Mind I*:

> there is a value in images quite apart from religious or emotional purposes: they, and they only, originally made us aware of the wholeness and over-all form of entities, acts and facts in the world; and little though we know it, only an image can hold us to a conception of a total phenomenon, against which we can measure the adequacy of the scientific terms wherewith we describe it. [...] It was the discovery that works of art are images of the forms of feeling, and that their expressiveness can rise to the presentation of all aspects of mind and human personality, which led me to the present undertaking of constructing a biological theory of feeling that should logically lead to an adequate concept of mind, with all that the possession of mind implies.[14]

The very basis of this discovery, as Langer explicitly calls it, is formed by the implications of the insight from *Feeling and Form* that works of art are expressive of feeling, objective and living forms. A lucid formulation of both the nature of works of art and the relation between *Feeling and Form* and the *Mind* trilogy can be found in an undated composition titled 'Philosophical Implications of the Theory of Art Contained in *Feeling and Form*' that can be consulted in Houghton Library of Harvard as it has been archived there as part of the Susanne Langer Papers, a 30-box, 38.75-linear-feet archive gifted to the library by Leonard C. R. Langer (1922–2009), Susanne's eldest son, in the period 1985–95. On four single-space typed pages, Langer provides a forward-looking summary of the approach to *Mind* (unbeknownst of the fact of it ending up being a trilogy), its total project, naturalist premises and her then-immediate reading-and-writing project. She writes under the subheading 'The Approach: From Art to Nature':

> We have come to regard 'life', today, as [...] a metabolic process, and consequently can make statements about it in exact chemical and physical terms. Under the new rubrics gathered from philosophy of art, we may view the 'life of the mind' as a process of essentially similar form. The fundamental rhythms of mentality and feeling are presented, not only in a vague way, but in amazing detail, by the fundamental rhythms of art. The inviolable character of the art symbol bespeaks the inviolability of organic structure. Art makes its abstraction not from rudimentary forms, as science tends to do, but from the highest efflorescence [*sic*] of life, the dynamic patterns of feeling and thought. But progressive study of art forms shows that these highest phenomena contain and express the entire gamut of vital events down to the basic anabolism and catabolism of physical organic existence.[15]

This summary is repeated in a more condensed form and from a slightly different angle in *Mind I* itself, where Langer writes:

> The fact that expressive form is always organic or 'living' form made the biological foundation of feeling probable. In the artist's projection, feeling is a heightened form of life; so any work expressing felt tensions, rhythms and activities expresses their unfelt substructure of vital processes, which is the whole of life.[16]

In both quotations we see immediately that Langer's philosophies of art and life are intimately connected. The premises are naturalist, indeed, and the very insight of expressive-form-as-living-form must be taken very seriously, albeit that the word 'living' is at times scare-quoted.[17]

Let me continue with a card from Langer's card-index file, a file that Langer worked on and used from 1916 until she had to give up philosophy entirely for reasons of growing blindness and old age.[18] The file consists of 37 iron drawers and roughly 25,000 paper cards, and can currently be consulted at the Houghton.[19] The card that I wish to single out here provides a view of the typically Langerian entanglement of art and life, and their philosophies, in a vignette about a motif that was found, first, in a tree living and dying across the road from the house where Langer lived in either Old Lyme or around Hurley and, second, as the Indian stupa. She used this vignette to muse on 'clues to feeling in art', that is, on 'what is expressed' by works of art.[20] The card reads verbatim as follows:

> Note – clues to feeling in art [↵ Return] Across the road from my house is a pile-up of vegetation: a red cedar completely overgrown with vines. The deepest mass of them is honeysuckle, at present dark green; over that, climbing more on the honeysuckle than on the cedar (though of course on both), a woodbine that has gone to the very top and turned down over itself, hanging in a curtain over the whole. In a few places, golden green bunches of bittersweet show through the dark red woodbine against the green honeysuckle and slightly different green bits of cedar that one can see. In front of the tree, on the wall, is a mass of poison ivy that sends its trailers to the foot of the tree and up the trunk inside the dead structure of choked twigs. This is not visible from outside at all. The whole setup has the form of an Indian stupa, *and the profusion of surface forms is reminiscent of Indian sculpture.* [↵ Return] The stupa is a fairly obvious phallic symbol. The cedar is a 'natural symbol', phallic in total form, but not only a symbol of generation; it also expresses the profusion of competing lives – overpopulation without the poverty we usually associate with it. It is overpopulation with immense wealth of living form, spreading all sorts of shapes over the exterior of the tree. The tree, of course, is dying. [↵ Return] Has the Indian stupa with

its mass of composed forms covering every inch of it a similar motif? What is the inside of it like? – *Usually empty, dead.* [↵ Return] India has lived so long with its vast population that the popular mind is shaped by it, and feeling has incorporated it. Art, the composition and expression of feeling, naturally reflects it. It has become the basis of style. *To us, who find it new, it is terrifying.* [↵ Return] *Motif is properly the localization of forms of feeling in actuality.* Many actual feelings are similar in form but quite different in value, even to the extent of being sad or happy.* Motif is their locus. [↵ Return] In good art, the play of values is greater than words make it. There is sense within sense. [↵ Return] All symbolism in art should be enrichment of the art symbol. [↵ Return] *See Ivy Campbell-Fisher.*[21]

Judging by the placement of this card in the file, safely stored in acid-free paper boxes in Houghton Library, it was used for the writing of chapter 4 of *Mind I*, titled 'The Projection of Feeling in Art'. Reading the card, we encounter a motif articulating phallicism in a combination of generation – which is a duplex concept consisting of actualized generational classes and generativity per se – and competition – representing here not poverty, but instead abundance. Competition comes to the fore as a duplex notion too as it ambiguously combines 'overpopulation with immense wealth of living form' that suffocates the cedar, just like the stupa that is, while abundantly decorated on the outside, regarded as 'empty, dead' inside. Langer reads the overgrown cedar (an actual living form studied by biologists) through the decorated stupa (an actual phenomenon of feeling expressed by artists and craftspeople and serving religious or emotional purposes) as a way to differentiate, not between actualized values such as sadness and happiness, but between such values and what could be called, for the time being and with the benefit of hindsight stemming from years of studying poststructuralist and new-materialist theories, 'valuing'. I consider Langer's combined philosophy of art and life a new-materialist theory *avant la lettre*, given that she works from a naturalist premise, and I read her as poststructuralist *avant la lettre* based on the following methodological choice she made: 'the principle that working concepts must be functional rather than substantive'.[22] The combination of new materialism and poststructuralism, here, is predicated on their shared non-reductive or inclusive premises that prefer to *study* instead of *presume to know* the workings of complex material, discursive and material-discursive apparatuses and systems across and within the spectrum of natures and cultures.[23] Admittedly, this combination of poststructuralism and new materialism may sound counterintuitive for some scholars.

Langer writes about 'valuing' in chapter 4 as part of a movement of taking the work of French writer Philippe Fauré-Fremiet (1889–1954) to the limit by reflecting on how 'works of art exhibit the morphology of feeling'. She continues: 'the matrix of a work is always an idea, a single idea whereof all apparently separate ideas in the work are further articulations ([art theorist Gustav] Britsch [(1879–1923)] would say, further differentiations). [. . .] In a work of art, the idea has to be embodied in a perceptible creation, worked out coherently as an organic form.'[24] Valuing, here, points at a threshold; it is the threshold between biology and psychology. How can the leap to such an abstract claim be made following a discussion of cedars and stupas, and of the work of a writer, Fauré-Fremiet, whose embryonal formulation of the threshold must be pushed beyond its terms?

In *Mind I*, the topic of valuing materializes in a discussion of respectively ordinary (i.e. everyday) projections of feeling that are incoherent and, let's say, free-floating, the limited and limiting power of discursive expression (literal language meant for direct communication), and the matrixial projection of feeling in art. Langer writes:

> The tensions of living constitute an organic pattern, and those which rise to a psychical phase – that is to say, felt tensions – can be coherently apprehended only in so far as their whole non-psychical organic background is implied by their appearance. That is why every work of art has to seem 'organic' and 'living' to be expressive of feeling. Its elements, like the dynamic elements in nature, have no existence apart from situations in which they arise; but where they exist they tend to figure in many relationships at once. . . . This multiplicity of functions is reflected in any symbolic form that can express the morphology of feeling [. . .] the non-discursive structure of artistic presentation prevents art from ever being a symbolism which can be manipulated by general rules to make significant compositions, but at the same time is the secret of its great potentiality.[25]

Valuing thus points at the shift from every day and discursive entities (the one, the many; possibly incoherent) to the artistic event (unity in multiplicity). The point, also to be found in poststructuralist philosophy and new-materialist theory, is that events can explain entities (as actualizations, articulations, differentiations), whereas entities never accrue to the level of the explanatory event.[26] In Langer's comprehensive formulation in the introduction to *Mind I*, this discussion, abstracted again, comes down to the following theorization:

> If vitality and feeling are conceived in this way there is no sharp break, let alone metaphysical gap, between physical and mental realities, yet there are thresholds

where mentality begins, and especially where human mentality transcends the animal level, and mind, *sensu strictu*, emerges.[27]

Whereas there exist entity-like physical and mental realities, we must not understand them as different in kind. We must say, though, that human and animal mentalities differ in degree. A similar threshold exists between the world of plants and the animal kingdom. The important point here is that the index card about a tree and the stupa opens a discussion about the virus, an *actual* living form that is *messier* than plant, animal and human entities and which is akin, perhaps, not to the cedar from the vignette above, but rather to its creeping vines.

Attention is paid to viruses in chapters 8 ('The Act Concept and Its Principle Derivatives') and 9 ('On Individuation and Involvement') of *Mind I*. In chapter 8, the virus is explicitly named a 'borderline case',[28] a characterization that is continued in chapter 9 where Langer mentions in passing that 'the status of viruses is uncertain'.[29] In both cases, Langer footnotes the work she builds on by referencing American geneticist and co-winner of a Nobel Prize in 1958, George W. Beadle (1903–89); Australian virologist and winner of a 1960 Nobel Prize, Frank Macfarlane Burnet (1899–1985); American microbiologist and virologist Lloyd M. Kozloff (1923–2012); and American biophysicist and virologist Robley C. Williams (1908–95).[30] The virus pops up immediately upon turning attention away from art and towards life itself: that is, upon '[t]urning from the symbolic presentation of life to the phenomena of its actual occurrence'.[31] In this move towards literature that is unconventional for the traditional humanist, a literature that is meticulously referenced, summarized and cross-referenced in her card-index file and masterfully integrated in the *Mind* trilogy itself, Langer shows herself struck, first, by the differences between living and non-living entities, and between animate and inanimate nature, and, second, by the difficulties of maintaining established biological differentiations. She writes:

> upon closer inspection, the boundaries between those two categories appear less and less sharp; there are borderline cases, such as viruses, which are hard to assign to one or the other, [. . .] 'Life' is obviously not easy to define.[32]

And, indeed, viruses defy classification as they neither obey the laws of mechanics, as the non-living and the inanimate do, nor behave in wholly incalculable and unpredictable ways like the living and animate. This insight brings Langer to the realization 'that all [biological] categories tend to have imperfect boundaries'[33] and to developing the concept of 'acts' with which she sets out to deal 'not [. . .] with material parts of a living thing, but with elements [that is, acts] in the continuum of life'.[34] These acts are Langer's way of philosophically 'approaching living form in nature' from the situated event upward, downward or sidewise, and on all levels of life's complexity. Given the project of also providing the grounds for a psychology on its own terms, and approaching the forms of mental life philosophically, it is important for us readers of Langer's work to immediately realize that *Mind I*'s subsequent chapter (chapter 9) opens with a discussion of acts-without-agents, driven instead by 'vital activity' or 'agency'.[35] One could summarize that for avant-gardist Langer, presupposing an entity-like doer behind a consciously executed deed is too easy a theory. Rather, deeds are eventful.

The lines from chapter 8 that follow the introduction of the 'act' concept form the very beginning of Langer's unique philosophy of life developed from her philosophy of art:

> [Natural] events arise where there is already some fairly constant movement going on. They normally show a phase of acceleration, or intensification of a distinguishable dynamic pattern, then reach a point at which the pattern changes, whereupon the movement subsides. That point of general change is the consummation of the act. The subsequent phase, the conclusion or cadence, is the most variable aspect of the total process.[36]

Langer then lists the varieties of change that may occur (e.g. gradual or abrupt) as well as the possible relations among acts (e.g. horizontal or vertical) thus keeping activity ontologically prior. She continues as follows by very precisely formulating the crossing of the threshold towards human mentality:

> These and many other relations among acts form the intricate dynamism of life which becomes more and more articulated, more and more concentrated and intense, until some of its elements attain the phase of being felt, which I have termed 'psychical', and the domain of psychology develops within the wider reals of biology, especially zoology.[37]

Chapter 9 then brings in 'individuation' and 'involvement' as the two mirroring concepts with which a philosophical approach to psychology can materialize. As a true avant-gardist thinker, Langer, *as if* inspired by posthumanism and anti-anthropocentrism, develops a theory of mental or psychical reality from within, and as part of, physical or biological/zoological reality.[38] Individuation is the functional notion that conceptualizes the process of events producing entities, all occurring in a series of differentiating acts motivated by a 'vital situation': that is, 'a phase of the total life, the matrix from which motivation constantly arises'.[39] Involvement is the relational function.[40] Individuation and involvement are complexly interconnected, and their interconnecting is at work almost everywhere in life.

Let us now return to borderline cases, because the fact that the borderline case of the virus defies standard biological classification got Langer going in the first place. Certainly, these cases are *involved* as Langer mentions the 'physically connected populations (plants conjoined in rhizoids, stolons or rhizophores, colonial animals by a coenoecium or a coenosarc)' as exemplary for involvement in chapter 9, and these populations (the plant populations) are indeed the vines from the index card discussed earlier.[41] Involvement is how borderline cases work: relationally. Langer also writes about the case of the parasite: 'what makes the parasite an organism in an environment is that it has fine control of the exchange of matter, whereas the organism it has invaded has, with respect to it, only gross or indefinite control of the contract transaction.'[42] The relevant point here, for a precise philosophy of life as well as for a biology and a psychology established on their own terms, is that as organisms-in-environments that engage in a process of individuating-in-involvement, borderline cases such as parasites and viruses and, indeed, creeping vines too, contribute to the ongoing 'patterning' (my word) that is life itself. Langer writes:

> An organism is a continuous dynamism, a pattern of activity, basically electrochemical, but capable also of large, concerted forms of action with further principles of organization. [. . .] The organism, *in toto* and in every one of its parts, has to 'keep going'. Every act of a living unit transforms its situation and necessitates action under the impact of that new development as well as of any fortuitous changes coinciding with it. This is what Whitehead called the 'creative advance' of nature. It is certainly the pattern of life.[43]

Whitehead, in *Process and Reality*, uses 'creative advance into novelty' for what I just called patterning,[44] so the influence of Langer's PhD supervisor even on the *Mind* trilogy, the pinnacle of a very independent career, to say the least, is hard to miss.[45]

And this is also how chapter 9, the chapter that clears the conceptual ground for a philosophical approach to psychology to materialize, closes: vital activity moves forward by individuation, by involvement, by mixtures of the two, and even by the two processes moving in opposite direction or directly clashing. These 'dialectical dynamisms' between individuation and involvement are driven by 'the great rhythm of evolution', says Langer, 'which moves between them in a direction of its own, always toward more intense activity and gradually increasing ambients of the generic lines that survive.'[46] There is creativity in the opportunism of all of this, Langer seems to suggest, in both non-human and in human life. 'Life is so opportunistic', she argues, 'that every possible avenue of implementation and continuation is exploited [. . .]'.[47] And regarding human life in particular, she ends on a quite critical note:

> In human life, corporate acts are the most spectacular assertions of the species, extending its ambient even beyond the terrestrial surface; but they spring from the most individuating element in each brief life, the mind, and as soon as individuation is seriously frustrated, they also fall apart.[48]

Evolution is the process that is responsible for integrating such literal and figurative highs and lows in its ongoing, dynamic patterning. Survival is often a matter of pushing back against an organism's falling apart by re-establishing itself in an environment, in an involved manner. This is a viral politics, one could argue, because, as Langer writes, 'under such conditions the organism can persist only by being involved with others of its own kind or of alien kinds that vicariously perform its waning function'.[49]

It does not do justice to the comprehensive understanding formulated in the *Mind* trilogy to end on this note. And besides that, now that creativity is on the agenda, we are invited to fold the discussion back to art and the philosophy of art as vantage points for Langer's discussions of life, of philosophy of life, and of the sciences of biology and of psychology. The integrative approach of Langer's project as a whole is the approach that Langer takes herself, both in the *Mind* trilogy and in the individual and cross-referenced index cards. The current ordering of the cards appears as frozen in the early 1980s as the period in which the near-blind Langer was working on her archive with her dedicated research assistant Linda M. D. Legassie (dates unknown) after the completion of *Mind III*. This makes them appear even more as the building blocks of the trilogy. Let me, therefore, as a final step in this chapter pick out a second index card, a card that I found in a drawer in close proximity to a card referencing aforementioned American philosopher and psychologist Ivy G. Campbell-Fisher (1888–1948), the former professor in Aesthetics at Wells College in Aurora, NY, who featured on the first index card that I discussed earlier. The new card, filed behind a salmon-pink tab dedicated to the introduction to the *Mind* trilogy, reads verbatim as follows:

> Note – principles of biological +artistic 'life' [↵ Return] The fact that vital functions, organic patterns, and physical tensions do not have direct counterparts in artistic functions, design, and illusory tensions is that there is a mediate transformation – the projection of life into the dynamic pattern of

feeling. It is this 'psychical' version of life that is objectified in art. *(The psychical phase of vital processes)* [↵ Return] The counterparts of physical organic factors and esp. biological principles are, therefore, often doubly transformed, and integrated past easy recognition in the structure of artworks. But they can usually be found if you know what you are tracing.[50]

This index card is about thresholding and discusses the phase transitions between life (as vital), feelings (as subjective) and art (as objective) as a series of two transitions between, first, the physical and the psychological or 'psychical' and, second, the psychological and the artistic.[51] Campbell-Fisher, who died before she finished the two articles 'to which [Langer] can subscribe almost without reservation', is staged in chapter 4 of *Mind I*.[52] Langer enthusiastically celebrates Campbell-Fisher's work for the distinction it makes between 'referential, associational meaning' and 'intrinsic expression'. She criticizes her colleague, however, for blackboxing the distinction in the same stroke upon calling it 'the art miracle of fusing the two'.[53] Langer herself cracks open the black box:

> The secret of the 'fusion' is the fact that the artist's eye sees in nature, and even in human nature betraying itself in action, an inexhaustible wealth of tensions, rhythms, continuities and contrasts which can be rendered in line and color; and those are the 'internal forms' which the 'external forms' – paintings, musical or poetic compositions or any other works of art – express for us.[54]

Sharpening Campbell-Fisher's philosophical toolbox by building on the philosophy of art as she, herself, provided it in *Feeling and Form*, which is concerned with how 'works of art exhibit the morphology of feeling',[55] Langer characteristically continues her discussion by moving into the direction of a philosophy of life (as implied in her philosophy of art):

> The connection with the natural world is close, and easy to understand; for the essential function of art has the dual character of almost all life functions, which are usually dialectical. Art is the objectification of feeling; and in developing our intuition teaching eye and ear to perceive expressive form, it makes form expressive for us wherever we confront it, in actuality as well as in art. Natural forms become articulate and seem like projections of the 'inner forms' of feeling, as people influenced (whether consciously or not) by all the art that surrounds them develop something of the artist's vision. Art is the objectification of feeling, and the subjectification of nature.[56]

This dialectics between objectification and subjectification provides the clue perhaps to how art can prefigure as-yet-unknown ways of living both among humans and in the more-than-human world. Let me explain.

For the clue provided by Langer to be found and worked with, I want to turn to Langer's plea for taking 'some analytic effort to distinguish between an emotion directly felt and one that is contemplated and imaginatively grasped'.[57] Both Campbell-Fisher and Langer criticize the commonsensical move to interpret art as representational: that is, as self-expression and direct communication of the emotions of the artist and as absorbed in the contingencies of the receiver's personal, emotion-filled life. The two women complicate common sense in aesthetics, psychology and epistemology. Campbell-Fisher, the aesthetician, writes about 'the emotions unnamed perhaps, but expressible and realizable in art' and argues: 'Those, and not personal emotional excitements, are what great artists give.'[58] Langer, the inter-disciplinarian, pushes Campbell-Fisher's non-representational or performative philosophy of art to a philosophy of life developed from such a philosophy of art. The former accomplished this task, first, by pushing Campbell-Fisher's work to the limit. Langer exchanges the emotional register that is limiting even when generalized for the more encompassing register of *feeling*. Second, she brings in her training in logic. Langer argues: 'The intuition of artistic import is a high human function which so far both psychology and epistemology have completely by-passed. Yet its roots lie at the same depth as those of discursive reason, and are, indeed, largely the same.'[59] And then she states: 'The analysis of spirited, noble or moving work is always retrospective; and, furthermore, it is never definitive, nor exhaustive. [. . .] The explanation of its peculiar resistance to systematic treatment lies in the nature of the symbolic projection effected in art.'[60] Great art, too, defies classification.

Notes

1   Susanne K. Langer, *Mind: An Essay on Human Feeling*, vol. 1 (Baltimore, MD and London: The Johns Hopkins Press, [1967] 1970); *Mind: An Essay on Human Feeling*, vol. 2 (Baltimore, MD and London: The Johns Hopkins Press, [1972] 1974; and *Mind: An Essay on Human Feeling*, vol. 3 (Baltimore, MD and London: The Johns Hopkins Press, [1982] 1984).

2   Susanne K. Langer, *Philosophy in a New Key: A Study in the Symbolism of Reason, Rite and Art*, 3rd edn (Cambridge, MA and London: Harvard University Press, [1942] 1957). For information about the publication history of *Philosophy in a New Key*, see Adrienne Dengerink Chaplin, *The Philosophy of Susanne Langer: Embodied Meaning in Logic, Art and Feeling* (London: Bloomsbury Academic, 2020), 18.

3   See, for example, Howard Gardner, *Art, Mind, and Brain: A Cognitive Approach to Creativity* (New York: Basic Books, 1982), 48.

4 Susanne K. Langer, *Feeling and Form: A Theory of Art* (London: Routledge & Kegan Paul, 1953).

5 The three currently available monographs on Langer are: Rolf Lachmann, *Susanne K. Langer: Die lebendige Form menschlichen Fühlens und Verstehens* (München: Wilhelm Fink Verlag, 2000), Robert E. Innis, *Susanne Langer in Focus: The Symbolic Mind* (Bloomington and Indianapolis, IN: Indiana University Press, 2009) and abovementioned Dengerink Chaplin, *The Philosophy of Susanne Langer*. For the growing interest in Langer's work, see Lona Gaikis, 'Susanne Langer,' *Oxford Bibliographies* (2020); available online: https://www.oxfordbibliographies.com/view/document/obo-9780195396577/obo-9780195396577-0401.xml (accessed 15 January 2021). See also the website of the international and interdisciplinary Susanne K. Langer Circle, founded in 2020: https://langercircle.sites.uu.nl/ (same access date).

6 For 'integrative interdisciplinarity', see Allen F. Repko and Rick Szostak, *Interdisciplinary Research: Process and Theory*, 4th edn (Thousand Oaks: Sage, 2021). In the language of this type of interdisciplinarity, 'common ground' refers to the concepts and/or models with which knowledge and (possibly conflicting) insights from at least two disciplines or fields of study can be integrated and a 'more comprehensive understanding' refers to the integrated result. Langer herself has reflected on integration and/as interdisciplinarity; see some index cards in box 20 of the Susanne Langer Papers, 1895–1985 (MS Am 3110). Houghton Library, Harvard University.

7 Langer, *Mind*, vol. 1, 26; Donna J. Haraway, 'Situated Knowledges: *The Science Question in Feminism* and the Privilege of Partial Perspective,' *Feminist Studies* 14 (1988), 595. The third volume of Langer's *Mind* trilogy and Haraway's article 'Situated Knowledges' are only four years apart.

8 Karen Barad, *Meeting the Universe Halfway: Quantum Physics and the Entanglement of Matter and Meaning* (Durham, NC and London: Duke University Press, 2007); Gilles Deleuze and Félix Guattari, *A Thousand Plateaus: Capitalism and Schizophrenia*, trans. Brian Massumi (Minneapolis, MN: University of Minnesota Press, [1980] 1987).

9 Langer, *Mind*, vol. 1, 55. The internal quotation is from Shakespeare's *Julius Caesar* from around 1600, a bibliographical fact that goes unmentioned in *Mind I*.

10 See, for instance, Susanne K. Langer, *An Introduction to Symbolic Logic*, 3rd rev. edn (New York: Dover Publications Inc., 1967).

11 Langer had received a Rockefeller Foundation grant for *Feeling and Form* while teaching at Columbia University in New York in the second half of the 1940s.

12 Lachmann, *Susanne K. Langer*, 23.

13 For 'semblance', see Langer, *Feeling and Form*, 50–1 (and throughout the entire monograph): 'All forms in art [. . .] are abstracted forms; their content is only a

semblance, a pure appearance, whose function is to make them, too, apparent – more freely and wholly apparent than they could be if they were exemplified in a context of real circumstance and anxious interest. It is in this elementary sense that all art is abstract. Its very substance, quality without practical significance, is an abstraction from material existence; and exemplification in this illusory or quasi-illusory medium makes the forms of things (not only shapes, but logical forms, e.g. proportions among degrees of importance in events, or among different speeds in motions) present themselves *in abstracto*.' See also Brian Massumi, *Semblance and Event: Activist Philosophy and the Occurrent Arts* (Cambridge, MA and London: MIT Press, 2011).

14 Langer, *Mind*, vol. 1, xviii–xix.

15 'Philosophical Implications of the Theory of Art Contained in *Feeling and Form*' (undated), 5. The underlining is original. Box 5 of the Langer Papers.

16 Langer, *Mind*, vol. 1, xix.

17 See also ibid., 61ff.

18 Winthrop Sargeant, 'Profiles: Philosopher in a New Key,' *The New Yorker*, 3 December, 75.

19 I undertook what is likely to be the first, and currently only, extensive study of Langer's card-index file in January 2020, right before the global Covid-19 pandemic made intercontinental travel impossible. Personal e-mail communication Donald Dryden, 5 January 2021. Dryden is a scholar of Langer who also processed her archive.

20 Langer, *Mind*, vol. 1, 100.

21 Box 24 of the Langer Papers. The italicized parts of the quoted card have been added by Langer at three different (later) stages, after having completed the vignette. The underlinings are original; the *first* underlining, however, was added when working on, or with, the card (i.e. later). All this can be gleaned from the fact that not only Langer's typical fountain pen was used on the card (for the original vignette), but also both a pencil, a ballpoint and a red crayon (for the additions). The reference to Campbell-Fisher was also one of the later additions to the card. Campbell-Fisher's work is discussed in chapter 4 of *Mind I* and we will return to it in the final section of this chapter. For Langer on the stupa, see also *Mind*, vol. 3, 151ff.

22 'Philosophical Implications,' 3.

23 I wrote about non-reductive continental naturalism before in relation to another, rediscovered female scholar (French historian of science Hélène Metzger [1886–1944]), poststructuralism, and new materialism; see Iris van der Tuin, 'Non-Reductive Continental Naturalism in the Contemporary Humanities: Working with Hélène Metzger's Philosophical Reflections,' *History of the Human Sciences* 26 (2013).

24 Langer, *Mind*, vol. 1, 100. This, and the part referenced in note 13, was written while explicitly reviewing the work of Fauré-Fremiet. Langer is explicit about pushing this work to the limit, thus explaining the method behind the project of the entire *Mind* trilogy: 'works of art exhibit the morphology of feeling. I think Fauré-Fremiet would have agreed to it, though he did not really exploit its implications, which were blurred for him by the usual difficulty of distinguishing between the occurrence of feelings and the conception of them' (Ibid.).

25 Langer, *Mind*, vol. 1, 103–4.

26 Cf. the slogan 'Beings do not pre exist their relatings', explicitly introduced as Whitehead-inspired, from Donna J. Haraway, *The Companion Species Manifesto: Dogs, People, and Significant Otherness* (Chicago, IL: Prickly Paradigm Press, 2003), 6. I wrote about entities and events together with Nanna Verhoeff in the article 'Interfaces (for) Diffracting Technobodies: A Science-Humanities-Design Perspective for an Algorithmic Somatechnics,' *Somatechnics: Journal of Bodies – Technologies – Power* 10 (2020).

27 Langer, *Mind*, vol. 1, xix.

28 Ibid., 258. The composition 'Philosophical Implications' already hints at the possibility of 'transitional forms' that do not fit into the three biological "kingdoms" of plants, animals and humans on page 3 (scare quotes around the word 'kingdom' in original).

29 Langer, *Mind*, vol. 1, 338.

30 George W. Beadle, 'Genes and Biological Enigmas', in *Science in Progress VI*, ed. George A. Baitsell (New Haven etc.: Yale University Press, 1949), 184–249; Frank Macfarlane Burnet, *Virus as Organism: Evolutionary and Ecological Aspects of Some Human Virus Diseases* (Cambridge: Harvard University Press, 1945); Lloyd M. Kozloff, 'Virus Reproduction and Replication of Protoplasmic Units,' in *Dynamics of Growth Processes*, ed. Edgar J. Boell (Princeton, NJ: Princeton University Press, 1954), 3-20; Robley C. Williams, 'Relations between Structure and Biological Activity of Certain Viruses,' *Proceedings of the National Academy of Sciences of the United States of America* 42 (1956).

31 Langer, *Mind*, vol. 1, 257.

32 Ibid., 258.

33 Ibid., 259.

34 Ibid., 261.

35 See ibid. for 'approaching living form in nature.' See ibid., 305 for 'vital activity' and ibid., 307 for 'agency.' Chapter 9 starts on page 307.

36 Ibid., 261.

37 Ibid.

38 Cf. Rosi Braidotti and Maria Hlavajova, 'Introduction,' in *Posthuman Glossary* (London, etc: Bloomsbury Academic, 2018), 2. They state on the indicated page that

posthumanist and anti-anthropocentric theory 'assumes that the human is always partially constituted by the non- human and that their interaction is too complex to be reduced to a mere dialectical opposition'.

39 Ibid., 311–12.

40 Ibid., 312.

41 Ibid., 312. See also ibid., 337 about symbiotic relationship as best characterized via involvement, not as an anomaly in relation to individuation.

42 Ibid., 26.

43 Ibid., 26-7.

44 Alfred North Whitehead, *Process and Reality*, corrected ed. David Ray Griffin and Donald W. Sherburne (New York: Free Press, [1929/1978] 1985), 35, 128, 222, 349.

45 Langer scholar Adrienne Dengerink Chaplin writes: 'Although Whitehead's supervision of [Langer's] thesis was minimal, his ideas and teaching were to have a major influence her own thinking.' See Dengerink Chaplin, *The Philosophy of Susanne Langer*, 15. See also Langer, *Mind*, vol. 1, 336, n. 53 for 'our great inspirer, A.N. Whitehead'; and Iris van der Tuin, 'Bergson before Bergsonism: Traversing 'Bergson's Failing' in Susanne K. Langer's Philosophy of Art,' *Journal of French and Francophone Philosophy* 24 (2016).

46 Langer, *Mind*, vol. 1, 355.

47 Ibid.

48 Ibid.

49 Ibid.

50 Box 25 of the Langer Papers. See note 17 for the key to underlining, italicization and so on.

51 'Thresholding' is, just like 'valuing' and 'patterning,' my choice of words.

52 Langer, *Mind*, vol. 1, 85-90. The two articles discussed by Langer are: Ivy G. Campbell-Fisher, 'Aesthetics and the Logic of Sense,' *The Journal of General Psychology* 43 (1950) and 'Intrinsic Expressiveness,' *The Journal of General Psychology* 45 (1951). The posthumously published articles were delivered by Campbell-Fisher's husband.

53 Langer, *Mind*, vol. 1, 86.

54 Ibid., 86–7; 'internal form' and 'external form' are used (according to Langer: wrongly) by Campbell-Fisher.

55 See note 19.

56 Langer, *Mind*, vol. 1, 87.

57 Ibid., 89.

58 Campbell-Fisher, 'Aesthetics', 268 in Langer, *Mind*, vol. 1, 88.

59 Langer, *Mind*, vol. 1, 89.

60 Ibid., 90.

3

Dead, alive

Deconstruction, biopolitics and life death

Stefan Herbrechter

Then, what is life? I cried

– Shelley, 'The Triumph of Life', l. 544

The virus is all the rage

Viruses are fascinating because they are unclassifiable. They are, strictly speaking, neither alive nor dead. They are somehow in between micro*organism* and *dead* matter, a biological entity without its own metabolism, a *parasite* that needs a host to develop a form of life. Like a *supplement* that *grafts* itself onto its host organism it *rewrites* its genetic *programme*, for better or for worse. It is a major factor in biological evolution, maybe even its cause, its beginning and its end. As one standard textbook of microbiology states:

> a virus is a noncellular particle that must infect a host cell, where it reproduces. . . . Viruses are ubiquitous, infecting every taxonomic group of organisms, including bacteria, eukaryotes, and archaea. . . . Some viruses introduce copies of their own genomes into the host's genome, a process that can mediate evolution of the host genome. Indeed, studies of molecular evolution reveal that viral genomes are the ancestral source of about a tenth of the human genome.[1]

The virus and its virality have also become powerful *metaphors* in postmodernist and posthumanist theory, especially since the virus not only transgresses the boundary between life and death but also between life and technology, especially under the condition of digitalization where computer viruses function analogically to biological ones,[2] namely by recoding patterns of information through 'sabotage', as Brigitte Weingart explains.[3] It is the virus's ability to *learn* or *imitate* the code or 'language' of its host that constitutes its subversive potential, its danger in circumventing and 'fooling' the host body's immune system, sometimes to a point where this immune system turns against itself (i.e. in an 'autoimmunitarian' reaction).[4] It is therefore no coincidence that the subversive power of the virus has served as an analogy for subversive thought, especially thought of the kind that turns against established forms of classification while itself remaining or claiming to be unclassifiable. The names of Jacques Derrida and deconstruction inevitably spring to mind here, especially since Derrida himself dwells on this analogy or metaphor (Derridean deconstruction = virus):

> I often tell myself, and I must have written it somewhere – I am sure I wrote it somewhere – that all I have done, to summarize it very reductively, is dominated by the thought of a virus, what could be called a parasitology, a virology, the virus being many things.[5]

The virus 'being many things' thus refers to a number of hidden analogies between the virus and deconstruction – understood as a recoding of the language of (Western) metaphysics and its fundamental semantic *programme* (of which the opposition between *bios* and *technē* is one primary example). Both the virus and deconstruction problematize the distinction between life and death, between inside or outside. They undermine chronology and teleology (who was first, parasite or host?). They function according to a logic of the trace (undermining the notion of (self-)presence and (self-)identity).[6] No wonder the virus evokes such ambiguous feelings, between fear and danger, desire and anxiety. Due to its power of *contagion*, it threatens to undermine both physical and philosophical indemnity, both individual and social identity, as well as ideas of political autonomy and sovereignty. It transgresses physical and virtual boundaries, especially in the age of bio-informatics, biotechnology and biopolitics.[7]

This usage of the virus, and contagion more generally, under the condition of globalization and digitalization, can therefore no longer be seen as purely metaphorical (if it ever could).[8] Like Haraway's cyborg figure in the 1980s and 1990s,[9] the virus has become 'our' biopolitical ontology and Covid-19, in a sense, its logical consequence. So while the virologist Luis P. Villarreal posed the (then still) provocative question 'can viruses make us human?',[10] the current posthumanist climate raises the question about the human and 'its' future as such – either in the form of 'have we ever been human?', or 'who or what comes after the human?'

Bios: Biopolitics/biophilosophy/bioh umanities/biomedia/bioart

The rise of biology and its intensifying co-implication with technology is one of the main characteristics of modernity. The argument about modernity being characterized by a fundamental shift towards 'biopolitics' – the idea that power exercised over life and death, life-death is becoming the main focus of politics, from Foucault, to Agamben, via Mbembe's notion of 'necropolitics', and Esposito and Timothy Campbell's call for an 'affirmative' biopolitics[11] as an attempt to overcome the inherent death-drive of technology – is too well rehearsed by now to reiterate it here. Suffice it to say, maybe, that the Covid-19 pandemic happens in and to a global system of (neoliberal)[12] biopolitical governance (of life and death) that, as Clough and Willse explain, 'has turned the legitimacy of governance over to technical systems of compliance and efficiency that underwrite the relationship of the state and the economy with a biopolitics of war, terror, and surveillance'.[13]

The centrality and ubiquity of a politics that centres on the *meaning* of life, that subjects the question of life *itself* to fundamental technoscientific scrutiny and for which the *decoding* of life has become a primary source of economic development as well as the main future-oriented ontology of the species and life on this planet in general cannot be overstated. It is legible in the pro-*life*-ration of *bios* (and its prefix bio-) from biopolitics to bioart, and in the 're-problematization of life: what is it that makes something *living* or *non-living* and what, after all, is *life* itself?'[14] The age of biopolitics and biotechnology – technobiopolitics one might say – is therefore a time when life becomes both the most precious resource (both at an individual and at a social, global, economic level) and the most 'precarious', to use Judith Butler's term,[15] where the human and non-human alike are subject to extreme biotechnological (self?) scrutiny while life *itself* is in danger of 'dehumanization', in the sense that humans are no longer the central life form, nor that biological life is the only life thinkable.[16]

The time of *bios* is therefore also already the time 'after life', as Eugene Thacker writes,[17] namely when biology and (digital) technology, or information, are integrated – what Thacker refers to as 'biomedia'[18] – and when 'life (*bios*) can no longer be separated from technology (*technē*), nature from artifice, the living from the non-living'.[19] What has been decisive within the process of techno-biopoliticization coincides with what Richard Doyle and others have called biology's 'molecularization', 'the molecule overtaking or territorializing the organism and getting plugged into the computer', thus giving birth to the 'postvital body or organism'.[20] Nicholas Rose also writes of 'molecularization' as the first of five 'mutations' that have occurred in contemporary biocapitalism and biopolitics.[21] While most humans still operate in everyday life at the level of the body, biopolitics and bioeconomics have become 'molecular' and operate at, what one might call, the level of microbiopolitics.[22]

In a time when 'biology is not destiny but opportunity',[23] and when biology may be manipulated at a molecular (DNA-RNA, biomedical) level,[24] *synthetic* biology challenges classical distinctions like animal, vegetable and mineral; nature and technology; organic and inorganic. It also questions any idea of bodily or organismic integrity, as we have already seen earlier, as well as a clear distinction between life and death. Even though viruses like Covid-19 are strictly speaking no micro*organisms* (see earlier; they have no cell structure or metabolism) what they share with bacteria (that are in fact their primary victims) is both their ancestrality and their vital importance for life and its evolution. They are thus also part of what might be called the 'microbial turn' that has occurred at the interface between the bio- or posthumanities and the life sciences, especially microbiology.[25]

It is no surprise, therefore, that the state of ontological co-implication of *bios*, *techne* and *polis* also has profound aesthetic consequences for investigating the meaning of life *itself*. The aim of *bio*art, in this context, according to Nicole Anderson, is 'to challenge and attempt to break down the respective boundaries between nature (that is, biology) and art; science and art; function and aesthetics, humans and animals, animals and plants, and so on'.[26] Bioart critically and aesthetically shadows the microbial turn and also provides an important interface of its own between (bio)philosophy, the (bio)humanities and what is going on in the life science lab. In this sense, it represents a critical intervention of biopolitics itself – 'tactical biopolitics' one might say[27] – which provides new perspectives on the 'molecular gaze'[28] and 'molecular aesthetics'.[29]

Biodeconstruction

The biocentrism of the biological age calls for 'biodeconstruction'. It is thus no surprise that in Derridean circles, concerned with the afterlife of deconstruction after Derrida's death, in 2007, as well as with the 'post-theoretical' backlash that has been gaining strength ever since, authors have been focusing on an understanding on deconstruction as a philosophy both *of* and *for* life. Derrida himself encouraged this focus, for example, in his final interview 'Learning to Live, Finally', which he concludes by saying that:

> I would not want to encourage an interpretation that situates surviving on the side of death and the past rather than life and the future. No, deconstruction is always on the side of the yes, on the side of the affirmation of life. Everything I say – at least from 'Pas' (in *Parages*) on – about survival as a complication of the opposition life/death proceeds in me from an unconditional affirmation of life.[30]

We will return to the question life affirmation and being on 'the side of life' later. The way Derrida and a number of prominent Derrideans after him seek to 'immunize' deconstruction against the reproach of it dying, and of it being – like most Western metaphysical philosophy (to use Montaigne's famous phrase and essay title) basically about 'learning to die'[31] – goes through a movement in 'ana-' one might say. It consists in showing deconstruction has always (already) been about life, from its *inception*. This, in turn, is connected to the structure of the *trace* and of its hauntological status of *survival*. To understand (Derridean) deconstruction as a merely *textual* approach to reading literature (*à la* Paul de Man, for example) can thus be said to miss the point that, for Derrida, *text* and *writing* are not to be taken *literally*, but as *organic* (or necessary) metaphors.[32] Life (itself), in the Derridean sense of *survival*, has the structure of a trace – it is neither present nor absent, but always deferred and differing from itself, like *différance*. In fact, life is (in)*différance*, a point that Jean-Luc Nancy makes in a comment on Juan-Manuel Garrido's proposal to use life as a synonym for 'différance':[33] 'It is possible, I believe, to take hold of *différance* in life or as life.'[34] Within such a re-inscribed understanding of life, death is not *outside* of life, rather 'it is that through which life relates to life, and thus to life as *différance*, or to life as structurally traversed by *différance*'.[35]

One of the earliest reminders of Derrida's long-standing, maybe even *originary*, interest in biology can be found in Christopher Johnson's 'La vie, le vivant: biologie et autobiographie', where he recalls Derrida's early engagement with François Jacob's *The Logic of Life* and molecular biology in the 1970s, without however mentioning Derrida's (until quite recently) unpublished seminar *La vie la mort* (1975–6).[36] It is the publication of this seminar – parts of which had nevertheless appeared, for example, in *Otobiographies* (first 1982) and *Post Card* (first 1980) – that has brought on the (somewhat belated) 'turn to life' and 'biodeconstruction' as a new 'strain' in Derrida studies.[37] Johnson rightly stresses that one can find an interest in biology in Derrida in his earliest writings, especially in *Of Grammatology* (1967) which already discusses the notions of code, writing and programme as they were taking over the new cybernetic and biological (what today would be called 'life') sciences, which at the time was causing a general shift, as Jacob explains, from 'life' [*vie*] to 'the living' [*vivants*] and its boundaries.

This is of course not the place for a detailed commentary or close reading of Derrida's seminar – which has already received some very detailed analysis, even in its unpublished form, based on Derrida's manuscripts held at the University of California, Irvine.[38] As the title of the seminar suggests, Derrida is interested here in life-death *before* any syntax so to speak, outside of any dialectical relation between these two 'concepts': that is not life *versus* death (an opposition between dead *or* alive), nor life before, after or beyond death, life first, then death and so on, but a radical entanglement between life (and) death: *la-vie-la-mort*.[39] In typical Derridean fashion what follows in the seminar is a carefully woven string of arguments of intertwined readings of the 'usual suspects', one might say: Hegel, Nietzsche, Freud, Husserl, Heidegger, Blanchot, Canguilhem – and François Jacob's *La logique du vivant*. It is thus an argument that weaves together philosophy, psychoanalysis and biology. The most important aspect here is Derrida's focus on Jacob's (and the life science's) use of the notion of 'programme', 'writing' and 'text', which he uses to further illustrate the necessity and centrality of grammatology as a general science of writing, at a time when both biology and informatics increasingly rely on writing as an arch-metaphor in the form of ideas like 'rewriting the *book* of life', 'writing software pro*gram*mes', 'genetic and digital *code*', etc. In doing so, Derrida shows that the deconstruction of logo- and phono-centrism was never merely or purely a linguistic argument (often misunderstood as nihilistic 'textualism' or radical 'constructivism'). *Of Grammatology* and the idea that 'there is no outside-text' rather insist on and problematize the very fusion of life and text, text and tissue, genetic technological writing, trace and inscription. The entire argument rests on some passages in *Of Grammatology* whose implications outside philosophy, linguistics or literature have often been underestimated:[40]

> we say 'writing' for all that gives rise to an inscription in general. . . . It is also in this sense that the contemporary biologist speaks of writing and *pro-gram* in relation to the most elementary processes of information within the living cell. And, finally, whether it has essential limits or not, the entire field covered by the cybernetic *program* will be the field of writing. If the theory of cybernetics is by itself to oust all metaphysical concepts-including the concepts of soul, of life, of value, of choice, of memory-which until recently served to separate the machine from man, it must conserve the notion of writing, trace, grammè [written mark],

or grapheme, until its own historico-metaphysical character is also exposed. Even before being determined as human (with all the distinctive characteristics that have always been attributed to man and the entire system of significations that they imply) or nonhuman, the grammè – or the grapheme – would thus name the element.[41]

The beginning of biodeconstruction, but also of postanthropocentric or critical posthumanism and animal studies, one might argue, can already be found in this passage, which spells out the centrality of the notion of inscription as a 'biotechnology' before or outside the distinction between human and non-human, thus challenging and deconstructing their opposition.[42]

Vitale says the following on biodeconstruction's project or programme: 'We shall consider the investigation of *life* not only an issue of deconstruction but the latter's very matrix; we shall think *différance* as the irreducible and structural condition of the life of the living, and thus *trace* and *text* as the structures of the organization of life.'[43] This follows Derrida in his critique of Jacob's and biology's more widely held 'metaphysical' view that arises out of 'preformationism', which understands life as 'germinal' process, programmed to unfold and merely (temporarily) interrupted by death (or death as a necessary supplement to life, associated with sexual reproduction).[44] It is precisely against this (vitalist) notion that Derrida sets his own concept of 'life death' and 'survival' [*survivance*].[45]

Survival and the originary technicity of life

As explains in 'Learning to Live, Finally':

> [S]urvival is an originary concept that constitutes the very structure of what we call existence, *Dasein*, if you will. We are structurally survivors, marked by this structure of the trace and of the testament. . . . This surviving is life beyond life, life more than life, and my discourse is not a discourse of death, but, on the contrary, the affirmation of a living being who prefers living and thus surviving to death, because survival is not simply that which remains but the most intense life possible.[46]

This 'logic of *survivance*' that underpins Derrida's deconstruction of life death could be summarized thus: for a metaphysical thinking of the relationship between life and death, death is the *end* of life, both in a temporal as well as a teleological sense,[47] which means that it develops a kind of *supplementary* structure[48] – it completes but also complements life. As a supplement it subverts from the start the idea of life's self-sufficiency and indemnity. Death is thus *inscribed* into life (physically as well as symbolically, philosophically) as a *trace*. It is, in fact, life's secret *script*, in the sense of Heidegger's 'Being-towards-death', which gives meaning to life, *in the first place*. Vicki Kirby summarizes this neatly in the following passage:

> When we think of division, we think of some*thing* that precedes its separation from itself. In conventional terms, we might think of a life lived, and then the cut of death that in the end divides that life . . . from life. If divisibility is originary, however, then we do not begin with the integrity of an entity that is *then* divided from itself. Strangely, Death would be internal to the very possibility of an entity's being itself, not simply at its birth, but throughout its ongoing re-production/ othering of itself. If we begin with an algorithm of pluripotentiality in which the emergence of every individuation is an articulation of the whole system (general writing), then the system remains in constant touch with itself *because* it is divided from itself, because it is pure divisibility, pure contamination.[49]

It is this systemic (self)division that Derrida thinks of as *survivance*, as life surviving itself as an originary trace, so to speak, of death's inscription or its self-interruption. It is also this very logic of originary division of life that is associated with the idea of the *technicity* of the trace. Before Life (the metaphysical concept) and its separation into life in all its forms [*vivants*] and (their) death(s), there is necessarily a moment of inscription, a 'pro-gramming'.[50] However, this writing only remains as a structuring trace and, since we are talking about writing (in a general, 'biotechnological', sense), we arrive at a point where the distinction between life and death, living and non-living, *bios* and *technē* and so on starts to disintegrate: we arrive at the very *technicity* of the trace in everything *alive*.[51]

The idea of originary technicity[52] has given rise to what might be called a deconstructive posthumanism, or maybe an 'inhumanism', that sees the technical inscription of life as a subversion of the animate-inanimate dichotomy that is used to distinguish between what is alive (animate, animal, animism) and what is machinic (inanimate, automatic, mechanical, artificial, inorganic and so on).[53] It is also the starting point of Bernard Stiegler's work on technics, which follows Derrida in applying the idea of originary technicity (of the human) to a rereading of paleoanthropology and the evolutionary process of 'hominization' through an *originary* co-implication of *anthropos* and *technē*.[54] While it is clearly possible (and maybe still strategically necessary) to stress the technicity of the trace to show that human evolution cannot be separated from technical evolution, and, so to counter the humanist phantasm of a *sovereign*

or *immune* human body by privileging a purely utilitarian idea of technology –
that is technology as merely a *tool* or as a *prosthesis*[55] – Derrida's notion of the
technicity of the trace at the beginning of or even *before* life, thought to its logical
conclusion, of course also challenges any reading of the unfolding of (human
and non-human) evolution as an unfolding of a kind of metaphysics of *technē*.[56]
The difference between Stiegler and Derrida, rather than merely concerning
'the different evaluation of the emergence of technical difference in the history
of life understood as the differing deferral of the genetic program', as Vitale
states, or merely as 'two different ways' of 'thinking . . . technology as the other
of life',[57] is maybe more accurately, and certainly more radically, described by
Deborah Goldgaber in the following terms: '[r]ather than marking a break with
the organic, as on Stiegler's account, the history of grammē, of grammatization,
implies the radical continuity between life and technē, a continuity in and across
heterogeneous domains.'[58] This emphasizes a thinking that stresses the idea of
general writing as the 'history of life . . . as *différance*'.[59] And it is precisely this
emphasis that allows Derrida to claim that deconstruction is affirmative of life
(and not, as philosophy more generally maybe, on the side of death, in the sense
of being a thanato-educational praxis: that is a 'learning how to die', as opposed
to 'learning to live', finally).[60]

Anim(al)ism – Derrida, Cixous and the 'side' of life

It is somewhat surprising that Derrida's *H.C. For Life, That Is to Say. . .*[61] has
so far been more or less ignored in the discussion around biodeconstruction.[62]
This is surprising in two respects: in *H.C. For Life*, Derrida is at pains to agree,
although not entirely, with his lifelong friend Hélène Cixous and her feminist
materialist, radically affirmative, arguably proto-vitalist, take on deconstruction;
second, because it contains a fascinating, if not fully developed, engagement
with the question of animism and Freud's discussion of the notion of *Belebtheit*
(livingness, *vivance*) in his chapter on 'Animism, Magic, The Omnipotence of
Thought',[63] which clearly links back to Derrida's discussion of biologism and
biocentrism in *La vie la mort*.[64]

Derrida develops the theme of animism in Cixous's work[65] in connection
with her use of the telephone in her novel *Jours de l'an*:

> She is on the telephone [*parle au telephone*]. But she does not speak *on the
> telephone*, as one says *to speak on the telephone*. No, she really speaks *to* the

telephone; she speaks in its direction [*à son adresse*], addresses it, says: 'O telephone. . .' She even asks it for forgiveness, for 'telephone' not only represents an animal life, even when there is an answering machine; telephone is somebody who must forgive her when she asks him to let her sleep, not to ring anymore. And we will see later why this is no zoo-anthropomorphic animism.[66]

The way Derrida takes up this recurring motif of anim(al)ism (or 'non-zoo-morphic animism') in Cixous's work is by way of critiquing Freud's analysis of 'the omnipotence of thought' in *Totem and Taboo*, in which he identifies what he calls some problematic 'snags' with regard to Freud's understanding of animism.[67] To summarize an extremely complex and dense deconstructive reading that combines Cixous's notion of life's 'omnipotence' and Freud's idea of animism as (a primitive, even originary, form of) narcissism, Derrida focuses on these aspects: Freud's exception granted to art in relation to animism; Freud's compulsion to introduce what he calls a 'pre-animism' (or 'animatism'); and Freud's gesture of 'denegation' regarding the 'necessity' of death.[68]

For the purpose of our argument here, we can focus on the second 'snag', where Derrida focuses on Freud's curious move which, on the one hand, acknowledges the logical necessity of a 'pre-animistic' phase, 'more ancient than the doctrine of spirits . . . which form the kernel of animism'[69] and which Freud calls 'animatism', but about which, on the other hand, Freud remains completely silent. Animatism – if it exists – Derrida concludes, '[i]s something like a theory of living, of being-alive, of livingness [*vivance*], of universal being-for-life (*Lehre von der allgemeinen Belebtheit* [a notion that Derrida places within the proximity of Jankélévitch's "universal hylozoism", and which of course would be the ultimate philosophical consequence of a "biological" animism])'. It would thus be a kind of *originary* and most importantly, a 'pre-religious', 'non-spiritual' or non-metaphysical form of life affirmation that must be prior to any known (including the most 'primitive') culture: 'a quasi-originary *Belebtheit* that must, if not present itself, at least announce itself to some pre-empirical or pre-positive experience.'[70] In short, what is sketched in these few very dense pages of Derrida's reading of primary narcissism via Cixous and via a return to Freud is nothing short of what may be called the beginning of a 'deconstruction of animism'. Or, in other words, a way of insisting on the inevitability and necessity of animism as an explanation for life in our and in any time, as well as a demonstration that, *at the same time*, one cannot, one *must* not, take animism *literally*, as a *system of belief*, but rather as a life *force* that is more originary than life *itself*, which has nothing to do with an intrinsic and problematic privileging of spiritualism of some *anima* (the animate, but also the animal), but implies instead that the idea of animalism should make us wary and maybe prompt a search for a *Belebtheit* that lies *before* or outside any anthropocentric remainders in the notion of animism.[71] In short, it would be the place in which the ancestrality of the virus would have to be located and thought.

And it is here also that bioart has its role to play, namely as a critical mediator in the time of pandemics. As a concluding example may serve Tagny Duff's work on 'viral tattoos', in which she uses Lentivirus (a synthetic retrovirus) 'as an artistic medium and subject . . . to explore how perceptions and tensions around infection and contagion might be re-imagined and rearticulated by engaging with viral vectors'.[72] Even if the perceptions of Covid-19 are currently (and understandably) ruled by fear and anxiety it should also become clear that:

> Viruses remind us that there is something more than the 'code' of life based on the presupposition that life operates similarly to a computational algorithm, without falling into [a] vitalist position that privileges cellular life above all else.[73]

As a specific discourse and practice engaged in mediating the question of life death, bioart can have an 'ecological' function, in the context of contemporary biopolitics, as Cary Wolfe argues, and can thus become a locus of critique and resistance to the totalization and technicization of Life (itself).[74]

Notes

1 Joan L. Slonczewski and John W. Foster, *Microbiology: An Evolving Science* (New York: Norton, 2011), 182–4.

2 The following quotation from Slonczewski and Foster (183–4) clearly shows the inextricability of biological and digital viruses due to their shared *tertium comparationis* – information: 'Viral propagation exemplifies the central role of information in biological reproduction. The propagation of viruses is mimicked by the spread of "computer viruses", whose information "infects" computer memory. . . . When a biological virus infects a host cell, the information in its genome subverts the host cell machinery to produce multiple copies of the virus; the multiple copies then escape to infect more host cells. Similarly, when a computer virus infects a host computer, its program code subverts the host to produce multiple copies of the virus, which then escapes to infect more host computers. Computer viruses generate epidemics analogous to those of biological viruses. The virus's code can even be designed to "mutate" in order to foil the "immune system" of antivirus software.'

The central notion in the viral logic here is 'programming', based on the idea of the 'gram': that is, writing, which will be discussed later in connection with Derridean deconstruction. The basic claim that Derrida makes, as discussed later, is that the 'mimicking' (referred to in the quote earlier) cannot be contained. It is not merely the result of 'technological' developments (i.e. digital information) that is based on some prior 'natural' genetic phenomena. Re-programming or re-writing is more than 'just a metaphor' in this context. It is a *necessary* or 'dead' metaphor, a catachresis, one might say.

For a more detailed medical account of the connection between parasite mimicry and autoimmunity, see also Irun R. Cohen, 'Principles of Molecular Mimicry and Autoimmune Disease', in *Molecular Mimicry, Microbes, and Autoimmunity*, ed. Madeleine W. Cunningham and Robert S. Fujinami (Washington: ASM Press, 2000), 17–26.

3 Brigitte Weingart, 'Parasitäre Praktiken. Zur Topik des Viralen', in *Über Grenzen: Limitation und Transgression in Literatur und Ästhetik*, ed. Claudia Benthien and Irmela Marei Krüger-Fürhoff (Stuttgart: Metzler, 1999), 212.

4 On the notion of autoimmunity in Derrida's work and in theory more generally, see Stefan Herbrechter and Michelle Jamieson (eds), *Autoimmunities* (London: Routledge, 2018). See also Ed Cohen's ground-breaking work *A Body Worth Defending: Immunity, Biopolitics, and the Apotheosis of the Modern Body* (Durham: Duke University Press, 2010).

5 Jacques Derrida, 'The Spatial Arts: An Interview with Jacques Derrida', in *Deconstruction and the Visual Arts: Art, Media, Architecture*, ed. Peter Brunette and David Wills (Cambridge: MIT Press, 1994), 12.

6 Cf. Weingart, "Parasitäre Praktiken", 217–18.

7 See Peta Mitchell's illuminating essay 'Contagion, Virology, Autoimmunity: Derrida's Rhetoric of Contamination', *Parallax* 23, no. 1 (2017): 77–93, and her *Contagious Metaphor* (London: Bloomsbury, 2012).

8 This is Mitchell's argument in *Contagious Metaphor*.

9 Donna Haraway established the connection between cyborg and micro-organic symbionts (of which the virus might be said to be an extreme case, if one accepts that parasitism can also be seen as a form of symbiosis, even though in some cases this leads to illness and death for either host or virus) in her contribution to the *Cyborg Handbook*, where she writes: 'cyborg figures have a way of transfecting, infecting, everything' (Haraway, 'Cyborgs and Symbionts: Living Together in the New World Order', *The Cyborg Handbook*, ed. Chris Hables Gray, New York: Routledge, 1995, pp. xi-xx; here p. xix). On Lynn Margulis's and Dorion Sagan's notion of 'symbiogenesis' that informs Haraway and the shift in current microbiological thinking more widely, see Margulis and Sagan, *Microcosmos: Four Billion Years of Evolution from Our Microbial Ancestors*, New York: Stone Books,

1986; *What Is Life?* Berkeley: University of California Press, 1995 and Dorion Sagan's *Cosmic Apprentice: Dispatches from the Edges of Science* (Minneapolis: University of Minnesota Press, 2013).

10   Luis P. Villareal, 'Can Viruses Make Us Human?' *Proceedings of the American Philosophical Society* 148, no. 3 (2003): 296–323.

11   Cf. Michel Foucault, *The Birth of Biopolitics: Lectures at the Collège de France (1978-1979)* (Houndmills: Palgrave Macmillan, 2008); Giorgio Agamben, *Homo Sacer: Sovereign Power and Bare Life* (Stanford: Stanford University Press, 1998); Achile Mbembe, 'Necropolitics', *Public Culture* 15.1 (2003): 11–40; Roberto Esposito, *Terms of the Political: Community, Immunity, Biopolitics* (New York: Fordham University Press, 2013); Timothy C. Cambell, *Improper Life: Technology and Biopolitics from Heidegger to Agamben* (Minneapolis: University of Minnesota Press, 2011). See also my commentary on Campbell in 'Afterword: The Other Side of Life', *Posthumanism: A Critical Analysis* (London: Bloomsbury, 2013), 207–13.

12   The connection between biotechnology and neoliberal capitalism – that is 'the realms of biological (re)production and capital accumulation mov[ing] closer together' – is analysed in Melinda Cooper's well-known study *Life as Surplus: Biotechnology and Capitalism in the Neoliberal Era* (Seattle: University of Washington Press, 2008), 3.

13   Patricia Ticineto Clough and Craig Willse, 'Beyond Biopolitics', in *Beyond Biopolitics: Essays on the Governance of Life and Death*, ed. Clough and Willse (Durham: Duke University Press, 2011), ix.

14   Sebastian Olma and Kostas Koukouzelis, 'Introduction: Life's (Re-)Emergences', *Theory, Culture and Society* (special issue on Life) 24, no. 6 (2007): 2.

15   Judith Butler, *Precarious Life: The Powers of Mourning and Violence* (London: Verso).

16   On this point specifically, see Scott Lash, 'Technological Forms of Life', *Theory, Culture and Society* 18, no. 1 (2001): 105–20.

17   Eugene Thacker, *After Life* (Chicago: University of Chicago Press, 2010).

18   Eugene Thacker, *Biomedia* (Minneapolis: University of Minnesota Press, 2004).

19   Eugene Thacker, 'Biomedia', in *Critical Terms for Media Studies*, ed. W. J. T. Mitchell and Mark B.N. Hansen (Chicago: University of Chicago Press, 2010), 117.

20   Richard Doyle, *On Beyond Living: Rhetorical Transformations of the Life Sciences* (Stanford: Stanford University Press, 1997), 1, 8–17.

21   Nicholas Rose, *The Politics of Life Itself: Biomedicine, Power, and Subjectivity in the Twenty-First Century* (Princeton: Princeton University Press, 2007), 5–6; the other 'mutations' being 'optimization', 'subjectification', 'somatic expertise' and 'economies of vitality' (6–7). For a prescient account of the implications of contemporary biopolitics for 'biophilsophy' in the humanities and the social sciences, see Rose's, 'The Human Sciences in a Biological Age', *Theory, Culture and Society* 30, no. 1

(2013): 3–34. On the notion of 'biohumanities', see my forthcoming essay in Daniele Sands, ed., *Bioethics and the Posthumanities*, London: Routledge, 2020.

22 Cf. Stefan Herbrechter, 'Microbe', in *The Edinburgh Companion to Animal Studies*, ed. Lynn Turner, Undine Sellbach and Ron Broglio (Edinburgh: Edinburgh University Press, 2018), 354–66.

23 Rose, *The Politics of Life Itself*, 51.

24 Cf. the overview the editors provide of the implications of this process of 'biomedicalization', in their 'Introduction', in *Biomedicalization: Technoscience, Health, and Illness in the U.S.*, ed. Adele E. Clarke et al. (Durham: Duke University Press), 1–44.

25 Again, see Herbrechter, 'Microbe'. On 'microbiology', see for example Maureen A. O'Malley and John Dupré, 'Introduction: Towards a philosophy of microbiology', *Studies in History and Philosophy of Biological and Biomedical Sciences* 38 (2007): 775–9.

26 Nicole Anderson, '(Auto)Immunity: The Deconstruction and Politics of Bio-art and Criticism', *Parallax* 16, no. 4 (2010): 101.

27 This is the title of a landmark collection which contains work that combines aspects of media theory, critical science studies and bioaesthetics, edited by Beatriz da Costa and Kavita Philip, *Tactical Biopolitics: Art, Activism, and Technoscience* (Cambridge: MIT Press, 2008).

28 Cf. Suzanne Anker and Dorothy Nelkin, *The Molecular Gaze: Art in the Genetic Age*, New York: Cold Spring Harbor Laboratory Press, 2004.

29 Peter Weibel and Ljiljana Fruk (eds), *Molecular Aesthetics* (Cambridge: MIT Press, 2013).

30 Jacques Derrida, *Learning to Live Finally: The Last Interview*, an interview with Jean Birnbaum, trans. Pascale-Anne Brault and Michael Naas (Houndmills: Palgrave Macmillan, 2007), 51–2.
Maebh Long, in 'Derrida Interviewing Derrida: Autoimmunity and the Laws of the Interview', *Australian Humanities Review* 54 (2013): 103–19, establishes an interesting (and provocative) connection between autoimmunity as 'self-deconstruction' (of life) and Derrida's use of the genre of the interview as an attempt to 'immunize' deconstruction against its own deconstruction – and in doing so, ironically, jeopardizes deconstruction's own 'survival'.

31 Montaigne, in his essay number twenty 'Que philosopher c'est apprendre à mourir', refers back to Cicero's idea that to philosophize is to prepare oneself for death; Michel de Montaigne, *Oeuvres Completes* (Seuil (*L'Intégrale*): Paris, 1967), 47–53.

32 Cf. for example Martin Hägglund's characterization of the 'life turn' in (post)theory in his 'The Trace of Time: A Critique of Vitalism', *Derrida Today* 9, no. 1 (2016): 36: 'The revival of "life" as a central category during the last decade of continental philosophy belongs to a more general turn away from questions of language

and discourse, in the name of a return to the real, material, and the biological. If Saussure and linguistics once were an obligatory reference point, Darwin and evolutionary theory have increasingly come to occupy a similar position. Alongside this development, the status of deconstruction has been downgraded. Derrida's work is largely seen as limited to questions of language or as mortgaged to an ethical and religious piety'.

33 Cf. Juan-Manuel Garrido, *Chances de la pensée – À partir de Jean-Luc Nancy* (Paris: Galilée, 2011), 15.

34 Jean-Luc Nancy, 'The Different Life [*La vie différante*]', trans. Matthew H. Anderson, *CR: The New Centennial Review* 10, no. 3 (2010): 56.

35 Ibid., 58.

36 Cf. Christopher Johnson, 'La vie, le vivant: biologie et autobiographie', in Marie-Louise Mallet, *L'animal autobiographique – Autour de Jacques Derrida* (Paris: Galilée, 1999), 353–68. François Jacob, *The Logic of Life: A History of Heredity*, trans. Betty E. Spillmann (New York: Pantheon, 1973). Jacques Derrida, *La vie la mort – Séminaire (1975-1976)*, ed. Pascale-Anne Brault and Peggy Kamuf (Paris: Seuil, 2019); translated as *Life Death*, trans. Pascale-Anne Brault and Michael Naas (Chicago: University of Chicago Press, 2020).

37 'Biodeconstruction' is Francesco Vitale's term. See his *Biodeconstruction: Jacques Derrida and the Life Sciences*, trans. Mauro Senatore, New York: SUNY Press, 2018. Vitale's work has 'spawned' extensive discussion, for example in the form of special journal issues dedicated to it by *Postmodern Culture* 28.3 (2018) and 29.1 (2018), and *CR: The New Centennial Review* 19, no. 3 (2019). One could argue that other recent 'strains' in Derrida studies include a new materialist, an animal studies and an environmental or ecological one.

38 There is Vicki Kirby's article 'Tracing Life: "La Vie La Mort"', *CR: The New Centennial Review* 9, no. 1 (2009): 107–26; Vitale's volume *Biodeconstruction*, 2018, which also contains large parts of the English translation of the seminar; and there is also Dawne McCance's *The Reproduction of Life Death: Derrida's La vie la Mort* (New York: Fordham University Press, 2019), which provides a close reading and a critical and genealogical contextualization of Derrida's seminar.

39 This is what occupies the first part of the first session in Derrida's seminar; cf. Derrida, *La vie la mort*, 19–26.

40 Christopher Johnson's *System and Writing in the Philosophy of Jacques Derrida* (Cambridge: Cambridge University Press, 1993), is a notable and early exception; see also Sean Gaston's excellent chapter 10 ('La vie la mort, la mort la vie') of *Derrida and Disinterest* (London: Continuum, 2005), 109–25. Even though the validity of Derrida's notion of grammatology as a general science of writing has been challenged by Catherine Malabou (see her 'The End of Writing? Grammatology and Plasticity', *European Legacy* 12, no. 4 [2007]: 431–41), I would

concur with Deborah Goldgaber that Derrida's notion of writing was always 'plastic' (i.e. 'nongraphic'), see Goldgaber, 'Programmed to Fail? On the Limits of Inscription and the generality of Writing', *Journal of Speculative Philosophy* 31, no. 3 (2017): 444–56. See also Vitale, *Biodeconstruction*, 73, on this point.

41 Derrida, *Of Grammatology*, trans. Gayatri Chakravorty Spivak, corrected ed. (Baltimore: Johns Hopkins University Press, 1997), 9.

42 Vicki Kirby's work is in many ways emblematic and also seminal in this respect; cf. her entry, 'Deconstruction', in *The Routledge Companion to Literature and Science*, ed. Bruce Clarke and Manuela Rossini (London: Routledge, 2011), 287–97, which already spells out many of the aspects of Vitale's 'biodeconstruction', and establishes a link between deconstruction and feminist new materialism and the 'nonhuman turn' more generally. See also her 'Original Science: Nature Deconstructing Itself', *Derrida Today* 3, no. 2 (2010): 201–20; *Quantum Anthropologies: Life at Large* (Durham: Duke University Press, 2011); and 'Grammatology: A Vital Science', *Derrida Today* 9, no. 1 (2016): 47–67.

43 Vitale, *Biodecontstruction*, p. 1; Vitale underlines life, trace and text in this passage. I would be inclined to underline 'matrix', and 'structures', too, for reasons that will become clear later.

44 This is the subject of session 4 in Derrida's *La vie la mort*, 109–31, and discussed in Vitale's *Biodeconstruction*, 47–9. See also Deborah Goldhaber's review of *Biodeconstruction* in *Derrida Today* 13, no. 1 (2020): 119–21. It is Derrida's aim to deconstruct this vitalist metaphysics by showing that death is a necessary inscription in life's 'programme'. Vitale illustrates this idea by referring to the scientific and philosophical discussion around the notion of *apoptosis* (or 'programmed cell death') in chapters 5 and 6 of his *Biodeconstruction*, where he uses Jean-Claude Ameisen's seminal, *La Sculpture du vivant – Le suicide cellulaire ou la mort créatrice*, Paris: Seuil, 1999. See also Astrid Schrader, 'Microbial Suicide: Towards a Less Anthropocentric Ontology of Life and Death', *Body and Society* 23, no. 2 (2017): 48–74.

45 See also Philippe Lynes's reading of *survivance* through what he calls 'general ecology', esp. chapter 1 of his *Futures of Life Death on Earth: Derrida's General Ecology* (London: Rowman & Littlefield, 2018), 1–42.

46 Derrida, *Learning to Live Finally*, 51–2.

47 The 'ends' of life, one might say, in many ways function analogous to the 'ends of man', in Derrida's eponymous essay in *Margins of Philosophy*, trans. Alan Bass (Chicago: University of Chicago Press, 1982), 109–36, and the discussion in Jean-Luc Nancy and Philippe Lacoue-Labarthe (eds), *Les Fins de l'homme – à partir du travail de Jacques Derrida* (Paris: Galilée, 1981).

48 Cf. Derrida, '. . .That Dangerous Supplement. . .', *Of Grammatology*, 141–64.

49 Kirby, 'Tracing Life', 120.

50 See note 185, on apoptosis as programmed cell death, discussed earlier.

51 For an excellent summary, see Laurent Milesi, 'Almost Nothing at the Beginning: The Technicity of the Trace in Deconstruction', in *Language Systems: After Prague Structuralism*, ed. Louis Armand and Pavel Černovsky (Prague: Litteraria Pragensia, 2007), 22–41. See also Milesi's 'triptych' of genealogies on 'Derrida and Posthumanism' ('From Sign to Trace'; 'The Technicity of the Trace'; 'The Animality of the Trace', *Genealogy of the Posthuman*, available online at: criticalposthumanism .net/derridaandposthumanism (forthcoming).

52 For an excellent overview, see Arthur Bradley, *Originary Technicity: The Theory of Technology from Marx to Derrida* (Houndmills: Palgrave Macmillan, 2011); see also the conclusion to Richard Beardsworth's *Derrida and the Political* (London: Routledge, 1996), 145–64.

53 Apart from the obvious reference to Donna Haraway's early work focusing on the figure of the 'cyborg', there is, closer to Derridean deconstruction, David Wills's work, esp. his *Inanimation: Theories of Inorganic Life* (Minneapolis: University of Minnesota Press, 2016), which asks: 'if human life is originally technological, then what particular artificial, automatic, inanimate, or inorganic forms of life might be identified "within" it or produced by it?' (xi).

54 See Bernard Stiegler, *Technics and Time*, 3 volumes, Stanford: Stanford University Press, 1998–2010; for a competing paleoanthropological account of the role of technology for hominization, namely through the notion of 'anthropotechnics', see Peter Sloterdijk, *You Must Change Your Life*, trans. Wieland Hoban (Cambridge: Polity, 2014).

55 On the deconstructive 'supplementary' logic of the prosthetic, see David Wills, *Prosthesis* (Stanford: Stanford University Press), 1995.

56 The latest manifestation of which would be all forms of transhumanism, understood as the continuation of evolution through technology, going through a phase of accelerated and intensified interfacing between humans and machines, 'enhancement' and eventual 'replacement' and, ultimately, transcendence of the human bodily form (i.e. the 'animal', organic, biological human body) by some form of AI or superintelligence.

57 Franceso 'Vitale, Making the Différance: Between Derrida and Stiegler', *Derrida Today* 13, no. 1 (2020): 12.

58 Deborah Goldgaber, 'Plasticity, Technicity, Writing', *Parallax* 25, no. 2 (2019): 144.

59 Ibid.

60 It is also the starting point of a posthumanism 'without' technology (but maybe not without *technē*) which, arguably, would be the best interpretation today of Heidegger's famous claim that 'the essence of technology is by no means anything technological' (cf. Martin Heidegger, 'The Question Concerning Technology', *Basic Writings* [New York: Harper & Row, 1977, 287]). See Stefan Herbrechter and

Ivan Callus, 'Critical posthumanism or, the *inventio* of a posthumanism without technology', *Subject Matters* 3.2/4.1 (2007): 15–29.

61 Jacques Derrida, *H.C. For Life, That Is to Say. . .*, trans. Laurent Milesi and Stefan Herbrechter (Stanford: Stanford University Press, 2006).

62 With the exception of Michael Naas, who briefly refers to *H.C. For Life* in his 'Learning to Read 'Life Death' Finally: Francesco Vitale's Epigenetic Criticism', *CR: The New Centennial Review* 19, no. 3 (2019): 31.

63 Sigmund Freud, *Totem and Taboo, Standard Edition of the Complete Psychological Works*, trans. and ed. James Strachey, vol. 13 (London: Hogarth press, 1955), 75–99.

64 For the first aspect of why it is impossible to be on the side of death even though Derrida cannot unreservedly countersign Cixous's radically affirmative stance of 'being on the side of life', please see my 'Theory . . . for life', in *Style in Theory: Between Literature and Philosophy*, eds. Ivan Callus, James Corby and Gloria Lauri-Lucente (London: Bloomsbury, 2013), 303–21.

65 See esp. *H.C. For Life*, 76–7.

66 Derrida, *H.C. For Life*, 105.

67 Ibid., 110–20.

68 Ibid., 108–20.

69 Ibid., 112.

70 Ibid., 114.

71 This is maybe what David Wills refers to when he speaks of 'inanimation' as a 'nonspecific vitalization of matter' (cf. Wills, *Inanimation*, 17).

72 Tagny Duff et al. 'How to Make Living Viral Tatoos', *Leonardo* 44, no. 2 (2011): 164.

73 Tagny Duff, 'Living Viral Tatoos? Crisis Alert!', *Total Art* 1, no. 1. (2011): n.p.; available online at: http://totalartjournal.com/wp-content/uploads/2011/08/Duff_LivingViralTattoos_TotalArtJournal_Vol.1_No.1_Summer2011.pdf.

74 Cf. Cary Wolfe, 'Ecologizing Biopolitics, or, What Is the 'Bio' of Bioart?' in *General Ecology: The New Ecological Paradigm*, ed. Erich Hörl and James Burton (London: Bloomsbury, 2017), 217–34.

Part II

Politics

4

Contagious politics

Posthuman anarchism

Saul Newman

The Covid-19 pandemic is not only a global public health crisis, but also it presents a major crisis of legitimacy for our political institutions and, indeed, for the existing structure of our society; and it is likely to have far-reaching and long-lasting consequences. Most obviously, we think about the extraordinary emergency powers employed by governments around the world, democratic and authoritarian alike, to lock down millions of their citizens and to impose unprecedented restrictions on social life and economic activity. Will this become a permanent feature of life, where routinely and with very little democratic oversight, states of emergency will be declared in the name of protecting public health? Surely this verifies Foucault's thesis about the way that the biopolitical management of life displaces or, rather, overwrites sovereignty in the modern period.

The pandemic is not only testing democratic regimes to breaking point, but has led to a fundamental questioning of the legitimacy of neoliberal forms of governance, as we rediscover the importance of public services and, indeed, of social solidarity. It has also intensified and accelerated political antagonisms between left and right, with 'culture wars' now being fought over the symbolism of mask wearing or the legitimacy of lockdowns. Such antagonisms have given further impetus to right-wing populism, which, fuelled by outlandish conspiracy theories (which have also spread like a virus in recent times) in some cases now takes the form of open insurgency. We have also witnessed protests and spontaneous mobilizations around the world against police violence, racial and economic injustice and ecological destruction. All these forms of politics, despite their differences, can be understood as a reaction to a (neo)liberal global economic order that has lost any sense of symbolic efficacy. What is revealed is the 'anarchy' at its core, as it is increasingly incapable of managing the crises – economic and ecological – that it generates. No wonder the prevailing condition today is a deeply nihilistic one. This crisis of legitimacy produces what I call contagious politics, characterized by unpredictable irruptions, unstable political forms and unlikely ideological affinities: the way, for instance, that many anti-lockdown protests involve conspiracy theorists and new age antivaxxers, and people on the Far Left and the Far Right. Political issues and struggles instantaneously 'go viral', and traverse borders, much like the virus itself. There is also a breakdown of trust in traditional political institutions and once accepted sources of political and epistemological authority; the political class and parliamentary institutions, along with the mainstream media, are openly held in disdain. Covid-19 has released, after a long period of incubation, political viruses that are transforming the social landscape.

These new antagonisms may also be seen as symptomatic of the posthuman political condition. If the pandemic has revealed anything, it is the vulnerability of our bodies and the permeability of our societies to unpredictable natural and biological forces, which we once believed we could control. It has brought home to us our dependence upon natural ecosystems which we have seriously disrupted. The fact that this global pandemic spread through a chance encounter between human and animal, emerging as a result of our commercial exploitation and domination of non-human species, ought to remind us not only of the disastrous consequences of our activity on the natural environment but also of our interconnectedness with broader networks of relations which we have made dangerously unstable. The astonishing way in which a microscopic biological organism (apparently all the virus particles that exist in the world take up the same space as a can of Coke) can bring human activity to a grinding halt symbolizes, in a dramatic fashion, the decentring of the figure of Man characteristic of the posthuman condition.[1] It is perhaps not surprising that this traumatic experience produces such divergent political reactions, from the climate-change denialism of the right-wing populists, who seek to cling onto the anthropocentric illusion of our dominion over the natural world, to movements for climate justice like Extinction Rebellion, which demand governments declare a climate emergency.

The sense of crisis and emergency – of the loss of control over our destiny – opens up a new and unpredictable horizon, a shifting and 'anarchic' ontological ground, which no longer provides a secure foundation for political experience. This is an uncertain ground which we now have to navigate, and in which are forced to think 'without a bannister', as Hannah Arendt would say.

How, then, can we make sense of this political horizon opened up by the pandemic? What kinds of theoretical and conceptual tools are available to us to grasp what is essentially a new political condition? And how might we respond? One way to understand this 'anarchic' condition – by which I mean the absence of central, dominant or founding signifier – is through anarchist theory itself. Anarchism, I would argue, has some important things to say about our contemporary political moment. Much has been written about the anarchist currents and influences in radical political mobilizations over the past decade, from Occupy Wall Street to forms of 'networked' politics and new social movements characterized by decentralized decision-making and a resistance to the usual channels of political representation and communication.[2] This is a new kind of insurrectionary politics, where the goal is no longer the revolutionary seizure of state power – as in the Marxist–Leninist model – but rather the deposing or de-legitimizing of existing political institutions; what Giorgio Agamben refers to as 'de-instituting' or 'destituent power'.[3]

In making reference to the ontological anarchy characteristic of the posthuman experience, I am also pointing to something beyond the conceptual confines of classical anarchist theory – the revolutionary anarchist philosophies and projects that emerged from nineteenth-century thinkers like Pierre-Joseph Proudhon, Mikhail Bakunin and Peter Kropotkin. Instead, a more apt way to grasp the politics of the posthuman condition is through what I call postanarchism.

Postanarchism

Postanarchism has emerged as a central genre in contemporary radical political thought. While it has followed different paths and trajectories, it can generally be understood as a reformulation of the classical doctrine of anarchism through an engagement with poststructuralist theory. It acknowledges many of the key insights from thinkers like Michel Foucault, Jacques Derrida, Gilles Deleuze, Félix Guattari and Jacques Lacan, among others. In this sense, postanarchism can be understood as 'poststructuralist' anarchism. As I have argued elsewhere, poststructural theory has important consequences for contemporary anarchism.[4] While it presents a central challenge to the foundationalist ontology of the classical anarchism of the eighteenth and nineteenth centuries – particularly in terms of its assumptions about human nature and the possibilities of a rational social order – it also fosters a renewal of anarchism in ways that make it more relevant to contemporary forms of radical politics.

Some time ago, Jean-Francois Lyotard announced the 'postmodern condition': a condition characterized by the collapse of the 'metanarrative', in which people no longer believed in the grand narratives of modernity and expressed an increasing scepticism towards traditional sources of epistemic authority, and even scientific knowledge.[5] No doubt this has ambiguous consequences. On the one hand, it seems to resonate with the contemporary 'post-truth' condition, in which competing narratives and 'alternative facts' obfuscate and decentre the symbolic order of truth; a condition which is manipulated by right-wing populists who, in a paradoxical fashion, use it to impose their own alternative order of truth on the world.[6] At the same time, the postmodern condition, in its challenge to the dominant philosophical narratives – like modernity, the Enlightenment and humanism – also has, I would argue, potentially emancipatory consequences, coinciding with the posthuman political experience.

As I have suggested, we are seeing the exhaustion of a particular way of experiencing the world and our place within it. This paradigm was founded on anthropological certainties and a Promethean faith in human progress, technological development and limitless economic growth. Yet today, as we are faced with imminent ecological collapse, we are forced to question not only our relationship with the natural world, but also our own centrality and significance in a world that increasingly takes the form of a network, an entangled series of relations in which we are inexorably bound to one another, as well as to non-human life forms and ecosystems, and even to material objects. As Cary Wolfe explains, posthumanism is the acknowledgement of the embeddedness of the human within broader social systems – natural, communicative, cultural, technological and so on – which blurs the binary division between the human and non-human, while at the same time giving greater meaning and specificity to the human condition.[7] It is to acknowledge that we are, as he puts it, fundamentally prosthetic creatures who have evolved with non-human forms which, paradoxically, are also what define what it is to be human. Posthumanism refers to the recognition of the way we as humans are situated within, dependent upon and, to speak in Derridean terms, *supplemented* by networks, relations and life forms, both human and non-human, that are beyond our immediate control. This unsettles us, limits our sense of mastery and autonomy – or rather the illusion of autonomy in the strictly individualistic and anthropocentric sense – and forces an opening towards the other. This does not signify the end of the human experience as such, but rather an auto-critique or auto-deconstruction of the discursive limits of humanism. The ecological crisis and the threat of the collapse of ecosystems upon which all human life depends, is perhaps the clearest example of the decentring of Man from his world. Whether our long-term response to this will take the reactive or paranoid form that we are presently witnessing, or the invention of new forms of commonality and solidarity with the natural and non-human world[8] – which we are also seeing some signs of – remains an open question.

There are some important parallels, which I will draw out later, between posthumanism and postanarchism. Postanarchism is an attempt to reformulate anarchist theory in the wake of the end of Enlightenment humanism as the guiding narrative of modernity. It is a way of understanding anti-authoritarian politics and ethics in the context of what Foucault referred to as the disappearance of Man,[9] and without the ontological and epistemological guarantees that this figure once provided.

Deconstruction and reconstruction

Postanarchism involves two main theoretical moves. *First*, it is a critical deconstruction of some of the epistemological limits of the nineteenth-century paradigm of classical anarchism. This was an anarchism borne of the revolutionary optimism of Enlightenment modernity. It was an anarchism that believed that the revolution would emancipate the whole of humanity and transform the entirety of social relations, ushering in harmonious and cooperative forms of coexistence. Underlying this vision of social relations was the belief in an immanent rationality and morality – obscured and distorted by existing political and economic structures, as well as by religion and ideological mystification – that would nevertheless be revealed once these artificial institutions had been overthrown. There was a faith in the inherent sociability of mankind, which would form the basis of a self-governing community. This is why the sovereign political state was seen by anarchists as an unnecessary and destructive intrusion upon an otherwise rationally ordered society, why it was regarded as an obstacle to human progress and flourishing. What is central to classical anarchism is a kind of Manichean logic that assumes an ontological separation between humanity and power. Power, embodied in the state and in other social institutions, is seen as an alien coercive force that limits and distorts people's natural rational and moral capacities for freedom, development and sociability.

Poststructuralism sharpens an auto-critique already immanent within anarchism itself. Indeed, poststructuralism might be seen as a kind of continuation of the anti-authoritarian impulse of anarchism itself, but turning its critique on discursive and epistemological authority and fixed identities. For Derrida, poststructuralism is an attempt to break with the 'chain of substitutions' that reaffirms the authority and determining power of a centre – whether it is God, man, consciousness or even the structure of language itself.[10] In this sense, what unites the diverse strands of poststructuralism is the rejection of the discourse of essentialist humanism, or what Derrida would refer to as the metaphysics of presence: the idea that there is a fixed, determined and determining identity (whether it is Power, Man, Truth, the Good) behind, or at the origin of, the play of signifiers and social forces.

In view of this deconstructive approach, we must ask ourselves whether we can make the same assumptions about subjectivity held by the anarchists of the nineteenth century. Starting with the nineteenth-century thinker Max Stirner, who argued that human essence was an ideological illusion and a hangover from religion and metaphysics, through to Foucault, who rejected any idea of a universal Subject behind the various historically specific ways in which subjectivity is constituted by power and discursive regimes of truth, the unity of the subject as a transhistorical entity has been placed in doubt. One of the key points to be taken from Foucault, and other poststructuralist thinkers, is that there can be no ontological separation between the subject and external social forces, including power. The subject who resists power is also in part constituted by it: 'The man described for us, whom we are invited to free, is already in himself the effect of a subjection much more profound than himself.'[11] The decentring of the subject is also present in the psychoanalytic theories of Jacques Lacan, who claimed that the subject is the subject of language as an external order of signifiers and is, moreover, founded on a fundamental lack, an incompleteness that propels the dialectic of desire without fulfilment. In a different way, Gilles Deleuze and Félix Guattari saw desire as a multiplicity of social forces that cut across and fragment the individual, connecting the human and non-human, man, animal and machine.

Poststructuralism also places in doubt the very idea of revolution itself, if by revolution we understand a total transformation of social, political and economic relations and the liberation from power. Where and how a revolution can emerge from a field saturated and power relations, and what it is able to achieve, is a question we must ask ourselves today. The idea of a revolution, as a struggle aimed at overthrowing hierarchical power, evades the reality that, in late modernity, power relations are much more decentralized, complex and take the form of overlapping and all-pervasive networks of communication, surveillance and control, rather than a centralized and clearly identifiable political structure.[12] Moreover, the notion of revolution was part of a modernist paradigm, in which Man acts on the world in a Promethean way, and attempts to transform the entirety of social relations in a single totalizing and collective political event. Invested in this fantasy is the idea that the revolution would liberate humanity, once and for all, from all kinds of oppressions and artificial limitations and usher in an eternal state of freedom and harmony. Instead, postanarchism embraces Foucault's insight that, rather than speaking about 'liberation', we should think in terms of ongoing 'practices of freedom' that are engaged in a continual contestation with the power relations and limits, limits that will exist in *any* society.[13] Today, the invention of alternative communities, ways of living, non-capitalistic forms of exchange based on the idea of the commons and, above all, non-violent ways of relating to other living beings, human and non-human, can all be seen as ethical 'practices of freedom' in this sense.

The encounter with poststructuralist theory no doubt poses certain problems for anarchism, particularly regarding the humanist epistemological and ontological limits that it was initially framed within. At the same time, it presents the challenge to think what anarchism might mean as a political and ethical project, without the ontological certainties and moral and rational foundations it once relied upon. Therefore, the *second* move central to postanarchism is 'reconstructive': an understanding of postanarchism as a positive political and ethical strategy or series of strategies that can inform contemporary radical struggles and movements. Below I outline a number of ethical coordinates for thinking about these new modes of radical political engagement.

Voluntary (in)servitude[14]

Perhaps the main ethical and political problem that postanarchism grapples with is what Étienne de La Boétie termed, several centuries ago, 'servitude volontaire' – the phenomenon of voluntary obedience to tyrannical power. This is an obedience that was not coerced but freely given, and it was this which was, for La Boétie in the sixteenth century as it remains for us today, the fundamental enigma of politics. The paradox of our time is one in which the decline of traditional structures of patriarchal authority and centralized political power is accompanied by ever greater levels of conformity, docility and obedience. The problem of voluntary servitude to some extent overturns the humanist assumption that man always desires freedom; rather, the project of freedom becomes an ethical problem to be worked through.

However, the key insight to be taken from La Boétie's radical analysis of obedience is that power has no consistency or stability of its own, but is something entirely dependent on, indeed constituted by, our free acceptance of it. Power would not exist if we did not choose to obey it. Put more radically, power is an illusion created by our own identification with it; power, on its own, does not exist. This means that just as the constitution of power is a matter of will and free volition, so is its undoing. As La Boétie put it, 'Resolve to serve no more, and you are at once freed.'[15] We overcome power, not by destroying it as such, but by simply refusing to recognize it, by turning our backs upon it; the reflexive illusion of power, constituted by our own obedience, is thus dispelled.

Singularities

We need another way of thinking about subjectivity that is no longer confined to identity. As Foucault put it, 'maybe the target nowadays is not to discover who we are but to refuse who we are.'[16] Even though marginalized identities, whether cultural, religious, sexual or gender, are so often subject to violence and oppression, the problem is that in confining one's struggle to a demand for recognition and inclusion within existing legal and institutional structures is a limitation of our political experience. The demand for identity recognition is a form of (neo)liberal biopolitics that does little to challenge structures of domination, exploitation and violence. Instead, I suggest we think in terms of *singularities*. Singularities escape and slip between categories of identity. They are mutable, contingent and in a constant process of *becoming* – reconstituting themselves in relation to others and within networks of relations. Postanarchism places an emphasis on multiple forms of experimentation with different ways of living and relating to ourselves and to others. Here I am partly indebted to Stirner's radical concepts of 'ownness' and 'uniqueness'. While these are often wrongly conflated with a selfish egoism, Stirner understood the ego, or what he called the 'unique one', as an ongoing process of *flux, becoming* and *anarchic self-constitution*. However, rather than this being a solipsistic experience, Stirner believed that in clearing the ground of the ideological 'spooks' of humanism, it would open the way for new, more autonomous relations with the external world.

Yet, we need to think more carefully about the encounter between singularity and community. One of the most important political tasks today is to invent new ideas of community which do not destroy difference and uniqueness, but work to enhance it. Stirner's underdeveloped and paradoxical idea of the 'union of egoists' – a loose, rhizomatic collective association without any fixed identity or structure – points in this direction.[17] We could also consider more recent attempts within continental philosophy to rethink community in non-totalizing and non-exclusionary ways. Jean-Luc Nancy argued that, in the wake of the collapse of Communism, we could no longer return to some organic or essential idea of community based on nostalgia for shared traditions, culture and identity; precisely the vision of community invoked by right-wing populists today, which inevitably involves forms of exclusion and domination. Rather, we need to think about an alternative form of community that is constitutively open to singularity, and which resists the temptation to absorb differences into a totalizing collective identity.[18] Similarly, Roberto Esposito has critically explored the immunizing paradigms and rationalities of modernity, which seek to protect and secure the identity and integrity of the body politic from the threat of contamination, whether from immigrants and stateless people, or even from biological agents like viruses. However, the danger is that these immunizing impulses become 'auto-immunizing' and end up destroying what they seek to protect. Esposito attempts to think beyond this 'immunitarian' logic through alternative understandings of commonality defined by gift (*munus*) and even debt, implying reciprocity, mutuality and obligation.[19] Giorgio Agamben refers to 'whatever singularity' and 'the coming community', invoking the idea of gatherings and convergences that are not based on predefined identities (not based on 'who'), which are, in other words, *indifferent* to identity and are defined instead by their co-belonging. In strikingly anarchistic overtones, Agamben predicts, 'the novelty of the coming politics is that it will no longer be a struggle for the conquest or control of the State, but a struggle between the State and the non-State (humanity), an insurmountable disjunction between whatever singularity and the State organization.'[20]

Insurrection

We must also think about political action in new ways, and this is where the notion of the insurrection becomes important. Following on from a number of themes outlined earlier, the insurrection might be seen as a kind of revolt not so much against the external world of power – although that might be a consequence of it – but more so as a form ethical self-transformation, a revolt against fixed identities, modes of action and forms of life that power imposes upon us or which we have freely internalized. Again, I am indebted to Stirner here and his idea of the Empörung (*Uprising*):

Revolution and insurrection must not be looked upon as synonymous. The former consists in an overturning of conditions, of the established condition or *status*, the state or society, and is accordingly a *political* or *social* act; the latter has indeed for its unavoidable consequence a transformation of circumstances, yet does not start from it but from men's discontent with themselves, is not an armed rising but a rising of individuals, a getting up without regard to the *arrangements* that spring from it. The Revolution aimed at new arrangements; insurrection leads us no longer to *let* ourselves be arranged, but to arrange ourselves, and sets no glittering hopes on 'institutions'. It is not a fight against the established, since, if it prospers, the established collapses of itself; it is only a working forth of me out of the established.[21]

While the revolution works to transform external social and political conditions and institutions, the insurrection is aimed at one's own self-transformation. To engage in an insurrection means placing oneself *above* external conditions and constraints, whereupon these constraints simply disintegrate. It starts from the affirmation of the self, and the political consequences flow from this. The insurrection, unlike the revolution, is radically anti-institutional; not necessarily in the sense of seeking to get rid of all institutions, as this would lead simply to different kinds of institutions emerging in their place, but rather in the sense of asserting one's power over institutions and, indeed, one's indifference to them. This notion of insurrection is radically different from most understandings of radical political action. It eschews the idea of an overarching project of social transformation. Freedom is not the end goal of the insurrection but, rather, its starting point. What Stirner's notion of insurrection highlights is the extent to which we are often complicit with the systems of power that we see as dominating.

Prefigurative politics

Perhaps we need to understand power not as a substance or a thing, but as a relationship we forge and renew everyday through our actions and our relations with others. As the anarchist Gustav Landauer put it: 'The state is a social relationship; a certain way of people relating to one another. It can be destroyed by creating new social relationships; i.e., by people relating to one another differently.'[22] He places the emphasis not so much on the revolutionary seizure or destruction of the external system of power, but rather on a micropolitical and ethical transformation of the self and its relation to others, and the creation of alternative and more autonomous relations; the result of which is the transcendence of state power. Here Landauer touches on one of the key ethical principles of anarchism, one also shared by postanarchism: prefiguration. Prefiguration is the idea that the type of politics one engages in should already reflect or *prefigure* the type of society, the kinds of social relations, one wishes to create. Prefiguration is therefore a kind of anti-strategic and, indeed, ethical impulse. It is the idea that one's moral principles should not be sacrificed to the exigencies of politics, that the ends do not always justify the means. For instance, if you aim to build a society without violence, then you should not use violent means to achieve this; if you want a society without domination, then you should not employ authoritarian or vanguardist measures in your revolutionary strategy. Understood in this way, prefiguration also means acting on the present, in the *here and now*, working to modify, at a micropolitical level, one's immediate environment and one's relations with others. As Bakunin warned in his debates with Marx and his followers in the First International, the use of authoritarian measures in a revolutionary struggle, and the instrumentalization of state power to build socialism, would only lead to a replication of the structures of state authority and an intensification of its power.

In considering prefigurative practices in the context of the posthuman political condition, we have much to learn from thinkers like Ivan Illich, who argued as early as the 1970s that modern institutions and technologies – schooling, corporate health care, mass transit systems and industrial technology generally – had reached a point of crisis in efficiency and effectiveness, robbing people of their autonomy and their capacity to manage their own lives. Modern medicine made people less healthy and more vulnerable to sickness, with more iatrogenic diseases and a greater reliance on drugs. Modern transportation – our reliance on cars – means that we spend more time travelling; the faster we can go, the slower we become. Modern education had diminished our capacity for self-learning. Today we could make the same point about faster connectivity of communication networks and devices, which is supposed to save time but which actually means we waste greater amounts of time 'staying connected'. Our over-reliance on antibiotics, as a result of our dependence on the pharmaceutical industry to administer our health-care needs, has led to our greater susceptibility to new strains drug resistant bacteria. And so on. In place of these systems, Illich proposed 'tools of conviviality' – human scaled technologies and systems designed to empower people to manage their own lives and wean them off their dependency on big institutions: 'I choose the term "conviviality" to designate the opposite of industrial productivity. I intend it to mean autonomous and creative intercourse among persons, and the intercourse of persons with their environment . . . I consider conviviality to be individual freedom realized in personal interdependence and, as such, an intrinsic ethical value.'[23]

Important here also is the emphasis on human limitation: not only will industrial and technological development and economic growth run up against their own internal limit (what is called entropy), but also, in order to live sustainably and for society to achieve homeostasis, people will need to limit their own activity and consumption. However, rather than this being a miserable condition, it is something to be welcomed. Illich talks about a 'right to frugality'. He proposes that reducing our needless consumption and learning to live with simpler, but more useful, technology, coupled with a more just distribution of resources and power, would free up time for self-expression and for more convivial relations with others. Perhaps this might be one of the positive outcomes of the current pandemic. Today we see many such experiments in autonomy and conviviality, forms of practical anarchy, where people in transnational networks or local and regional communities try to foster more sustainable ways of working, farming, consuming and living, organizing movements and networks in defence of common natural resources, indigenous lands and the local environment against corporate and state enclosure and development; or, more recently, forms of mutual aid and networks of solidarity springing up in response to the pandemic. The current crisis has shown us the destructive hubris of our current way of living, with its obsession with work, productivity and economic growth, and our exploitation of the natural world and non-human species. It has hopefully taught us the value of a different way of life, one that is more autonomous and sustainable.

Ecological entanglement

Postanarchism rejects an anthropocentric view of the world, and embraces instead an ethics and politics of entanglement with the non-human natural world. Of course, an ecological sensibility has never been alien to anarchist theory or practice. We think of the variants of anarchism which take into account our connections with the natural world: from Murray Bookchin's theory of social ecology, which explored the interrelationship between ecological and social domination,[24] to even more radical elements of deep green ecology and 'anti-civilizational' or 'primitivist' anarchism.[25] However, where postanarchism departs, particularly from Bookchin's 'dialectical naturalism', is in rejecting the idea of a rational totality or wholeness that is somehow immanent within social relations and whose emergence will bring about a rational harmonization of social forces and the full humanization of Man. Bookchin says: 'By wholeness, I mean varying levels of actualization, an unfolding of a wealth of particularities, that are latent in an as-yet-undeveloped potentiality. This potentiality may be a newly planted seed, a newly born infant, a newly born community, or a newly born society.'[26] However, can we assume that the possibilities of human freedom lie rooted in the natural order, as a secret waiting to be discovered, as a flower waiting to blossom, to use Bookchin's metaphor? Can we assume that there is a rational unfolding of possibilities, driven, in a Hegelian manner, by a unified historical and social logic? This would seem to fall into the trap of essentialism, whereby there is a rational essence or being at the foundation of society whose truth we must perceive. There is an implicit positivism here, in which political and social phenomena are seen as conditioned by natural principles and scientifically observable conditions. A postanarchist perspective is sceptical of this view of a social order founded on deep rational principles. Indeed, this is part of the very anthropocentric/anthropomorphic paradigm that has contributed to the objectification and instrumentalization of the natural world. Rather than nature providing the basis for a stable and rational social order, ecological entanglement embodies indeterminacy and contingency; it means that all social identities now have to be considered as part of an unstable, unpredictable network of relations, of ecosystems that are constantly changing and adapting and therefore disrupting any fixed or consistent image of a social order. A similar point is made by Bruno Latour, who develops an alternative idea of 'political ecology' based on our place within unstable and unpredictable *assemblages* of relations with non-human entities, in which 'nature' acts upon and shapes the meaning of politics, just as politics acts upon and shapes the natural world.[27]

Yet, while classical anarchism, in its assumptions about human nature, is in many ways part of the humanist paradigm of modernity, it also goes beyond this. For instance, in Peter Kropotkin's idea of 'mutual aid'[28] we find ideas of solidarity and cooperation based on shared biological and evolutionary instincts between humans and non-humans – something that challenged the anthropocentric view of the world as well as a crude articulation of Darwinian theory that saw the natural (and social) world only in terms of the 'survival of the fittest'. The philosopher Catherine Malabou has recently sought to rethink Kropotkin's idea of mutual aid as a basis for social solidarity and political mutuality. Importantly, she argues – in contradistinction to postanarchist critiques of Kropotkin's biological determinism[29] – that his evolutionary theory, which he derives from observations of animal species, disrupts the boundaries between philosophy, politics and biology; between the human and natural worlds. She says in an interview:

> This would also give me the opportunity of questioning the frontier between traditional anarchism and what has been called post-anarchism, a grouping of several trends and lines of thought that seek to reconcile libertarianism with post-structuralism. Post-anarchism is very critical of thinkers like Kropotkin, whom they judge essentialist and rationalist because of his use of biology and evolutionism. Such a rejection is what I intend to challenge, thus renewing also Kropotkin's definition of mutual aid. In his work, mutual aid appears as the other trend of evolution, along with natural selection. Living beings do not only compete, they also help each other. Political mutuality keeps something of this biological memory. Mutual help is not only support and solidarity; it is self-management, cooperative economy, organic symbiosis or ecological bioregionalism. So this is what I am currently exploring, showing that mutual help, or aid, does not constitute a *telos* in the traditional sense, but an emancipatory orientation.[30]

While I would insist that there is a rational *telos* at the heart of Kropotkin's evolutionary theory – something that at the same time drives its emancipatory politics – what I think is interesting in Malabou's interpretation of mutual aid is the way that it is oriented towards a posthuman terrain of interspecies cooperation and disrupts the neat boundaries between human and non-human lifeworlds.

Ontological anarchy, or 'anarchaeology'

Many of the ideas and themes I have been outlining here are reflective of a condition that can be referred to as *ontological anarchy*. The Heideggerian thinker Reiner Schürmann defines anarchy as the withering away of the epochal first principles, the *arché* that defined metaphysical thinking:

> The anarchy that will be at issue here is the name of a history affecting the ground or foundation of action, a history where the bedrock yields and where it becomes obvious that the principle of cohesion, be it authoritarian or 'rational', is no longer anything more than a blank space deprived of legislative, normative, power.[31]

For Schürmann, this is an experience of freedom: it frees action from its *telos*, from fixed normative frameworks, from the rule of ends that hitherto sought to determine it. Action becomes 'anarchic', that is to say groundless and without a predetermined end. Importantly, he differentiates this idea of anarchy from the political ideas and programmes of anarchist theoreticians like Bakunin, Proudhon and Kropotkin, who, on Schürmann's reading, simply sought to replace one founding principle, the political authority of the state (*princeps*), with another, rationality (*principium*): 'as metaphysical an operation as there has ever been'.[32]

Foucault, in one of his lectures at the College de France from 1979 to 1980, described his methodological approach as 'anarchaeological'. It starts from the presupposition that 'there is no universal, immediate, and obvious right that can everywhere and always support any kind of relation of power'.[33] This is not the same as saying that all power is bad; rather it means that no form of power is *automatically* admissible or incontestable. This ethico-political standpoint is one that is largely consistent with most forms of anarchism. However, where it differs is in making the non-acceptability of power one's *point of departure* rather than one's end point. In other words, perhaps we need to think of anarchism today not so much as a specific revolutionary project, but rather as an open and contingent form of action that takes the non-acceptance of power as its starting point. Can we understand anarchism as a politics that starts, rather than (necessarily) ends up with, anarchy? To quote Foucault:

> it is not a question of having in view, at the end of a project, a society without power relations. It is rather a matter of putting non-power or the non-acceptability of power, not at the end of the enterprise, but rather at the beginning of the work in the form a questioning of all the ways in which power is in actual fact accepted.[34]

So, perhaps contemporary forms of anarchism should be seen not as predetermined by fixed objectives, but rather as based on a certain contingency, open-endedness and freedom of thought and action. It does not have a predetermined ideological shape, but may take different forms and follow different courses of action at different moments. It might resist and contest specific relations of power at localized points of intensity, on the basis of their illegitimacy and violence; it might work against certain institutions and institutional practices by either working within and in support of other kinds of institutions, or through creating alternative practices and forms of organization. In other words, taking anarchy or non-power as its starting point, postanarchism, as a form of experimental and autonomous thinking and acting, can work on multiple fronts, in a variety of different settings, institutional and non-institutional, producing reversals and interruptions of existing relations of domination.

Conclusion

This flexibility in anarchism refers to what Malabou calls its *plasticity*. She said in an interview, in response to a question about how she thinks her theoretical concept of plasticity should be received:

> What would interest me is to see how we can solve the contradiction, philosophically and politically, of why we resist plasticity. How is it that some people can still be in control in a very non-plastic way of plasticity itself? How does this lead to fascisms and the new forms of extreme authoritarian regimes which all define themselves as anti-plastic? I would expect different ways of exploring what I now call the possibility of 'anarchy'.[35]

It would seem, then, that the implications of ontological anarchy – or plasticity – for radical politics today are highly ambiguous. On the one hand, anarchism must embrace the experience of anarchy and no longer rely on firm ontological foundations once provided by humanism. The experience of the contemporary world suggests that the tectonic plates of our age are shifting, that familiar and once hegemonic institutions, principles and philosophical categories – economic, political and above all anthropological – appear increasingly empty, lifeless and obsolete, or at the very least are in a state of crisis. Never has political and financial power been in a more precarious position. Never before have we been confronted in such a dramatic way with the extreme consequences of the Anthropocene condition, whereby the survival of all species, including our own, is threatened. This makes possible, indeed *necessitates*, new and more autonomous forms of action, communication, economic exchange and being in common. On the other hand, this sense we all have of an increasingly dislocated world, spinning off its hinges, fragmenting before our very eyes, confronts us with immense and unparalleled dangers: the empty nihilism and destructiveness of the global capitalist machine (and here the Anthropocene can only be understood in relation to the Capitalocene)[36] and the appearance of apocalyptic and fascistic forms of politics that seem intent on hastening the coming disorder. The condition of ontological anarchy is always accompanied by the temptation to restore the principle of authority, to fill in its empty place with new proliferations of power. We realize that power itself has become dangerously anarchic.

Against this blind and nihilistic drive, anarchism today must affirm a kind of ethical care or even conservation of the networks and ecosystems in which we are entangled, for a natural world faced with ecological collapse, as well as cultivate and affirm new forms of life, community and autonomy which are already being made possible by the ontological rift opening before us.

Notes

1 Francesca Ferrando, *Philosophical Posthumanism* (London: Bloomsbury, 2019).

2 See for instance: Richard J. F Day, *Gramsci is Dead: Anarchist Currents in the Newest Social Movements* (London: Pluto Press, 2005); David Graeber, *The Democracy Project: A History, a Crisis, a Movement* (New York: Spiegel & Grau, 2013); Paolo Gerbaudo, *The Mask and the Flag: Populism, Citizenism and Global Protest* (Oxford: Oxford University Press, 2017); Mark Bray, *Translating Anarchy: The Anarchism of Occupy Wall Street* (London: Zero Books, 2013); Marianne Maeckelbergh, *The Will of the Many: How the Alterglobalisation Movement Is Changing the Face of Democracy* (London: Pluto Press, 2009).

3 Saul Newman, 'What Is an Insurrection?' *Political Studies* 5, no. 2 (2017): 284–99.

4 Saul Newman, *From Bakunin to Lacan: Anti-authoritarianism and the Dislocation of Power* (Maryland, MD: Lexington Books, 2001); and *Postanarchism* (Cambridge: Polity Press, 2016).

5 Jean-Francois Lyotard, *The Postmodern Condition: A Report on Knowledge,* trans., Geoff Bennington and Brian Massumi (Manchester: Manchester University Press, 1979).

6 Saul Newman, 'Post-Truth and the Crisis of the Political', *Soft Power* 6, no. 2 (2019): 91–108.

7 Cary Wolfe, *What Is Posthumanism?* (Minneapolis: University of Minnesota Press, 2010), xxv.

8 See Erika Cudworth and Stephen Hobden, *The Emancipatory Project of Posthumanism* (London and New York: Routledge 2018).

9 Michel Foucault, *The Order of Things: an Archaeology of the Human Sciences* (London and New York: Routledge), 2005.

10 Jacques Derrida, *Writing and Difference*, trans. A. Bass (Chicago: University of Chicago Press, 1978).

11 Michel Foucault, *Discipline and Punish: the Birth of the Prison*, trans. A. Sheridan (London: Penguin Books, 1991), 30.

12 See, for instance, Gilles Deleuze's idea of the 'control society' in 'Postscript on the Societies of Control', *October* 59 (Winter 1992): 3–7.

13 Michel Foucault, 'The Ethics of the Concern for the Self as a Practice of Freedom', in *Ethics: Essential Works of Foucault 1954–1984*, vol. 1, ed. P. Rabinow, trans. R. Hurley et al. (London: Penguin, 2000), 281–302.

14 I borrow this term 'voluntary inservitude' from Foucault, who says that 'Critique will be the art of voluntary inservitude, of reflective indocility'. See Michel Foucault,

'What Is Critique?' in *What Is Enlightenment? Eighteenth Century Answers and Twentieth Century Questions,* ed. Schmidt, James (Berkeley, CA.: University of California Press, 1996), 382–98, 386.

15 Étienne de La Boétie, 'Discourse de la servitude volontaire' (*The Politics of Obedience: The Discourse of Voluntary Servitude,* trans., Harry Kurz, Auburn (Alabama: Ludwig von Mises Institute, 2008), 47.

16 Michel Foucault, 'The Subject and Power', in *Power: Essential Works of Foucault 1954–1984,* ed. James Faubion, trans. Roberty Hurley et al. (London: Penguin, 2000), 326–48.

17 Max Stirner, *The Ego and its Own,* ed. David Leopold, trans. S. Byington (Cambridge: Cambridge University Press, 1995), 161.

18 Jean-Luc Nancy, *The Inoperative Community,* trans. Peter Connor et al. (Minneapolis: University of Minnesota Press), 1991.

19 Roberto Esposito, *Communitas: the Origin and Destiny of Community,* trans. Timothy Campbell (Stanford: Stanford University Press, 2009).

20 Giorgio Agamben, *The Coming Community,* trans. Michael Hardt (Minneapolis: University of Minnesota Press, 1993).

21 Stirner, *The Ego and its Own,* 279–80.

22 Gustav Landauer, 'Weak State, Weaker People', in *Gustav Landauer: Revolution and Other Writings, a Political Reader,* ed. G. Kuhn (Oakland, CA: PM Press, 2010), 213–14.

23 Ivan Illich, *Tools for Conviviality* (New York: Fontana/ Collins, 1975), 24.

24 Murray Bookchin, *The Ecology of Freedom: The Emergence and Dissolution of Hierarchy* (Palo Alto, CA: Cheshire Books, 1982).

25 See, for instance, John Zerzan, *Elements of Refusal* (Columbia: CAL Press, 1999) and *Future Primitive and Other Essays* (New York: Autonomedia, 1994).

26 Bookchin, *The Ecology of Freedom,* 31.

27 Bruno Latour, *Politics of Nature: How to Bring the Sciences into Democracy,* trans. Catherine Porter (Cambridge, MA: Harvard University Press). See also, *Facing Gaia: Eight Lectures on the New Climactic Regime,* trans. Catherine Porter (Cambridge: Polity Press, 2017).

28 Peter Kropotkin, *Mutual Aid: A Factor of Evolution,* ed. Paul Avrich (New York: New York University Press, 1972).

29 Saul Newman, *The Politics of Postanarchism* (Edinburgh: Edinburgh University Press, 2010).

30 Interview with Catherine Malabou by Gerardo Flores Peña (25 July 2017) *Figure/ Ground* < http://figureground.org/interview-with-catherine-malabou/>

31 Reiner Schürmann, *Heidegger on Being and Acting: From Principles to Anarchy,* trans., C-M Gros, Bloomington: Indiana University Press, 1987, 6.

32 Ibid., 7.

33 Michel Foucault, *On the Government of the Living, Lectures at the College de France 1979-80,* ed. M. Senellart, trans. G. Burchell, Houndmills (Basingstoke: Palgrave Macmillan, 2014), 77.

34 Ibid., 78.

35 Benjamin Dalton, 'What should we do with plasticity? An Interview with Catherine Malabou', *Paragraph* 42, no. 2 (2020): 238–54. See also 'What Pleasure is there in Thinking Today?' (Interview with Catherine Malabou) *Spike Art Magazine #64* Summer 2020 < https://www.spikeartmagazine.com/articles/qa-catherine-malabou> (accessed 10 February 2021).

36 See Donna Haraway, *Staying with the Trouble: Making Kin in the Chthulucene* (Durham and London: Duke University Press, 2016).

5

Spectatorial splitting and transcultural seeing in the age of pandemics

Josephine Berry

Covid-19, like capital, is having its cake and eating it. Elizabeth Povinelli has expressed her mutual behaviour thus: 'Like the Virus that takes advantage but is not ultimately wedded to the difference between Life and Nonlife, Capital views all modes of existence as if they were vital *and* demands that not all modes of existence are the same from the point of view of the extraction of value.'[1] This paradox, I believe, is one that can also describe the emerging spectatorial regime that the Covid-19 pandemic has brought to light within the institutions and practices of Western art. The art viewer is increasingly addressed both as paradigmatic Life – the still Transcendent I/eye of Western reason – and as less than fully human, namely as the bare life whose thingification[2] has hitherto been reserved for the West's colonial Others. This conflation of ontological and biopolitical orders of the human within the pandemic museum is triggered by, but also mimics, the behaviour of the virus itself, which treats humans and objects interchangeably – while also exploiting the systems and behaviours that uphold these differences. Given how deeply invested Western ontology is in such a separation between Life and Nonlife, *bios*/zoë and *Thanatos/geos*,[3] and the associated universe of semantic, ethical, political and economic values produced on this basis, such a lack of recognition is profoundly destabilizing to the social order which presupposes it. Yet, crucially, we must acknowledge, together with Povinelli, that Capital has organized its extraction of value according to the very production of differentials in 'modes of existence' which, as a virus-like living-dead entity itself, it is also incapable of sensing or knowing – hence the paradox. The difference between life and death is, then, for capital, not an ontological but rather a strategic one. This separation that the discursive and violently practical techniques of colonialism perfected is constitutive of the regime of the racial.

Such a separation of (qualified) Life and (Non)life, *bios* and *zoë*/*Thanatos*, is also sustained by a way of seeing that Western art and its exhibition in public space have helped to produce; a way of seeing exchangeable with the transcendently universal I/eye which is premised on a non-seeing of Others. It is this non-seeing of Others, whose devalued labour has created the very production conditions of the universal, I argue, that the pandemic has rendered impossible. Later I consider the role played by Western art in co-constructing the racial regime, a political-symbolic order whose ethical justification of the unsustainable extraction of value from all other (Non)life has itself helped to create the destabilized conditions in which the zoonotic transmission of disease occurs. I argue that the virus compels art institutions, and by extension art itself, to address the spectator as the split subject of universal reason *and* bare life, thereby creating a rhizomatic link between different ontological states of humanness. While the virus has in so many ways retraced the differentials of race and class, its yoking together of post-Enlightenment and decolonial ways of seeing and being seen is shaking up the Western liberal regime of universality which produces such differentials in the first place. We might see in these tremors the prospect of a more truly transcultural perception that could help to dismantle the bourgeois liberal aesthetic regime and its reliance upon the delusion of universality.

Stepping to the side of the picture

The weekend before the second UK lockdown, I finally made it out of the house and into the centre of London to visit an actual bricks and mortar museum – the National Gallery – which stands at the tired old heart of this tired old former Empire. We didn't have long inside because one of our party had booked late and so couldn't share the same timeslot as us. In this new dystopia of public space, he had to sit outside in Trafalgar Square instead, contemplating Heather Philipson's sculpture *The End* – a fly and drone infested giant melting ice cream that sits on the Fourth Plinth gleefully spoiling the pomposity of Trafalgar Square.

'The End' sounds like a commentary on everything from the dream of endless consumption, to the self-aggrandizing mission of Western imperialism embodied in Nelson's Column, to the civic values of publicness, to the political subject of modernity which also corresponds to the aesthetic subject.

Back inside the gallery I felt like I was witnessing another ending, something more than just one more *petit mort* of Western art. But why should this be

Figure 5.1 View of Trafalgar Square with Heather Philipson's *The End* in the foreground, November 2020. Photo by Josephine Berry. © Josephine Berry.

when the gallery has remained relatively unchanged, give or take the Sainsbury Wing, since the 1970s when John Berger used its collection as the main target of his classic book and TV series *Ways of Seeing*? Or how, rather, is it ending in a way that's different from the obsolescence that Berger detected in European oil painting's complicity with patriarchal and racist capitalist power? After contemplating Gainsborough's 1750 double portrait of *Mr and Mrs Andrews*, Berger had concluded:

> If one studies European oil painting as a whole . . . it is not so much a framed window open on to the world as a safe let into the wall, a safe into which the visible has been deposited. . . . The relation between property and art in European culture appears natural to that culture.[4]

This way of seeing that Berger so effectively anatomized required a frontal mode of vision from the viewer. We need to stop in a central position and face the painting to achieve full absorption into its world, regardless of whether it employs single point perspective and the visual pyramid of Renaissance invention, or splinters into modernism's multiple spatialities. If European painting is a scopic regime in which the viewer is constructed as proprietor of the picture space, then this proprietorial mode also requires a model of subjecthood to which it refers. The viewer-proprietor should be upright, static, disembodied, concentrated and easily substituted by another equivalent eye-mind assemblage. This subject is a universal one, just as the structure of the political subject of the liberal West – endowed with rights, reason and self-determination – is also constructed as universal. The universal space of art which the National Gallery aims to embody by placing on display the chronologically ordered single story of civilizational development, its transcendental Spirit, demands an equally universally conceived viewer. But what happens to all this when such a subject of disinterested aesthetic judgement is required to follow a series of arrows stuck to the floor because her body may or may not be the bearer of a zoonotically contracted virus sweeping the global population in a technologically accelerated state of hyper-connection with effects varying from deadly to asymptomatic? What happens when the body of the viewer is addressed explicitly by the art institution outside of their capacity for judgement or even reason? Does the pandemic, like so many underlying fragilities, render explicit a tension within contemporary art's address of the subject as still both the locus of reason and yet also a bodily phenomenon whose interactions with objects and others are happening below the level of conscious thought? This dual address brings to the surface a tension running through the history of Western thought and aesthetics between the philosophical ideal of the freely self-determining subject of reason, and the subsequent scientific description of the human being as externally affected, shaped and determined; an object subject to forces like any other. Such a division, however, between those subjects of self-determination and those who are construed as externally determined and affected also demarcates a relation of power that decolonial thinkers understand to be integral to the production of the West's racial regime.

Needing to get back to our companion sitting out in the cold due to his late booking of a timeslot for entering the space of universality, we began to move at haste along the white floor arrows guiding us to the exit. Unexpectedly, this safety promoting arrow system sent us speed walking through most of the gallery, skimming past Caravaggios, Titians, Seurats, Monets, Manets, Degases, Gainsboroughs, Hogarths – so many cassocks and buttocks, bosoms and bludgeonings, white bodies engaged in lust, leisure or piety. In this sidelong blurring of each careful composition into a wave of picture-objects, the symbolic function of individual paintings started to give way, producing instead the sensation of misfiring representational and ideological stimuli. A new diagram of spectatorship and publicness seemed to emerge in this slightly breathless charge up and down the aisles of art's scrambling story. While access to the universal had been carved up and booked out, one was nevertheless there to complete the apex of the viewing pyramid, still the privileged surveyor of 'systematic space' first developed in the Renaissance and the dawn of colonial exploration. But now, just as Marx said of the worker in the accelerating industrial age, the spectator 'steps to the side of the production process instead of being its chief actor'.[5] No longer conceived as a subject of judgement and taste, a disinterested eye-mind, the spectator has become biological and potentially contagious, not to mention distracted, and needs to be acted upon as bare life at one level so she may be granted access to the universal at another. How do these two models of the subject relate to each other, and what does their convergence do to art?

What Marx means by 'stepping to the side' is that due to the development of fixed capital the worker's labour is no longer directly included into the production process, which is now built from assimilated general social knowledge that has become a 'monstrously' efficient 'direct force of production'. Instead, the human labourer is only required to act as a 'watchman or regulator':

> No longer does the worker insert a modified natural thing [*Naturgegenstand*] as middle link between the object and himself; rather, he inserts the process of nature, transformed into an industrial process, as a means between himself and inorganic nature, mastering it.[6]

We can easily see why this section of the *Grundrisse*, known as the 'fragment on machines', is famous for its prescience. Understanding technology as the production of processes, themselves modelled on nature, and the assimilation of general knowledge, rather than the mere automation of tools, is a capacious enough understanding of technology to accommodate our own computationally mimetic times. What I want to ask here is how Marx's image of the worker standing to the side of the machine, engaged in abstract gestures that depend upon the technological mimesis of natural processes, relates to the splitting of subjects of art into flesh and Spirit, *zoë* and *bios*, that we encounter in the pandemic institution. Is there in fact something missing from, or invisible within, this diagram that could help us understand the relationship better?

We are addressed frontally and laterally in the new institution of the zoonotic age, asked to be reasoning subjects, yet acted upon as mere bodies, herded as animals. Seeing pictures sideways on releases something that normally remains hidden within the frontal regime, something it has systematically obscured. This lateral seeing allows the viewer to perceive, perhaps for the first time, the construction of public exhibition space not as the egalitarian setting it purports to be, but as a space conditional upon a certain non-seeing – that of the perspective of a subject rendered bare life, a subjecthood whose creation was necessary in order to pay for the creation of such spaces in the first place. This connects to what Denise Ferreira da Silva has said about the patriarchal subject who always introduces another subject under His authority while claiming to be the only full one: that is, those less than human Others in contradistinction to which He constitutes himself.[7] The contemporary split subject of the zoonotic museum is in part still the surveyor of propertied and systematic classical space; a centred and self-transparent perspectival authority whose relations to Others are acquisitive and objectifying. Indeed, European painting's systematization of perspective is intimately bound up with the scientific, moral and legal tools that enabled its discovery, plunder and division of foreign territories *over which it held no sovereignty*. Speaking of Holbein the Younger's painting *The Ambassadors* (1497/8) held in the National Gallery's collection, Berger comments: 'To colonize a land it was necessary to convert its people to Christianity and accounting, and thus prove to them that European civilization was the most advanced in the world. Its art included' (1972, 95). The liberal European subject of politics and rights needed its Other, constructed as affectable, carnal and irrational, against whom to perfect its own embodiment of reason. One might add that the ability of the eighteenth-century couple Mr and Mrs Andrews to embody such an exemplary referentiality between identity and landownership depended not only upon the enclosures of common lands at home, which enabled the creation of the sweeping backdrop of landscape in their portrait, but upon the outsourcing of unsightly and intensively extracted agricultural labour to the colonies. The universal subject, like the increasingly abstracted factory worker, required the looted labour, resources and territories of racialized subjects to establish the global domination of capitalism and its unequal allocation of resources and life chances that continues undiminished to this day.

This capture of labour, reliant on the radical dehumanization of African slaves above all, was also made invisible as the self-same 'process of nature' referred to by Marx. The re-composition of imperialism's colonial subjects on a sliding scale of sub-humanity rendered their labour a free or devalued input of capitalism, comparable to the fertility of the soil or the energy locked up in carbon deposits. While Marx himself perceives the profound transformation of industrial labour through the assimilation of general social knowledge into fixed capital, as witnessed in the rapidly developing factories of Europe, he fails to acknowledge that what also stands between the worker and the machine at this time is slave labour or imperially extorted and racially devalued labour. We can conceive of this in the material form of the cotton derived from plantation slavery in the Americas and woven by the looms of Lancashire, or as the tea grown in colonized British India and drunk by their proletarian operators. But we can also think about this in terms of the direct subsumption of know-how, craft and cultural knowledge into the processes of capitalist production that facilitates its extraction of value and the acceleration of its technological processes.

Black and colonial labour is missing from Marx's diagram in its manual *and* mental forms and is also a part of what causes the European labourer to stand to the side of the machine, whose head and hands were needed less and less to work materials directly. The standing to the side of the machines that relies upon the looting of racialized labour in the colonies of the West is connected to the frontal regime of Renaissance perspective that creates the self-transparent subject at the apex of the visual pyramid and uses that self-positioning as an epistemological technique with which to dominate and plunder the rest of the planet. In her book *Potential History: Unlearning Imperialism* Ariella Aïsha Azoulay traces how the creation of the modern state depended upon the construction of neutral universal forms such as democratic sovereignty, citizenship, universal suffrage and the archival spaces of knowledge. Yet, in her words, 'Far from neutral, these imperial devices facilitated the plunder and appropriation of material wealth, cultures, resources, and documents, and generated the establishment of state institutions to preserve looted objects and produce a bygone past.'[8] It is the very universality of these forms that justifies the disavowal and disappearance of the genocidal violence of colonialism that was the condition of their creation. In a poignant example, she discusses a slave from South Carolina called Dave the Potter who produced exquisite clay pots that have subsequently become highly collectible and are included in a collection at the Museum of Fine Arts in Boston. Dave's work belongs to a type of handmade sculpted jar produced by slaves in the mid-nineteenth century working in Edgefield, South Carolina, a region famed for its pottery. What is also known, however, is that after the abolition of slavery in 1865, some 170 slaves of Congolese origin were illegally smuggled up the Savannah River by steamboat into the Edgefield plantation owned by a relative of the ship's owner. In other words, these craft skills were so sought after at the time that the plantation owner risked fine and arrest to procure them by kidnap. This story belies the caption in the Boston museum which states that their 'early history is unknown', both because this episode has been written about, but also because, in Azoulay's words, 'in order for these pieces to be sold in the late twentieth century, people must have believed that they were valuable and preserved them in excellent condition over the course of several generations to later sell them as "exceptionally rare examples". 'The recognition,' she continues, 'of Congolese people's skills as sculptors in materials such as clay or wood was not appreciation of an exceptionally talented individual but of a community where such knowledge was developed and transmitted over generations.'[9] It seems to be no contradiction for the 'Transcendental I' to enslave Congolese people, demean and destroy their living cultures, unsee the quality of their arts and then fill its own museums and workshops with their artefacts and skilled labour.

The nation building propelled by colonial violence drove the universal models of art and civilization embodied in places like the National Gallery or the Boston Museum of Fine Arts just as much as this violence helped power the cogs, belts and spinning jennies of factories in Cottonopolis. The extraction of resources and labour entailed the relegation and devastation of world cultures which were condemned to a bygone 'primitive' past, a separate temporality denied from co-existing in the same present as the bourgeois modernity that vampirically fed on them, rendering colonial subject worldless and their cultures valueless. This differential production of global subjects was needed to produce the ideal of Western modernity and what Sylvia Wynter has called the 'coloniality of Being'[10] – a self-transparent and latterly biologized 'descriptive statement' of humanness. Yet, the Western human descriptive statement is but one genre of humanness that sees itself, due to its scientific basis, as outside any genre whatsoever. The imposition of a biocentric Darwinian descriptive statement onto global humanity results in the dismantling of all other origin stories and all other ontologies but its own. Yet the Transcendental I escapes the consequences of its scientifically universalizing model that might threaten its privileged autonomous status by fusing the Darwinian model of biological evolution with a naturalization of Western economic domination. The market is thereby construed as an emergent evolutionary force which, like the Christian cosmogony it replaces, is fantasized to be beyond all social control and invested with the power to decide over life and death. It is no coincidence, of course, that the symbolic code of life and death instituted by this biocentric genre of being human and its attendant market logic retraces the self-same colour line drawn by colonialism between the economically saved and the 'economically damnés', in Wynter's paraphrase of Frantz Fanon.

Universal man and viral backchat

The eruption of zoonotic diseases is a direct consequence of the Western colonial construction 'Man', this genre-denying, self-transparent descriptive statement that relies upon the systematic degradation of all other forms of being human, not to mention life forms. The history of civilizational and biopolitical separations that produced the National Gallery merely culminate with the white arrows on the floor since, like the deracination of objects from colonized lifeworlds, the modern conception of art itself as the apotheosis of transhistorical Spirit necessitated the extraction of objects and practices from their living cultural milieus. This constitutes the splitting of Spirit from the Life it apparently epitomizes in the form of civilization's development and which it then comes to judge scientifically through the differential (read racial) comparison of global cultures.[11] As Rancière wrote of the eighteenth-century antiquarian art historian Johann Joachim Winkelmann, he was 'one of the first, if not the first, to invent the notion of art as we understand it: no longer as the skill of those who made paintings, statues or poems, but as *the sensible milieu* of the coexistence of these works'.[12] Reason, universality, Man, art and modernity are all synonyms for this sensible milieu, this way of seeing, as Berger called it. But if the modern museum organizes samples of deracinated species and cultural objects into teleological series, coronavirus hacks this space of rational combination by threatening humans with an animal pathogen derived from pangolins in an act of reverse colonization.

Written shortly after the first successful launch of a satellite into Earth's orbit in 1958, Hannah Arendt's proto-biopolitical work *The Human Condition*, speculates: 'The human artifice of the world separates human existence from all mere animal environment, but life itself is outside this artificial world, and through life man remains related to all other living organisms.'[13] Accordingly, the coronavirus levels the careful construction of racial hierarchies and sensible milieus by reminding us that 'through life' humans of whatever genre are related to all other living organisms. In the words of Deleuze and Guattari, 'the virus causes us to form a rhizome with other animals.'[14] Yet, with heavy sense of irony, it is modern society's phobic relation to all other life which triggers its strategies of immunization, propelling the development of an 'artificial world' that would intensify its incursions into so-called primary habitats. Ceaseless deforestation, industrial farming and trawling of the seas are the effect of the terrible success of the capitalist genre class of being human, one might say. These continuous capitalist expansions, entailing land-use changes, burgeoning human and livestock populations, climate change, global travel, biodiversity loss and habitat fragmentation, combined with random mutation and natural selection, are what cause viruses to get 'chatty', in the words of anthropologist Genese Marie Sodikoff.[15] Chatty viruses are liable not only to talk back but to jump species, including over the cordon sanitaire erected at the boundaries of human civilization, causing the laying of white arrows in the National Gallery that highlight the split contemporary subject of art.

How should we conceive of this subject of art today and how does this connect to the crisis of the universal subject and the rise of what Wynter calls a transcultural perspective – a perspective from which it is possible to perceive the edges, even the outside, of the culture-genre we inhabit? She quotes Mikhail Epstein to explain her use of the term: 'Culture frees us from nature, transculture frees us from culture, from any one culture.'[16] The virus creates a rhizomatic structure that crashes the systematic separations, thresholds and hierarchies produced by and productive of white Western bourgeois Man, freeing us from this single genre of life and manifesting our connectedness to all life. The world of artifice is thereby thrown into doubt and the poker face of civilization slips, at the cost of growing global mortalities. Visitors are addressed as infectable, vulnerable or contagious bodies as much as the universal eye-mind, the peculiarly modern subject of static attention. They are *zoë* as much as *bios*, and it is this politicization of bodily life and biologization of the political subject that is what Agamben means by 'bare life' or 'politically qualified life' (1998). Yet, unlike historical modernity's programme of self-immunization for which bare life is the inevitable and sacrificial remainder, now all such attempts at immunizations seem to increase death and threaten the conditions of life for everyone – not only the subaltern world. Bare life becomes the new universal.

The conflict between immunization and infection emerges everywhere. Top Glove, the Malaysian manufacturer of the National Health Service's (NHS) biggest supplier of rubber gloves, which has made a fortune from the pandemic, has been using forced migrant labour, forced overtime, debt bondage and passport confiscation, while housing its workers in overcrowded, unsanitary and highly contagious dormitory blocks. The manufacturers of a key component of protective equipment against this zoonotic virus employs the self-same racialized logic that sentences neo-colonial subjects to economic damnation and fracks the environment of the Global South, causing the virus bearing bats to leave their caves. This, in turn, has caused a large-scale Covid-19 outbreak across Top Glove's facilities, forcing it to close half of its factories, sending its share price tumbling and causing shortages of global glove supply.[17] Racialized capitalist extraction strategies and zoonotic outbreaks have been revealed to be continuous with each other, but now the circle has become a vortex, breaking apart multiple assemblages of separation. We can also think of these assemblages as including the techniques of systematic perspective that simultaneously produced highly focused modes of viewing and the world as a separate, scientifically knowable object.

Systematic perspective in Renaissance painting, according to the German art historian Erwin Panofsky, corresponds to a wider European understanding of space as universal and objective. In order to register the novelty of its development, he quotes Luca Gaurico (1475–1558), the Renaissance astrologer to Catherine de' Medici, who said that mathematical space is a 'continuous quantity consisting of three physical dimensions, existing by nature before all bodies and beyond all bodies, indifferently receiving everything'.[18] This neo-Platonic construction of space emerges, in Panofsky's account, with the supersession of 'divine omnipotence', producing a measurable world of continuous extension and objectification. This rationalization of space corresponds perfectly to what Ferreira da Silva calls the Western invention of the 'Transcendental I', the self-transparent subject of racialized modernity. Just as space is conceived as before and beyond 'all bodies', the Transcendental I is likewise self-grounding and thus not only unwilling, but unable to return its gaze upon itself. It presumes itself to be the universal and natural locus of reason, history and science, outside all genre types of being human.

Accordingly, for Panofsky, the price of spatial objectification in painterly representation is the replacement of 'psychophysiological space' with mathematical space, subjectivity with objectivity. If the universality of systematic space comes before *all* bodies, then this must also include the embodied eye of the observer despite the construction of that eye as omnipotent. Self-ignorance, one might say, is likewise the price to be paid by the autonomous subject of reason for rendering all other life as secondary to, or lesser than, itself. It bears emphasizing again that this Transcendental I takes on a proprietorial relation to all the fruits of the earth; its peoples and products become so many objects ripe for the taking or the crushing. Berger analyses the correspondence between the rise of colonial capitalism and the representation of new kinds of wealth in oil paintings. 'Thus painting itself,' he writes, 'had to be able to demonstrate the desirability of what money could buy. And the visual desirability of what can be bought lies in its tangibility, in how it will reward the touch, the hand, of the owner.'[19] But while objects are rendered conspicuously textured, tangible and graspable, the subjects of portraiture avoid reciprocating the viewer's gaze, they occupy the non-place of power. In his discussion of *The Ambassadors*, Berger says of the two men: 'There is in their gaze and their stance a curious lack of expectation of any recognition. It is as though in principle their worth cannot be recognized by others. They look as though they are looking at something of which they are not part. At something which surrounds them but from which they wish to exclude themselves.'[20] This is the very definition of the colonial gaze which the viewer necessarily and ideologically completes.

In Sylvia Wynter's discussion of Western ontoepistemology's production she describes the humanist turn in fifteenth-century theology that imagines mankind to stand between the physical and spiritual worlds, the natural and supernatural orders. It was, she explains,

> within this syncretized reinscription that the new criterion of Reason would come to take the place of the medieval criterion of the Redeemed Spirit as its transumed form – that the master code of symbolic life ('the name of what is good') and death ('the name of what is evil') would now become that of reason/ sensuality, rationality/irrationality in the reoccupied place of the matrix code of Redeemed Spirit/ Fallen Flesh.[21]

The nonreciprocity of the ambassadors' gaze can thus be read in these terms, as the transposition of God's invisible gaze into the new terms of human reason and its dominion over those affectable, fleshy forms of existence ascribed to racialized subjects. Now we visitors to the universal museum of Nationhood and Art are asked to occupy a double subject position – that of the subject of reason who completes and governs the visual/territorial field; and that of the affectable and scientifically knowable object of this same objectifying gaze. *We are both the name of what is good (Spirit) and the name of what is bad (Flesh).* We are also the subjects of a potentially fixed and productive attention, and those of an unbound, physiological and inattentive vision.

Unbound and doubled vision

This notion of weakened or unbound perception begun to be studied by the empirical sciences in the late 1870s as part of a wider decomposition of the perceptual field into units of sensation with the capacity for synthesis. In Jonathan Crary's account of this scientific expansion he focuses particularly on the new pathology of Agnosia that names the impairment of 'a hypothetical symbolic function', producing a 'purely visual awareness of an object'. Agnosia, in other words, is 'an inability to make any conceptual or symbolic identification of an object, a failure of recognition'.[22] The secularizing episteme of the Renaissance, which placed Man halfway between Spirit and Flesh, good and evil, rendering him invisible to himself, had the effect of unleashing the empirical sciences which cause Man himself to appear as the object of empirical study. Man, as such, is subject to this split mode of apprehension, as both the weak and fallible physiological object of the neutral scientific gaze *and* its transcendent operator who wields the techniques and taxonomies of pathologization. This paradoxical way of seeing has been accentuated by the pandemic in which we are addressed as law-comprehending subjects of reason and calculation on the one hand, and potentially pathogenic matter on the other. We all become agnosiacs who look distractedly sideways at frontally constructed pictures unable or less able to recognize them symbolically as we follow white arrows on the floor towards the exit. In this moment we have formed a rhizome between Enlightenment and decolonial seeing within the collapsing vision machine of the universal museum. In the words of Wynter, 'Christian becomes Man1 (as political subject), then as Man1 becomes Man2 (as a bio-economic subject) [. . .] in both cases, their epistemes will be, like their respective genres of being human, both discontinuous and continuous'.[23] When the switching between modes of being can no longer sustain this epistemic continuum, we can start to glimpse something of the transculturalism Wynter requires as a prerequisite for decolonization to begin.

Unbinding vision has in many respects been the constant work of modernist and contemporary art: from Manet's hyperreal yet psychologically absent subjects, to Pointillist experiments with the effects of the eye's physiological mixing of pure colour dots, from Jackson Pollock's laying the canvas on the floor to allow the gestural mark to relate as much to the manual as to the optical, to post-conceptual and performative experiments of all kinds that deemphasize retinality and incite the reappearance of bodies, material processes, social relations or situations.[24] We might say that this history already comprises the self-negation of the Transcendental I from within art's own matrix, and in many ways defines the last century of art historical development. Yet for all this, the spaces and institutions of art have been able to reconstitute the systematic negations of modernism and post-modernism into the guise of the public realm and its illusion of universality. This observation includes such direct interrogations of the artwork's apparent benevolence and the neutrality of spectatorial conditions as we see in a performance piece like Tania Bruguera's *Tatlin's Whisper #5*, 2008, at Tate Modern, in which mounted riot police performed crowd control exercises on the largely compliant crowd. As ever with institutional critique, such a challenging exposure of the artwork's conditions is unproblematically digested back into the institutional success story, strengthening rather than questioning its foundations. So, what has the virus brought that wasn't already present within art itself? How does it hack universality differently?

For one thing, a virus is also an agnosiac because it doesn't operate symbolically – although it makes copies. For another, unlike the diachronic journey from Man1 to Man2, it does not evolve by going from the least to the most differentiated state. Instead, in the explanation of Deleuze and Guattari, 'it develops a rhizome to jump from one already differentiated line to another.'[25] This they call an 'aparallel evolution' which by 'transversal communications between different lines scramble the genealogical trees'.[26] In the image of art theorist Filipa Ramos, the Covid-19 virus integrated the rhizome of late capitalist globalization, taking its desire to connect and network everything and running with it. 'Now it believes that you and me and them are us.' She writes, 'That "We" are one. That you and me and them are made of the same stuff.'[27] This, for Deleuze and Guattari, is how becoming works through a 'capture of code, a surplus value of code, an increase in valence'.[28] Networked globalization takes on a whole new significance and at last becomes fully legible to itself and to those subjects previously occupying the non-place of power: those who have long disavowed the black labour that causes Western workers to stand alongside, and now sit down in front of, the machine. The Ambassador turns his telescope around and catches a glimpse of his own flesh as determined by the external forces he thought he mastered. The picture has been caught into a new anamorphism adding to that of the skull painted in the foreground which Holbein used to signify the omnipresent spiritual domain that ruled over these *Uomo Universale*. The anamorphism brought on by the virus reveals the underworld of suffering blithely ignored by Man in the comfort of his non-place, as much as it reveals him as affectable flesh. It enables us to see how the virus captures racialized capitalism and crashes its logic of immunization and exploitation, turning the vectors of its first world sovereignty into the circuitry of sickness and death. In Aimé Césaire's words, 'death scythes widely', and not always along the race and class lines he was speaking of – although the pandemic state has been highly efficient at reterritorializing power along these differentials.[29]

Of course, racial capitalism itself is one of the most successful viruses of all time and, unlike Covid-19, isn't particularly threatened by killing its host. We saw this in 1929 and in 2008 – and no doubt we will see this again, perhaps as soon as 2021. Yet, as decolonial theory teaches us, its white Western bourgeois ontology never ceases to require the myth of its own self-determination and transparency. In Denise Ferreira da Siva's summary,

> While the others of Europe gaze on the horizon of death, facing certain obliteration, the racial keeps the transparent I in self-determination (interiority) alone before the horizon of life, oblivious to, because always already knowledgeable (controlling and emulating) of, how universal reason governs its existence.[30]

This myth requires that all Others appear as lacking reason, as mere bio-mechanisms to be plundered, enslaved, exploited, copied, consumed or destroyed. Capitalism obliviates its omnivorous consumption of all other ways of being human or animal, all other ways of living, all other cultures, all other genomes, all other bodies, and all other laws and rights. While abolitionist, civil rights, decolonial, feminist, environmental, animal rights and LGBTQI movements have long confronted the Transcendental I with the reflection of its disavowed violence, the virus addresses it in a language it understands – the non-symbolic form of death. Its symbolic fiction of Spirit/Flesh which creates the all too real sociogenic code of life/death cannot be perfectly sustained because the virus, as a living-dead assemblage of RNA (Ribonucleic Acid) and protein, cannot differentiate between the two. So, while the pictures continue to line the walls of the National Gallery, the body of the viewer has become a vector of disease and potential death; it can no longer complete the ideological and perspectival pyramid. What this shows, and what we/they cannot not see, is that we/they are just as externally determined as the colonial subjects whose living deaths paid for the erection of the museum in the first place.

As already noted, this split subjectivity has plagued Western Man since what Ferreira da Silva calls the 'refashioning of reason as the secular ruler and producer of the universe, as an exterior (constraining or regulative) force, [that] threatened to transform the mind into such an other thing of the world'.[31] Yet this potential externalization of reason from the mind of the Transcendent I precipitated multiple disavowals too various to compress in this brief space, but generally pivoting on some form of differentiation between the human body and the mind it houses. We can find a parallel history in art which, while attempting to negate its boundaries so as to escape its state of autonomy and return to the spaces of common experience (the bodily, the material, the situation, the libidinal, identity, local power relations), has found its rebellions sublated back into the separate ontology of art. We look at Olafur Eliason's melting icebergs at the Tate Modern as art spectacle as much as a fragment of our dying planet, and we cannot return them to the continuity of the landscape and climate that made them.[32] We also cannot see how the differential sovereignty that helps to construct art as an autonomous system participates in their melting. In this sense, Eliasson is reminiscent of Mr and Mrs Andrews, forging a proprietorial circuit between his own (creative) identity and the (anthropocenic) landscape it requires.[33] My proposal is rather that the rhizome slung, or hacked, between Enlightenment and decolonial ways of seeing produced in the museum as an inadvertent effect of the virus triggers something closer to the double consciousness referred to by W. E. B. du Bois in his 1903 book *The Souls of Black Folk*. In his words the 'American Negro' has a sort of second sight brought on by a split ontology:

> a world which yields him no self-consciousness, but only lets him see himself through the revelation of the other world. It is a peculiar sensation, this double-consciousness, this sense of always looking at one's self through the eyes of others, of measuring one's soul by the tape of a world that looks on in amused contempt and pity. One even feels this twoness – an American, a Negro; two souls, two thoughts, two unreconciled strivings; two warring ideals in one dark body, whose dogged strength alone keeps it from being torn asunder.[34]

The double consciousness brought on by Covid-19, in which a oneness of the living world smashes through the carefully constructed material-symbolic menagerie of racist separation and vision, gives us a glimpse of the transcultural perspectives long held by colonized peoples that Western hegemony has continuously and fairly successfully sought to suppress. While this 'peculiar sensation' may be the painful, yet self-seeing, consciousness borne through racial subjection, and while capitalism is doing all it can to prevent this self-seeing from becoming general because it threatens its necessary neutrality, the virus has momentarily shifted our perspective by planting our eyes back in our bodies, by turning the circuits of value extraction into the highways of contagion and by forcing 'us' privileged bourgeois subjects to understand how it is to be treated as contagious flesh. Perhaps an aparallel evolution of vision is occurring. What we now see is how truly universal is Life's relation to all other life, something that the constructed universals of the nation state, citizenship, and its spaces of art and knowledge actively threaten. To have universal validity, the rights of the political subject and the work of art can never be asserted at the expense of another's rights or an Other's cultural world but, like the virus itself, must constitute and be constituted together with all.

Acknowledgements

Thanks to Atau Tanaka and Dubravka Sekulic for their thoughtful comments on this chapter.

Notes

1 Elizabeth A. Povinelli, *Geontologies: A Requiem to Late Liberalism* (Durham and London: Duke University Press, 2016), 20.

2 In Aimé Césaire's original formulation, 'colonization = thingification', ([1955] 2000, 42).

3 Not to mention the Western ontoepistemological distinction within life itself, between *zoë* (the life common to all creatures) and *bios* (the form or way of life). This distinction is extended spatially within the ages of colonialism and post-colonial globality such that Western Europeans are seen as fulfilling the full potential of *bios* or the 'laws of nature' by achieving 'civilization' while the colonized, whose cultures have been deemed undeveloped within Western epistemics, are apprehended as *zoë* or bare life. In this sense the distinction *bios/zoë* can also be said to correspond to the social destiny of life or death. See Denise Ferreira da Silva (2007) for a detailed elaboration of this ontoepistemological trajectory.

4 John Berger, *Ways of Seeing* (London: British Broadcasting Corporation and Penguin Books, 1977), 109.

5 Karl Marx, *Grundrisse: Introduction to the Critique of Political Economy* (London: Penguin Books in association with the New Left Review, 1973), 705.

6 Ibid.

7 Denise Ferreira da Silva, *Toward a Global Idea of Race* (Minneapolis: University of Minnesota Press, 2007).

8 Ariella Aïsha Azoulay, *Potential History: Unlearning Imperialism* (London: Verso 2019), 39.

9 Ibid., 111.

10 'Man, which overrepresents itself as if it were the human itself, and that of securing the well-being, and therefore the full cognitive and behavioral autonomy of the human species itself/ourselves. Because of this overrepresentation, which is defined in the first part of the title as the Coloniality of Being/ Power/Truth/Freedom, any attempt to unsettle the coloniality of power will call for the unsettling of this overrepresentation.' Sylvia Wynter, 'Unsettling the Coloniality of Being/Power/Truth/Freedom: Towards the Human, After Man, Its Overrepresentation – An Argument', *CR: The New Centennial Review* 3, no. 3 (2003): 257–337, 260.

11 For an in-depth reading of the incorporation and preservation of the Western project of reason into the science of life and then subsequently anthropology which effected the transmutation of 'race' into the more acceptable signifier 'culture', while preserving the stratifications of the racial regime transcoded into the comparative measures of modernity and progress – see Ferreira da Silva (2007).

12 Jacques Rancière, *Aisthesis: Scenes from the Aesthetic Regime of Art*, trans. Zakir Paul (London: Verso, 2013), 12.

13 Hannah Arendt, *The Human Condition* (Chicago: University of Chicago Press, 1998), 1.

14 Gilles Deleuze and Félix Guattari, *A Thousand Plateaus: Capitalism and Schizophrenia*, trans. Brian Massumi (London: Continuum, 1987), 11.

15 Genese Maria Sodikoff, 'Zoonosis', *Anthropocene Unseen: A Lexicon*, Goleta (California: Punctum Books, 2020).

16 Epstein, cited in Wynter, 'Unsettling the Coloniality of Being/Power/Truth/Freedom', 286.

17 Hannah Beech, 'A Company Made P.P.E. for the World. Now Its Workers Have the Virus', *New York Times*, 20 December 2020, https://www.nytimes.com/2020/12/20/world/asia/top-glove-ppe-covid-malaysia-workers.html

18 Erwin Panofsky, *Perspective as Symbolic Form* [1927] (New York: Zone Books, 1991).

19 Berger, *Ways of Seeing* (1972), 90.

20 Ibid., 94.

21 Wynter, 'Unsettling the Coloniality of Being/Power/Truth/Freedom', 287.

22 Jonathan Crary, *Suspensions of Perception: Attention, Spectacle and Modern Culture*, Cambridge, Mass: October Books and MIT Press, 2001, 94.

23 Wynter, 'Unsettling the Coloniality of Being/Power/Truth/Freedom', 318.

24 For a biopolitical analysis of this historical trajectory see: Josephine Berry, *Art and (Bare) Life: A Biopolitical Inquiry, Sternberg Press*, 2018.

25 Deleuze and Guattari, *A Thousand Plateaus*, 11.

26 Ibid., 12.

27 Filipa Ramos, 'What the Virus Needs', *Artshock*, 28 April 2020.

28 Deleuze and Guattari, *A Thousand Plateaus*, 11.

29 'Guadeloupe, split in two down its dorsal line and equal in poverty to us,

Haiti where negritude rose for the first time and stated
> that it believed in its humanity and the funny tail of Florida
> where the strangulation of a nigger is being completed,
> and Africa gigantically caterpillaring up to the Hispanic foot of Europe,
> its nakedness where death scythes widely.'
> Aimé Césaire, *Discourse on Colonialism* [1955], trans. Joan Pinkham (New York: Monthly Review Press, 2000), 19.

30 Deleuze and Guattari, *A Thousand Plateaus*, 30.

31 Ibid., 40.

32 This is a reference to Olafur Eliason's project *Ice Watch* staged at Bankside, outside Tate Modern, London 2018.

33 Thanks to Dubravka Sekulic for this observation.

34 W. E. B. du Bois, *The Souls of Black Folk* [1903] (Oxford: Oxford University Press, 2007), xiii.

6

Posthuman vectors and the production of a common flesh

Amanda Boetzkes and Anna McWebb

'The coronavirus is us.'[1] This is the conclusion of philosopher Michael Marder in an initial reflection in the *New York Times* in March 2020, shortly after that virus had achieved the status of a global pandemic. Marder suggests that this robust microbiological entity reveals itself as a figure of sovereignty over passageways where power is otherwise dispersed across systems of media communication, exchange and transport. At a time when nation states are fortifying their borders against populations of stateless migrants, and global capital is held and circulated by invisible corporate entities, the coronavirus has discovered and infiltrated biomediatic channels.

Careening past such borders, catalysing the renewal of social justice movements and commanding the world's attention, the coronavirus reveals us humans to ourselves as an alienated vector of our planetary political ecology. The outbreak is an outcome of human territorialization, but it is also a posthuman recoil: an agent that spans the categories of the technological, natural, biological, economic, mediatic and political. It is an effect of the human that propels the human into a posthuman state. Or perhaps it is the other way around: the virus is an alienated posthuman entanglement that reminds us of the humanity we have not yet arrived at. This predicament, in which humans must grapple with a posthuman political ecology by way of a deadly virus, calls us to reflect on the human imbrication in a planetary flesh. In other words, the transgression of boundaries over which the coronavirus reigns sovereign calls forth a new consciousness of planetary embodiment.

This chapter will consider the case of Covid-19 in relation to the common flesh produced by factory farming with its corporate and pharmacological underpinnings. We consider the insights of Marxist evolutionary biologist Rob

Wallace who argues that every viral outbreak is preceded by an influx of capital.[2] Wallace comes to this conclusion through an understanding of viruses not as discrete microorganisms that are implicitly dangerous to humans, but rather as beings whose evolutionary trajectories are best understood in the context of forest ecologies, which, when perturbed by farming monopolies, result in contagions that are unrepresentable within the current spatio-temporal parameters that are predetermined by capitalist economic schemas. It is precisely because factory farming creates the ideal conditions for accelerated reproduction that Covid-19 has become a multi-scalar planetary agent.

It is only by reading the factory farm in terms of its yielding of human and non-human bodies as viral vectors that it becomes possible to imagine a posthuman perspective in the global pandemic. Posthumanism, we argue, must be reconsidered in terms of the management of bodily death and not merely the management of life. While early theorizations of posthumanism have been beholden to a Foucaultian paradigm of biopolitics, and an associated biomediatic perspective of ontology, we argue that the coronavirus identifies the limitations of the biopolitical account of posthumanism precisely by transgressing the abstract division between human and non-human animal, life and death. Drawing from Achille Mbembe's concept of necropolitics, and Syl Ko's history of Black veganism, we argue that what is precisely posthuman about contemporary pandemics is their way of collapsing bodily boundaries between ontological beings. The novel coronavirus pandemic is best conceptualized in necropolitical scenes in which labour, bodily suffering and death become the means by which privileged humans historically distinguished their lives as human per se. Pandemic conditions put pressure on such divisions and the bodily substructure that upholds them. The coronavirus is therefore a crucial fulcrum for rethinking the political pretences by which humanism and posthumanism are defined.

Insofar as the distinction between humanism and posthumanism has been considered as a matter of perspective of the visible world and a position with regards to invisible worlds – often in terms of the representability and mediation of the human world as distinct from the ontological realities that lie beyond our perception – we consider the politics of posthumanism at stake in the representational practices of British graphic artist Sue Coe. For decades, Coe has documented scenes of animal cruelty and slaughter, as well as the corporate, pharmacological and political regimes that produce factory farms, viral outbreaks and social misery. We suggest that Coe's work does not so much mediate a posthuman perspective – say an imagined or mediated perception of the coronavirus – but rather shows how this invisible agent effects a necropolitical situation in which human and non-human animals are united in a planetary condition of embodiment. In other words, her work does not succumb to a totalizing representation but rather discloses the effects of viral activity as a way to render a posthuman realism. Ultimately, we suggest that if the coronavirus is a posthuman recoil, while we cannot see it, we can still deduce that it does not distinguish between humans and non-human animals within the schemas of the factory farm. The posthuman perspective is no white, male biomediatic utopia of otherness; rather, it is the preclusion of complexity and the preservation of otherness. It registers in the outbreak of a totalizing necrosis afflicting planetary bodies.

Posthuman perspective, or the theatricality of masculinist modernism

In his essay on the question of the animal in contemporary art, Cary Wolfe identifies a difference between a purportedly undialectical obsession with content (artworks 'about' animals) and artistic strategies that gesture towards the unrepresentability of non-human animals – humanist and posthumanist practices respectively.[3] Where the former domain pictures and figures animals unproblematically, conflating the artistic representation of animals with the animals' own ontological expression, the latter poses the question of the unrepresentability of non-human animals' perspectives. Wolfe thus offers the critical insight that humanist art humanizes non-human animals, whereas posthuman art acknowledges the displacement of ontological others at stake in the very practice of (human) representation.

To illustrate his contradistinction between humanist and posthumanist visual regimes, and the dialectical bind between humanism and posthumanism more broadly, Wolfe establishes a comparison between the work of British graphic artist Sue Coe and American bioartist Eduardo Kac. For decades, Sue Coe has produced prints, lithographs, drawings and paintings of slaughterhouses, in a documentary style that recalls the political realism of Käthe Kollwitz and Mexican muralist Diego Rivera. The 'realism' of this tradition does not lie so much in their naturalism in a literal sense (why would it?), but rather in their inheritance of a political imperative to 'speak truth to power'. Coe's work stems from a daily practice of sketching at factory farms and slaughterhouses, the sites where non-human animals are subjected to unregulated sadistic abuse and death. Her mandate is to show what happens at such sites of legal invisibility, where the rights of non-human animals are not so much unthinkable as violently refused by the implicit misery of their situation and the explicit pain their bodies are forced to endure. As Wolfe points out, however, it is precisely in bringing attention to animal cruelty that Sue Coe's work locates itself in a paradox: while it appeals to the viewer directly, if not melodramatically, in such as a way as to make legible the acts of violence, does it not also then rely on the implicit disavowal of violence on which representation itself is predicated? In other words, Coe's work humanizes animals through representation in order to make their perspective knowable to the viewer, but in so doing, it displaces the question of the animal perspective altogether.

Biomedia artist Eduardo Kac's practice intervenes on the visibility of non-human animals from a different representational paradigm. Coining the concept of *transgenic* art, Kac has been recognized for his works in which he splices the DNA sequences of a variety of species (mice, zebra fish, tobacco plants and, most notoriously, a rabbit) with the green fluorescent protein of the jellyfish *Aequorea Victoria*). Most notoriously, Kac initiated a multiyear project called *GFP Bunny* (2000) in which he created a rabbit – which he named Alba – that glowed green in the dark, and publicly demonstrated her care as well as a care for her public representation. Despite the moral panic about genetic experimentation animating the public discourse of his practice, Wolfe insists that what is at stake in Kac's practice is not so much the fact of human intervention on the non-human animal body, and the anthropocentric mode of knowing at stake in genomic research, but rather his production of new forms of visuality by which the animal's perspective is proposed through a redistribution of sense and meaning. *GFP Bunny*, for example, presents a scopic reversal since the marker of her genomic difference is not manifest to the public eye but only appears in an artificial scenario in which one would see her in the dark. In a similar vein, Kac's robotic works, *Darker Than Night* (1999) and *Rara Avis* (1996) require that the viewer don a VR headset that interferes with human vision and instead translates bat sonar signals as well as the sounds the viewers themselves make into a visual display. What is visualized is not a human-centric representation, then, but rather the combined output of sense of bats and humans repositioned as recursive interplay.

In this way, Kac's practice overcomes the binary of human visibility and animal invisibility, by underscoring the specificity and finitude of the human sensorium and its correlative field of meaning, rather than evading it. Indeed, Wolfe suggests that Kac's posthumanism rests on his capacity to show not merely what we do not see but *that* we cannot see.[4] The posthumanist paradigm at play therefore rests on the way in which Kac problematizes vision and representation by surfacing its located-ness as specifically human indifference, but also in interplay with the perceptual system of non-human animals. The animal sensorium is indexed but not represented from an ontological divide.

Wolfe's argument is indebted to a Friedian (modernist) approach to art's representation of vision, the ethics of which rests on an acknowledgement of the disfigurative practice of representation itself and the resistance of zones of ontological difference to the possibility of representation. Representation disfigures fundamentally, and it is therefore the task of art to absorb the implicit theatricality of representation (the glaring difference between me and you, viewer and object, the capacity for visual recognition that the viewer brings to spectatorship and the visible world that the artwork draws the viewer into). Art 'should' efface the traces of its disfiguration of the other while airing the other's insolubility to that disfiguration. For Fried, the antithesis of art is its very theatricality, the way in which it airs its desire to be looked at (the way it screens 'look at me, look at my difference'). By contrast, an ethics of representation would internalize difference in such a way as to point or gesture to the irreducible reality of the other without presuming to lay that reality bare.

From Wolfe's perspective, what Kac achieves is a visual field in which the difference between bat vision and human vision is articulated. It foregoes anthropomorphism, the theatrical manoeuvre par excellence, which would presume to represent the perspective of the non-human animal for the human viewer in the language of human perspective. It perhaps risks theatricalizing the difference between bat vision and human vision, however, in its spatialization of a this-here and that-there. Nevertheless, in Wolfe's analysis, theatricality is put to work in the service of an expression of ontological difference within representation. Kac represents the recursive relation between the one and the other, as a reflexive interplay between bat and human vision *over time*. This theorization draws from Niklas Luhmann's systems theory approach to perception, which takes into account the self-referentiality of perception itself in and alongside the self-referential perception of others in the environment. In this respect, Wolfe diverges from a classic Friedian understanding of the theatricality of difference within the representational field, for, as he suggests,

> The point is not just, as Fried would have it, that Kac's work is 'theater' [which in his terms it would surely be] but that 'theater' is not doing the work Fried thinks it does. In Kac, the artwork does indeed 'play up' to the viewer, but only as Derrida would put it, to lead the viewer to the realization that the only place the meaning of the work may be found is no place, not where the viewer irresistibly

looks [eg. The glow-in-the-dark creatures] but rather. . .precisely where the viewer does not see – not 'refuses to look' or even 'is prevented from seeing,' but rather *cannot* see.[5]

Wolfe's analysis, however, is also founded on two flaws in argumentation, both of which are bound to a disingenuous setup of the difference between Sue Coe's and Kac's respective practices of visualization, whereby the former fails at a posthuman perspective and the latter achieves it. The first flaw is endemic to the comparison without acknowledgement of the obviously gendered basis of the differences he sets out to elaborate. Where Coe draws animal faces anthropomorphically, positioning the animal's face as a screen for human feelings in an attempt (Wolfe assumes) to cultivate empathy in the viewer, Kac does not presume to know the animal's different perspective. Coe's work undermines an ethics of the animal because it relies on a 'melodrama of visibility' – a phrase from Michael Fried that Wolfe applies to Coe – by which she pre-empts the animal's excess from the disfiguring effects of representation, and by which Coe plays the animal to the viewer in such a way as to ensure a 'surefire effect' of empathy. Essentially, following from Fried's logic, Wolfe accuses Coe of being literal about the ethics of her practice. He writes,

> If the ethical function of art is what Coe thinks it is, why not just show people photographs of stockyards, slaughterhouses, and the killing floor to achieve this end ? To put it another way, what does [her] art *add*? . . . The paradoxical result for Coe's work, then, is that it appeals to us to read it as directly (indeed melodramatically) legible of the content it represents, but the only way it achieves that end is *through* its figural excess, which is precisely *not* of the slaughterhouse but of the interposing materiality of representation itself.[6]

Ultimately, he concludes that in her dogged quest to make the animal visible – to *make* the viewer *see* – Coe replicates the Taylorist logic of the slaughterhouse itself, with its ideal mode of production to repeat without difference. The lifelong animal rights activist who on a daily basis records animals, killing floors and immigrant meat production workers alongside the politicians at the helm of this cultural regime falls short of the sensibility for preserving the animal's difference from human signification required by Wolfe for posthuman art.

Yet, the logic of Michael Fried's modernism, which is predicated on art's overcoming of theatricality, has been increasingly subject to criticism on the grounds of its exclusionary terms. As Christa Noel Robbins argues, drawing from the language of an especially offensive and homophobic comment in a personal note between Michael Fried and Philip Leider, an editor for *Art Forum*, Fried's modernism strove for a mode of representation of the anarchical otherness of *everything* in and through a sensibility (and especially a language) of defeating and overcoming theatricality, which he passionately articulated in terms of the perverse and corrupt desire of those objects to be looked at and desired.[7] Robbins links Fried's casting of theatricality to a surge of heteronormative anxiety over queer male sexuality (and the implicitly misogynist association of queer men with femininity at this time) in the wake of the Kinsey Reports and the Stonewall Uprisings. Fried's elaboration of theatricality and its absorption by modernist art was underpinned by his own homophobic and normative imperative to master and sublimate homosexual desire into a normative masculinist sensibility. In this account, Fried's modernism is nothing short of a melodrama of male panic and a theatre of phallocentrism that has become the origin of a phallocratic chain of meaning. Indeed, Robbins suggests that Fried's anti-queer (modernist) sensibility has been so compelling for acolytes and critics alike that his argument has the power of a discursive practice: a text that has the surplus effect of producing the possibilities and rules of other texts.[8] We do well to bear in mind the risk of this phallocratic repetition in our charting of the ethics and politics of posthumanist art. After all, what could be more human or more base than the compulsive repetition of sexism and homophobia, even if it masquerades as criticism, whether modernist or posthumanist?

The second flaw in Wolfe's argumentation, which follows from the first, is to position Coe's practice of drawing (inscription) against a biomediatic practice, without accounting for the gendered or ideological differences at stake in doing so. The gendered setup ignores the fact that Coe's drawings involve a representational process with a clear stylistic history connected to an entirely different genealogy of modernism than the one (re)canonized by Michael Fried – one that was always explicitly political and explicit about the politics of its realism. Further, it gives no account of the fact that Kac's biomediatic practice was always centrally concerned with the pedagogical imperative to represent technologies of genetic reproduction and the concern for transgenic animals to the public. Kac could not be more straightforward (literal) about wanting to demonstrate and model his care for his research commodity, the rabbit, Alba. On this point, it is worth recapitulating Nicole Shukin's critique of Derrida's reflections on his primary relationship with his (little) cat that he conspicuously refuses to think how she is 'an engineered product of material institutions'.[9] Wolfe's subtle gendering of the comparison of Coe to Kac leads to a conflation of the difference between the materialist imperatives of realist art and art's mediation of the structure – a difference in the modality of representation –

which inadvertently ushers in a not-so-silent history of exclusionary thinking for which Fried has been widely criticized.

The distinction between Coe and Kac is therefore (albeit unconsciously, one hopes) bound to a modernist understanding of theatricality and its overcoming in gendered terms, and risks hypostasizing an implicit misogyny and homophobia that closes off the potential to read the queerness of co-implication and the politics of care that might be elaborated precisely through the artistic representation of non-human animals, whether or not it is anthropomorphic or 'politically' motivated. Wolfe's comparison, established on the terms of Fried's modernism, effects a gendering of posthuman perspective by failing to articulate the assumption of male mastery of both visuality and ethics at stake in his positioning of Kac contra Coe. By assuming the neutrality of the former against the compromising femininity of the latter, he sets up a straw man argument, vis-à-vis Coe's work, while presenting Kac's work as a more successful redistribution of the senses using a language by which to 'explain' both. It is as though Coe's humanism is distinctly feminine and fails at a true ethics in its espousal of a different tradition of realism, whereas Kac's posthumanism succeeds at a truly free articulation of the question of the animal as such.

In light of this risk of reproducing a masculinist posthumanism, one must ask, 'Why is Wolfe so confident in Fried's logic that he can presume to know what Coe thinks the ethical function of art is?' How does he know what Coe wants, and why would Fried give us any insight in this regard? As Alice Kuzniar argues, the casting of Coe as 'deeply idealistic' and 'playing to the audience' hardly constitutes a satisfactory critique of her work given its painful grappling with animal exploitation.[10] Especially when Coe is being set up to fail at art while striving to succeed in a politics of representation in this argument, it behoves us to wonder, what are the terms of posthumanism such that politics itself is feminized, theatrical, ranges from the melodramatic to the sentimental and (we are to assume) is *therefore* disclosive of anthropomorphism? One must wonder whether it is possible to represent a sphere of commonality and common sensibility with animals at all without it betraying the post-Derridean gambit of 'the animal in theory'. Kuzniar appropriately suggests that we can properly understand Coe's practice as shattering the viewer's sovereign gaze, and as reopening the question of the animal by depicting the abyssal gulf between human and non-human species even while maintaining their relationality, in her 'modalities of following the animal' and by specifically foregrounding the animal body.[11] Coe's oeuvre gives the non-human animal a bodily mass, weightiness, groundedness and, we would argue, a specific fleshiness as its very means of 'facing' the animal. Indeed, we will suggest that it is the very fleshiness of exploited farm animals that points towards a deeply troubling and anarchical unfolding of biopolitics in the form of viral dumping and, consequently, a global pandemic.

Sue Coe's realism: The inscription of dead animals onto human 'life'

Coe's specific form of realism and its relevance to posthuman perspective becomes clear in a study of her oeuvre over time. Her serial practice demonstrates how forms and scales of non-human death and life are (barely) managed and disavowed within the biopolitical regime, and tracks the surge of anarchical biopolitical agents: from uniformed racialized workers, to white corporate profiteers, politicians and, importantly, corrupt pharmaceutical companies and viruses amid this assemblage. Her work visualizes how corruption is not merely played out in scenes of sadistic human figures who exert their violence against animals, but that this sadism is a symptom of a broader paradigm to which many scales of life are subjected. Where Wolfe suggests that the artist situates animals within a capitalist scene of exploitation with a view to depicting that structure as accurately as possible – a biopolitical regime from which the animal cannot register its irreducibility and irreproducibility – what remains latent in his argument is the extent to which these scenes are also permeated by an active and unseen microbial world, which Coe *has* inferred in its very alien difference precisely because of her long-standing concern with the corporate underpinnings of the factory farm, the slaughterhouse and a practice that attempts to cope with its unseen effects. In other words, it is by following the political arc of Coe's series that the scope of her practice and its representational integrity can be understood to lead the viewer to a sense of the secret economy of life in and through the visible machinations of cruelty and death in the political sphere. These forms of unseen life originate from, but are also exacerbated by, the Taylorist assemblage that requires humans to be desensitized to the cruelty of factory farms and slaughterhouses and by which they are also desensitized to the connection between viral outbreaks and the meat industry. More importantly, Coe shows the obscenity of the slaughterhouse – what is *ob*-scene about the nourishment of human life on the mechanized liquidation of animal lives within this paradigm. Her practice is so profoundly mimetic (born of the sites whose lines she traces daily) that it captures the system in which humans disfigure themselves – inscribe, overwrite and render human bodies and humanism itself – in and through our interpolation of the biopolitical assemblage and its abuse of animal bodies. The factory farm is the implosion of the human as such, and the explosion of bodies into a totalizing biosphere through influenza outbreaks. We might call this posthumanism, but this version has no predilection for the 'genohype' of bioart.[12] Coe traces the limit and anarchical delimitation of biopolitical control. The unseen Other that is inferred from the margins of Coe's tracery – from the obscenity of the killing floors – is viral.

A posthuman reality appears by subtraction in and through the caricatured disfigurations that are so central to Coe's practice. Posthumanism is the outcome of the collapse of a biopolitical utopia into a dystopian corporate pharmacon, or a 'factory pharm,' as Coe titles one of her capstone prints published in her collection *Cruel: Bearing Witness to Animal Exploitation* (2012). In *Factory Pharm* (2001) Coe presents a doubled space in which the farm (where animals are bred) and the slaughterhouse (where they are killed) are linked together as a mechanized digestive system where animals are killed and then consumed by other animals in an endless circularity (Figure 6.1). In this Escher-like space, seemingly limitless floors of animal faces joined together by conveyor belts that carry an unending supply of animals which they dump into vats that grind their bodies into a slurry. To the left of the composition, the viewer sees a vat dumping its liquefied contents into a pen of living animals on a lower floor, closing the cycle of killing and (re)consumption. Looming cogs broach the tiered space suggesting the continuous movement of circulation within this closed system. The centre of the image is dominated by the eye of one of the round vats that

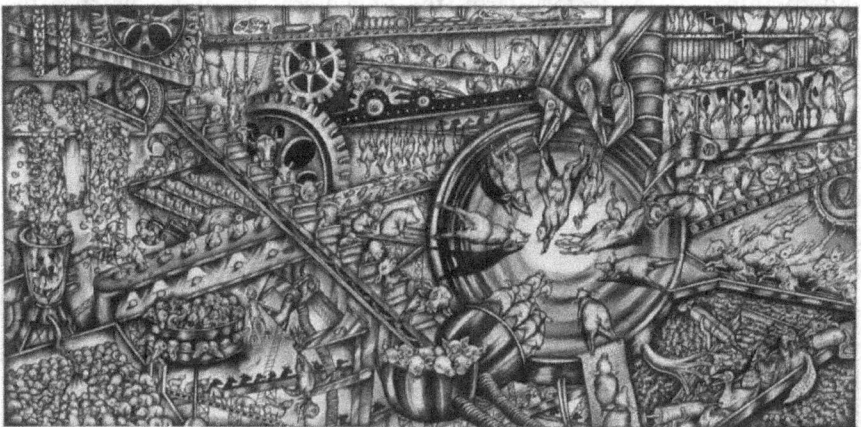

Figure 6.1 Sue Coe, *Factory Pharm*, 2001.

opens into a white abyss. Giant pincers hover above to extricate any animals that might cling to its edge. Not only are the animals killed for human consumption, but the factory farm has become a digestive system, fuelled by its own return of animal flesh as feed; it runs on its own auto-ingestion. But the farm as such gives way to another kind of system that is driven by pharmacology, hence the inference at stake in the titling of this scene as a factory *pharm* per se.

This cycle in which animals are forced to self-cannibalize before being rendered as food themselves is precisely the condition by which this closed system collapses into an unwieldy and invisible reality. It is not surprising, then, that Coe has also undertaken print series devoted to the rise of big farm viruses such as the avian flu virus, the swine flu (H1N1), SARS and the novel Covid-19. Coe maintains that 'factory farming and zoonotic viruses are one and the same', an idea she has elaborated further over the course of the Covid-19 pandemic.[13] It is in this context that we might consider her engraving *Carnivorous Coronavirus* (Figure 6.2). The titular terms are anagrams of one another, and activate a mirroring of visual analogies. The work summarizes Coe's perspective on the unseen origin of the coronavirus pandemic at the site of systematized killing and eating of non-human animals. The factory farm is the genesis of a larger system of self-cannibalism. The food source for humans has generated an agent of self-consumption. Coe's scenes of animal cruelty are now refigured in a broader framework of generalized zoonotic consumption.

The top register depicts a slaughterhouse worker holding up a cow haunch that dangles from a hook. His thick arm echoes the cut of beef which he hugs to his chest, leaning his head against its weight having just reached around it to slice a piece off the carcass. Coe dwells on the close proximity – one might even call it the quasi-intimacy of this embrace. His face touches the flesh, his mouth is open and he seems to breathe heavily against it. Indeed, the beef appears as an extension of the worker's chest, like an exposed beating heart. To the left, a solitary calf dangles on a hook from its neck; it is next in line for the butcher's knife. In the upper corner, a group of three bears huddle together. Their frightened eyes appear to witness the scene in its entirety. Significantly, these are wild animals, not farm animals: their wide paws tug at the chain link that imprisons them. The spatial logic of the factory farm thus threatens to encroach on other animals, a situation that became more public as scientists tried to locate the cause of the coronavirus pandemic in wet markets where exotic animals are held, sold and killed.

The lower register of the engraving redistributes the figures in the upper half: in a reiteration of the worker-beef pairing, a dying coronavirus patient lies in

Figure 6.2 Sue Coe, *Carnivorous Coronavirus,* 2020.

a hospital bed with a breathing tube inserted into his mouth and a cluster of equipment that emulates the heart-like pattern of the beef in the upper register. His skeletal hands recall the withered limbs of the hanging calf. The patient is tended by a health-care worker wearing a mask, hairnet and face shield. A banner spans the middle ground of the work upon which is written 'CARNIVOROUS' and 'CORONAVIRUS', separated horizontally by a tangle of lines that connotes barbed wire and mimics the cords of the respiratory equipment in the bottom half of the image. The lines bind together the common letters that make up the anagram. A visual pattern comes forward since the last two letters of both words are identical and line up one above the other: US—US. The viewer, the artist, the figures (human and non-human animals; wild and domestic), the invisible virus, and the equipment that ties us carnivores to us victims of coronavirus: the image shows 'us' who we are at the cusp of life and death, two sides of the same assemblage of consumption.

As much as posthumanism is concerned with the biopolitical subject and the perspective elaborated through this paradigm, so also must it consider its underlying necropolitics. The management of life and the sovereignty of the human invokes the management of animal death at the juncture of human life. But, as Achille Mbembe argues, the sovereignty of life in the biopolitical regime has been irrevocably joined to the torture, immiseration and death of racialized slaves.[14] In his account of necropolitics, not only does the intimate tie between race, slavery and the disposability of lives become clear, but so too does the logic of necropolitical sites such as plantations, concentration camps, genocides and terrorism begin to take shape. For example, he argues that the plantation is both a political-juridical structure and a space in which death itself is wielded on the body of the slave as a continuous threat and presence of the power of the sovereign and the economy of the master–slave relation. The slave is alive but is always kept in a state of injury, in a 'phantom-life world of horrors and intense cruelty and profanity. . . . Violence, here becomes an element in manners, like whipping or taking of the slave's life itself. . . . Slave life, in many ways, is a form of death-in-life'.[15]

We might extrapolate from Mbembe's reading of the spaces in which death becomes a presence within life through the cruel treatment of bodies, that the factory farm is another prime site at which the necropolitical regime unfolds. Where the presence of animal torture and death is only ordinarily visible in the ubiquity of meat commodities, it is only through a visual practice such as Coe's that the jointure of animal death to human life is visualized. The politics of representing cruelty to animals is less a matter of a politics of literalism (as though Coe not only wants to show what we know but adds an unwanted affective surplus) than it is a matter of showing the investment of animal cruelty and death into human embodiment as its form of life and nourishment. It is from this perspective that philosopher and activist Syl Ko argues that the category of 'the animal' is in and of itself rooted in a racist and colonial categorization of living beings that is driven towards the justification of the exploitation, violation and elimination of non-white humans and non-human animals.[16] Racialization and animalization have therefore been axiomatic instruments of the biopolitical regime. Taking into account that excessively sadistic bodily death underlies the management of bodily life, posthumanism must consider how the global pandemic reveals their often unseen intersection. Further, it shows how the necropolitical regime is becoming a broader planetary necrosis that is now a sovereign vector. The coronavirus originates from the factory farm and tears through human lives, exacerbating the hierarchies that underpin biopolitics, but threatening to topple them as well.

Sue Coe shows the enmeshment of non-human animal death in human bodies that arise from factory farms and slaughterhouses. Further, she shows this enmeshment as a ruptured system, where animal death gives rise to human suffering, precarity and death as well. While the coronavirus itself remains invisible, it has nevertheless penetrated what were once conceptualized as discrete and exclusively human systems: the food supply chain, labour, the economy and human health care. In Coe's work, this co-enfleshment is visible not as a causal chain, nor as an anthropomorphized representation of the virus, but rather in the analogous misery and death of humans and non-human animals, in scenes of their imprisonment and death. The virus is an unseen vector that registers in representation only by its exacerbation of the necropolitical logic that binds humans and non-human animals together.

Virus dumping into the common flesh

Insofar as the coronavirus introduces into the closed system of the factory farm an invisible ontological reality that exists at an unseen spatio-temporal scale, it requires an alternative theorization. For it is not merely the case that posthumanism can be captured through a deconstruction of the difference between human and non-human animals; rather, the materialization of their difference within a necropolitical regime produces a spillover from the factory farm into a global political ecology. It is this systemic excess – one that is explicitly enfleshed – that opens the way to a questioning of the ontology of posthuman (co-)existence from the anarchical core of the pandemic.

In his book *Big Farms Make Big Flu*, Rob Wallace provides an account of the genesis of the global pandemic in the spillover from the factory farm.[17] He names this excess 'virus dumping' and charts its underpinning in corporate agriculture. For Wallace, the coronavirus appears out of the techniques of bioeconomic warfare used by multinational agribusinesses to colonize developing countries. Virus dumping occurs when a multinational agribusiness, such as Smithfield Foods, dumps grain or other farm goods into another country's market. When borders are open, such corporations can legally dump goods in that other country and offer competitive pricing below production costs. While on the surface it appears that the corporation will take a loss, ultimately it is a cutthroat manoeuvre to recuperate its profit by outselling the competition, collapsing all competing businesses and creating a monopoly. From the 1990s until 2005, in large part due to the North American Free Trade Association, major goods such as corn, soybeans, wheat, rice, cotton, beef, pork and poultry were dumped in Mexico, creating an increase in the gap between the cost of an item and pricing from 12 per cent to 38 per cent, and costing Mexican producers about 6.6 billion dollars in production costs.[18] Smithfield Foods dumped major agriculture commodities related to pork farming, thus priming Mexico as a pork producer that would supply the United States. But these agricultural monopolies also produce side-effects that have to be accounted for: a series of factory farm-based pathogens that thrive from the genetic homogeneity of mass reproduced factory farm animals coupled with the uniform industrial spaces of the farm itself. As Wallace charts, the dumping of agriculture commodities in foreign countries is tantamount to virus dumping in those same countries.

To offer an example of virus dumping in the context of an outbreak, Wallace focuses on the 2009 outbreak of swine flu (H1N1), the first strain of its kind to reach pandemic proportions in forty years. While Mexico's pork industry is considered to be the H1N1 source of origin, it was tracked to Smithfield Food's subsidiary, Granjas Carroll. The area had been seized for grain and hog imports through the cheap commodity ploy, and consequently it was primed for a virus dump that left it financially and environmentally devastated. The example of Granjas Carroll perfectly illustrates the correlation between corporate factory farming, virus dumping and the emergence of proto-pandemic pathogens. To add insult to injury, bioeconomic warfare has almost no consequences for multinational agribusiness. In fact, corporations can prosper when influenza strains emerge from their own operations because they spread out to any remaining competition, and the corporation can skirt economic punishments with the horizontal integration of the surrounding farms. Small operations often suffer catastrophically in the face of virus outbreaks because they cannot afford the repercussions of virus prevention plans for their animals. Legal accountability and moral responsibility is elided by the sheer capaciousness of the possibilities of economic growth. As Wallace comments, 'The financial tab for these outbreaks is routinely picked up by governments and taxpayers worldwide. So why should agribusiness bother with ending practices that repeatedly interrupt economies and will someday produce a virus that kills hundreds of millions of people?'[19]

Wallace's explanation of virus dumping captures the way in which the global economy obscures a shared condition of embodiment between human and non-human animals, and that this shared condition gives rise to unseen viral agents. Viral evolution which arises from aggressive capitalist parlay is rendered invisible by the market itself; its causal connection to the economy is obscured, while the global vectors of viral contagion are visualized exclusively through the lens of microbiology and pharmaceutical corporations. The coronavirus pandemic is an excessive outcome that arises from corporate territorialization and appears as an alienated being from the human world that ushered it in precisely by displacing it from its ecology. But it is precisely the difference between a being and its ecology that produces a difference between a pathogen and an outbreak.

In his recent analysis of the global pandemic, Wallace charts the vectors of Covid-19, arguing that the virus emerged as a result of factory-farming practices pushing the site of its food production land too close to rapidly urbanized spaces. Factory farming collapses the barriers between forests and urban areas and provides the perfect conditions for the infiltration of pathogens into Chinese farming industries.[20] Viruses, which originate in forested hinterlands, are released into the food supply chain when those hinterlands are razed for massive farms and plantations. In his analysis of the Ebola outbreak, Wallace argues that the Ebola pathogen and its effects were treated in isolation from the forest complexity that slowed its evolution and rendered it largely inconsequential to humans. But the corporate seizure of land for rubber plantations by Firestone eliminated the forest ecology that held Ebola in a symbiotic relationship with humans.[21]

Wallace and his research team discovered that the forest ecology balances the evolution of viruses with a stochastic differential: a level of 'noise'.[22] If the stochastic level is below a certain level, a virus can have a sudden population explosion. But if forest noise is above a certain level, it frustrates the virus's attempt to find 'susceptibles', vectors that foster its reproduction and evolution. Forest noise cloaks possible viral pathways so that pathogens simply burn out on their own. Thus, Wallace argues, 'The formalism [of the stoachastic differential] implies that under certain conditions the forest acts as its own epidemiological protection and we risk the next deadly pandemic when we destroy that capacity. When the forest's functional noise is stripped out, the epidemiological consequences are explosive.'[23] It is for this reason, he argues, that pandemics are preceded by the influx of capital. Once the market has been mobilized by the corporation, and land mobilized for farming, the epidemiological protection of forest noise is eliminated, and viral outbreaks ensue. Such outbreaks are expensive, and the costs must be borne by the countries that have been mobilized by the market. Thus, Wallace establishes that the corporate dumping of agricultural commodities onto the market leads to viral dumping and to new dependencies on pharmaceutical corporations, if not a pharmacological paradigm *tout court*.

Wallace's analysis brings new insight into the imagery at play in Coe's *Factory Pharm* (2001) and its explicit link between the dystopian spaces of factory farming and the pharmaceutical industry. While Coe does not show the antibiotics regimens by which corporations (barely) manage pathogen outbreaks, it is nevertheless underwritten in the equipment that does not merely section the animals for meat, but liquefies them and pours them through funnels. The factory farm doubles as a monstrous laboratory. Coe elaborates a similar visual lexicon in her linocut *Big Pharma* (2019; Figure 6.3) in which

Figure 6.3 Sue Coe, *Big Pharma*, 2019.

two anthropomorphized flies in lab coats stand over a dead human body, one holding a pipette and an aerosol spray can that sprays into the human's face, while the other holds a beaker of liquid. Coe began scrutinizing the merger of Bayer and Monsanto – a pharmaceutical manufacturer and a corporate agriculture developer – producing the image for Art Basel, in the city where the corporation has its headquarters. The lettering on the clock on the wall identifies the scene, 'Big Pharma, Basel', while a cloud issuing from the pipette on the left to the beaker on the right is marked with the words 'It doesn't hurt the beneficial humans'. The image does not lend itself to a reading with regards to an ethics of representation of the non-human animal; rather it caricatures the logic of the pharmaceutical corporation with a role reversal: insects who experiment on a human while evaluating which ones are beneficial. We are to presume a perverse logic: a dead body is beneficial to the flies that would consume the flesh, but, since they are disguised as scientists, we trust their evaluation of which 'ones' can live and which can be extinguished. Between the profit motive and scientific authority, the intersecting worlds of human and non-human animal relations is inaccessible. What is visualized, however, is the mediation of corporate science in determining the value of life and condemnation to death. The biopolitical animal, whether human or non-human, is split between an underlying will to cruelty and its surface will to knowledge.

What becomes apparent through Sue Coe's work is that politics is an impossible sphere of representation precisely because an infrastructure of cruelty pervades. Her ethical imperative lies in discovering ethics only in and through the representation of transgressive cruelty. Representation is not a matter of epistemology or social justice; it is a matter of locating the limit of possibility of tolerance for cruelty to the other, and the recognition that cruelty is the very posthuman recoil of human ethics. Through cruelty to non-human animals, humans find themselves in a common flesh with them. Thus, posthumanism is the very breach of the human subject and its recurrence as an imperative to see that shared condition.

As part of her recent series on the novel coronavirus, Coe's *Social Distancing* (2020) captures the shared corporeality of human and non-human animal as the very condition that seems to contradict the directives for 'social distancing' during the pandemic (See Figure 6.4). At the centre of the image is a body hung upside down in a slaughterhouse. While the torso has been cut open to expose a row of vertebrae, the spine also divides the body into two identifying parts, one

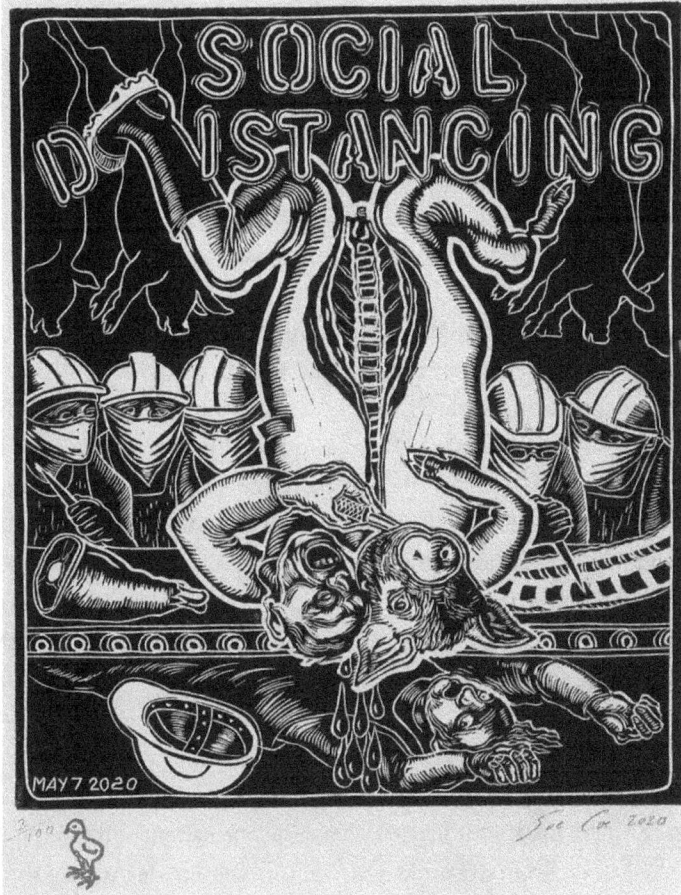

Figure 6.4 Sue Coe, *Social Distancing*, 2020.

human and the other porcine. The human side leans over to slit the pig's throat. But the mastery of the human position has been turned upside down; indeed, another human figure has fallen beneath the conveyor belt and is positioned as though ready to be hung up and sliced. On the right, two masked figures stand over an exposed midsection with a view to testing it. On the left, two others lean over a ham hock, while looking anxiously at the lower body of the fallen figure. Human body parts and pig body parts look uncannily similar when they have been sutured together under the conditions of the pandemic. Social distancing itself is re-pitched as the state of dissociation by which the mass killing of human and non-human animals is enabled. Coe does not need to represent the virus to show its effects on the corporate imaginary.

Consuming coronavirus

If the coronavirus is us, this is because it is the recoil of corporate meat manufacture. It is a microbial agent born of the encroachment on forested land, the construction of homogenous agricultural spaces and mass animal production and killing. It returns to human bodies to consume them, to liquify our bodies' refined respiratory and vascular systems with the same dissociated and unmitigated force by which humans consume land and animals alike. The coronavirus exacerbates the necropolitics of big farms, pharmaceutical companies and capitalist tyrannies. But Sue Coe is conscious that to represent the coronavirus is not necessarily to represent its figural nomenclature nor its microbial *Umwelt*, nor to fantasize that she possibly could. She does not have those representational desires. The coronavirus is a posthuman agent, best understood through its displaced effects on the economy of life and death from which it originated. Coe shows this economy, its spatial logic and its disciplining of bodies by which this agent travels.

Certainly, representation involves an implicit disfiguration of perceived realities. It precludes both a view of marginal beings and the perspective from the margins. But what Sue Coe's work demonstrates is the way in which the factory farm exists in a broader necropolitical regime in which animal death marks human life. Further, this regime is one that predetermines its margins by killing the complex life that it seeks to harvest. The sadistic killing of animals is the tip of the iceberg: one site amid a global topology of destroying the margins between life and death, living beings and dead beings altogether. Otherness as such is abolished as the bodily differences between humans, non-human animals, and their spaces of relation are homogenized and homologized within a corporate schema. We grow into a common flesh in a farm/pharmacon. Even anthropocentrism is disfigured as the human master falls victim to its alienated posthuman effects on the biosphere.

The coronavirus is one of many anarchical agents that arise from this necropolitical enfleshment. It exacerbates the necropolitical regime, bringing into visibility the shared embodied condition of human and non-human animals by effecting the death of both. If there is any other perspective that is preserved against the representational disfiguration, one that Sue Coe refuses to represent, it is a zone of infinite recession from imaginability: the chaos of ecological diversity that is destroyed by corporate dumping and spillover. For while the deadly global pandemic is at stake in our current condition and consumes our full attention, an absolute otherness is being negated – the differences between humans and non-human animals, the differences between humans and the differences between species: complexity itself. Such a situation can only be thought in terms of the disfigurative effects of a political sphere that has been predestined by sadism. Yet Coe shows us that there is no planetary ground on which we might take shelter from such disfigurations. Necropolitics is the *a priori* ground of representation. We do well to look again.

Notes

1 Michael Marder, 'The Coronavirus Is Us', *The New York Times*, 3 March 2020. https://www.nytimes.com/2020/03/03/opinion/the-coronavirus-is-us.html

2 Rob Wallace, 'Notes on a novel coronavirus', 29 January 2020. https://mronline.org/2020/01/29/notes-on-a-novel-coronavirus/. Accessed 19 April 2020.

3 Cary Wolfe, 'From Dead Meat to Glow-in-the-Dark Bunnies', *What Is Posthumanism?* (Minneapolis: University of Minnesota Press 2010), 145–68.

4 Ibid., 167.

5 Ibid., 166.

6 Ibid., 152.

7 Christa Noel Robbins, 'The Sensibility of Michael Fried', *Criticism* 60, no. 4 (Fall 2018): 429–54.

8 Michel Foucault, 'What Is an Author?' in *The Foucault Reader*, ed. Paul Rabinow (New York: Pantheon Books, 1984), 114.

9 Nicole Shukin, *Animal Capital: Rendering Life in Biopolitical Times* (Minneapolis: University of Minnesota Press, 2010), 38.

10 Alice Kuzniar, 'Where Is the Animal After Post-Humanism: Sue Coe and the Art of Quivering Life', *The New Centennial Review* 11, no. 2 (Fall 2011): 21.

11 Ibid., 22.

12 For a substantive critique of 'genohype', see Kate O'Riordan, *The Genome Incorporated: Constructing Biodigital Identity* (London: Ashgate Press, 2010): 71–98.

13 Hilarie M Sheets, 'Casting a Critical Eye, From the Slaughterhouse to the White House', The New York Times, 21 October 2020, https://www.nytimes.com/2020/10/21/arts/sue-coe-artist.html.

14 Achille Mbembe, 'Necropolitics', *Public Culture* 15, no. 1 (2003): 11–40.

15 Ibid., 21.

16 Aph Ko and Syl Ko, Aphro-ism: Essays on Pop Culture, Feminism and Black Veganism from Two Sisters (New York: Lantern Books, 2017), 11.

17 Rob Wallace, *Big Farms Make Big Flu: Dispatches on Influenza, Agribusiness and the Nature of Science* (New York: Monthly Review Press, 2016).

18 Ibid., 113.

19 Ibid., 115.

20 Rob Wallace, 'Notes on a novel coronavirus,' 29 January 2020. https://mronline.org
    /2020/01/29/notes-on-a-novel-coronavirus/. Accessed 19 April 2020.

21 Gregg Mitman, *The World That Firestone Built: Capitalism, American Empire and
    the Forgotten Promise of Liberia* (New York: The New Press, 2021).

22 Wallace, *Big Farms*, 332–3.

23 Ibid., 333.

7

While you were at home, confined

Control and technology after the city

Rick Dolphijn

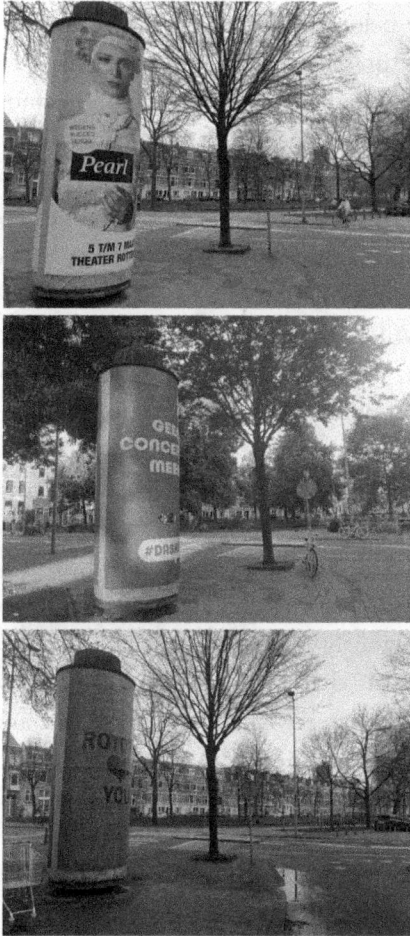

Figure 7.1 Advertising column, Rotterdam, near the city centre, the Netherlands. First picture taken in early April 2020, second one in June 2020 and third in January 2021.

To not resist

In the first paragraph of his magnum opus *My Struggle*, Karl Ove Knausgård talks of the death of his dominant father, which is the moment, we find out later, when he finds life himself. Death, for Knausgård, marks a moment of transition, in which 'a life' disappears, or better, *stops resisting others*:[1]

> The enormous hordes of bacteria that begin to spread through the body's innards cannot be halted. Had they tried only a few hours earlier they would have met with immediate resistance, but now everything around them is still, as they delve deeper and deeper into the moist darkness.

Being dead, the body belonging to his father perhaps evokes some memories with Karl Ove (the expression on his face, the shape of his hard hand, are recognized by him), but there is no confrontation anymore, 'it' is not resisting anymore; things that were stopped before can pass and continue their journey. From now on, his father doesn't matter.

During March and early April 2020, witnessing the coronavirus taking over Europe as it had paralysed East Asia first, I was too scared to leave the house, severely struck by the information bombs that had been dropped on us since early January already. In March, the Dutch government had announced an 'intelligent lockdown', which, in combination with the ongoing media wars, resulted in the fact that public life came to an abrupt halt. Not so much forced by the government policy, but all the more by a politics of fear, the city of Rotterdam, where I (now) spend most of my time, lost its energy, its flows, its warmth. I was confined close to its heart and could see from my window how the city surrendered, how life poured out, how it stopped resisting the forces that had been powerless before but that now, immediately, took control. At first, and most obviously of course, people noticed the rapid increase of wildlife in the city, birds that were not chased away by the traffic and the amount of people in the streets, plants in pavements and in parks that were given much more space than before. And in addition to that, we were told that pollution went down significantly, the sun was bright, the wind was crispy, and somehow everything smelled differently. As if we could smell the countryside again, in the city centre, as if these fragrances were no longer blocked anymore by the machines and the people of the city. Now they were free to flow anywhere.

In early April, after I 'celebrated' my birthday, I dared to walk just a few blocks from my prison cell/house, my 'site of confinement'. Wearing my face mask, with hand sanitizer in the pocket of my coat (in other words, taking all the precautions necessary to avoid contact with the unidentified life forms [viruses] that had virtually taken over the streets) I passed by several advertisements for theatre plays, concerts and other public events. My attention was caught by one large poster which mentioned the performances of a Rotterdam-based contemporary dance company. The poster claimed that the performances were to take place in March 2020 (see Figure 7.1). What was it doing there? Of course, posters like these inform us about an upcoming event, hoping that the people who see these announcements buy tickets for these events. The problem now was of course that the events advertised had not taken place in March. Also, as I passed these posters in early April, it was highly unusual that these particular posters were actually still hanging there. They should have been replaced with new posters, probably the day after the events they advertised took place. Posters like these are supposed to announce events that were to happen in the future, as we know. They are a vital element of the cities timing, informing its citizens about the life to come. Perhaps especially in a place like the Netherlands, where regular advertisement billboards can only be found next to main roads and freeways (rarely), but do not play a significant role in the cityscapes, the announcements of cultural events to come are important to the rhythm of the city.

Sometimes those posters (only the most memorable ones) are embalmed and mummified, collected and displayed at exhibitions. They not only evoke some memories of a shared history, but they also belong to something completely different now. They have become part of a style, an oeuvre, a historical event. Then, they have little to do with the life they belonged to before. Within the museum or an exhibition space, we may recognize the life it was part of before, we may feel some of the resonances of times long gone, and imagine the city, the life, as it once was; that particular energy that defined it, that rhythm that was so essential to it – seeing the things that could have happened in those days. But the style, the oeuvre or the historical event is more important now. The museum is not the space for personal histories. It is about what we have in common, what we share. The mummification (and embalming, etc.) did not happen with the posters I walked into. The posters were not taken into a new context, nor were they, in any other way, framed to tickle the imagination. Here, they were simply not included in the urban fabric in which they made sense before. Like the body that belonged to the father of Karl Ove Knausgård, the posters didn't matter anymore. Surely there were bacteria and fungi that saw opportunities (and perhaps had taken them), but to a large extent, it seemed these posters had been left to die.

Perhaps it was even worse. Perhaps I did not recognize another power, another life present in the posters. With the streets empty, or at least, emptied of human life, with all these other life forms (plants and animals) taking over the streets, I did not recognize the life of the city itself anymore. The city, as I knew it, did not matter.

After only one walk, since having spent a month in my house, this was what I realized: that this was *not* the city I lived in before. The city life that once resisted outside forces in order to persevere in being, the city life that had always embraced me, that gave me a gush of wind in my back and that would always introduce me to some unexpected excitement, something beautiful, something right, was gone now. If I try, I may be able to recognize some of the traces of its life, as perhaps some of the frames are still partly functional, but I couldn't say they were 'there' anymore. *Everything I saw grew cold*. It was as if I saw what the satellite images saw; the 'warmth' (the images were claimed to refer to the absence of the dust, the pollution, the movement) had already pulled back from the highways but had by now also left the city centre empty. Deserted.

The end of an era

The opening section of Knausgård's *My Struggle* with which I started this chapter is essential for all six volumes of this book. The death of his father caused a crack; it broke open a history and a future and laid bare the writer that Karl Ove had always been, as, from that moment on, he started writing his own history (3,600 pages long) while becoming the writer he had to be; the crack offered him a new history and a new future. Of course, this reminds us of Marcel Proust, for whom it was the *Madeleine* (the little almond flavoured cake) that not only brought back his memories of Aunt Leonié (and how she dipped the *Madeleine* in her tea or tisane), but that, in the end, realized a completely new history and a new future, a history of lost times and of times regained. The question is now; why did Knausgård (let us stick to him in this analysis) start writing his history only after his father passed away? Hadn't his struggle already happened, wasn't it already there? His timeline says it was, but somehow, it couldn't be realized as a book (or as a series of books). Somehow, it seems, this other history (because of this other present?) did not allow it to take place.

The life of the city I knew must have made other lives impossible. And here I am not just referring to 'the city itself' having many untold, unwritten and unrealized histories; it is perfectly reasonable that there are histories imaginable, in which the city 'as such' does not matter, does not function as one. Let me remind you of the best possible example of this (historically); when Genghis Khan realized his *Pax Mongolica*, it was not 'according to' the cities that he organized the Empire, as this happened in most empires before and after him. As Deleuze and Guattari put it: 'he [Genghis Khan, r.d.] "didn't understand" the phenomenon of the city.'[2] Genghis Kahn, the nomad, gave us the Mongol Empire, an unusual empire as it was not bound together by cities, but stretched out through routes and connections, sometimes referred to as the Silk Road. It is telling that the *Pax Mongolica* is so often referred to as 'an oddity' of history, by the textbooks that actually consider all of nomadic history inferior and that, in many ways, 'do not understand' the phenomenon of nomadology. The territories of an Empire have to be defined, it seems, by its lively centre and by its protected (walled) borders. Thinking an Empire through its (ever-changing) routes seems impossible, or at least incompatible with the dominant use of the term.

It is good to remember that the *Pax Mongolica* was the *first and only* empire to unite Eurasia to date (as it passed through Europe, the Middle East, the Indian subcontinent *and* East Asia). Also, very intriguing; it was not defeated because of an attack by a hostile (sedentary) state, the Mongol Empire 'disappeared' because of the plague. Suddenly it was not the merchant who travelled its silk roads, but the Black Death. The Black Death killed the Empire.

Of course, long before the corona crisis hit the city, the idea of the city, and how we make use of it, had already been under great pressure. Its unity may have seemed undisputed in modern times, but surely there have been many social organizations that have been unable to realize themselves because of the city, for all sorts of reasons. Yet they are there. And we could ask ourselves how the city has survived for so long, at what cost, and what its alternatives would have looked like. So little is known (still) about the *Pax Mongolica*, what it brought us and what it could have realized. And only so rarely people wonder whether this idea of the city itself, that we seem to cling on to, is not terribly outdated.

Fortunately, at least some of us placed question marks after institutions like the city. In his wonderful little booklet *Thumbelina*, Michel Serres[3] nicely summarizes that so many of the nineteenth-century modern or early capitalist ideas according to which we have organized our lives might still seem functional in today's society, but, in a way, resemble those stars that still lit up the sky at night, while having already been dead for 10,000 years. One of these ideas would no doubt be 'the city'; an idea with a long European (!) history, that might find its (mythological) origin in the eternal city (Rome), but that became an international phenomenon in due time. As the archetypical centre of power, its success allowed it to persevere in being. Two thousand years later, here we are.

One of its major victories was that the European city, since the Renaissance, invented the countryside. This proto capitalist/colonialist invention followed the invention of the printing press, which, as Marshall McLuhan[4] told us long ago, gave the European towns the tools to set up the bureaucracy needed for the rise of the city-state, as stricter rules and better legislation were now easily and uniformly spread. The new-born city invented the countryside as it was high on demand for the foods, garments and people, that the countryside could produce. However, it was especially in the nineteenth century, when modern technology gave rise to a much more rigid opposition, according to the capitalist rules of production, turning the countryside into the home of food production and the city into the place where the industries were located and where consumption took place. This bond between the city and the countryside by means of a trade would not just be practised in Europe, but, through colonization, would become the dominant model of socio-cultural organization of the world.

Since agriculture was very labour intensive in those days, the overwhelming majority of people would live and work in the countryside. It is crucial to notice that, probably since the 1920s when cities underwent enormous changes, this has changed completely, with enormous consequences to how we, as a society, relate to the earth. Michel Serres, interested in the lives and times of the millennials, the schoolchildren that populate our classes today, sums this up at the start of *Thumbelina*:[5]

> This young schoolgirl and new schoolboy have never seen a calf, a cow, a pig, or a brood of chicks. In 1900, most human beings on the planet worked on the land; by 2011, in France and in similar countries, the number of people working on the land has been reduced to one percent of the population. This has been one of the greatest revolutions in history since the Neolithic period. Our cultures, which used to be tied to pastoral practices, have suddenly changed. Of course, what we eat, on the planet, still comes from the earth. The children I am introducing here no longer live in the company of animals; they no longer inhabit the same earth; they no longer have the same relation to the world. The nature they admire is merely an Arcadian nature, the nature of vacation and tourism.

The words of Serres echoed in my mind, as I, back in confinement, listened to yet another televised speech from the prime minister of the Netherlands, where he was repeating the new decrees of the State in response to the ongoing corona crisis: people should keep on working from their homes and if everyone followed the guidelines, the borders would open up again in summertime and we could all enjoy our holidays in the French countryside, as usual. What an interesting – and new – opposition! Talking to his contemporaries, it is obvious that he assumed that work today was done by urban professionals (not anymore by farmers or industrial workers, but by those in the tertiary sector, who were not bound to the land to do what they were paid for). He also seemed to accept that 'the countryside', which perhaps included any form of nature, is to be visited during 'the summer vacation'. Interestingly enough, the summer vacation was originally free time designated for the kids to help their parents with the harvest. Now, it seems to refer to the time when the urban kids and their parents were released from their duties and were allowed to escape their urban lives, briefly.

Societies of control, the panopticon inverted

Similar to how death does not always coincide with the moment someone releases their last breath (it could have happened decades prior to that moment), Serres ensures us that the nineteenth-century institutions that still organize society have entered their 'zombie phase' long ago. In many ways they have even been replaced by other systems of knowledge, without the majority of us noticing it. *Thumbelina* is his homage to 'the millennials', a term he uses to describe the students in his class and his grandchildren in the first place. In the end, however, the term covers a large amount of his contemporaries. It could therefore also be read as a warning to the 'boomers' and actually all of us who are not digital natives, who, for some reason (could it be capital?), are blind to the forces that have already given shape to a whole other world. Gilles Deleuze, in his *Postscript on Control Societies*, published in 1990,[6] already foresaw that actually all of the nineteenth-century institutions that functioned as 'sites of confinement', were finished. Famously defined by Michel Foucault as 'disciplinary societies', the nineteenth century saw the institutionalization not just of the normal and the abnormal, by giving form to the sites where the abnormal could be 'cured' (think of hospitals, prisons, but also schools and barracks) before they were placed back in the normal.

It is important to note here that these changes from a disciplinary society to a society of control is not just about noticing how particular ideas of power are changing, but, all the more, about how a radically different *geometry* would come to dominate the organization of social life. In line with Foucault, Deleuze's ideas are materialist in that Deleuze too looks at systems of power first and foremost as a geometry, as a way of organizing the physical territory that is supposed to be governed. The sites of confinement of the disciplinary society should therefore be seen above all as constructions that are positioned and designed in order to spatially separate one group of people from the rest of society (the children, the sick, the mad, the delinquent, etc.). The biggest change occurring in the current transformation is thus a change in the use of space. The societies of control will not be organized by means of these sites of confinement; these are – as we speak – being replaced by what Deleuze foresaw as 'free floating forms of control'.

It is often said that Foucault had already claimed that the systems of power in the disciplinary societies became operational by means of the changes realized in discourse. This is to say that being powerful does not mean one has the ability to 'make a new law', or 'set up a new institute'. Power, on the contrary, has always been about *bending* the discourse, about understanding how dominance works and having the tools to do so. Foucault famously introduced us to the term 'governmentality', which he simply defined as the 'techniques and procedures for directing human behaviour'.[7] The advantage of the term 'discourse', in analysing the practices of power, is that, as mentioned before, Foucault could use this term to emphasize how power is at work in both the words and the things; how changes in ideas of justice and legal discourse were concomitant with changes in actual practices of punishment and even prison architecture.[8]

In our days, to continue the analysis, 'discourse' allows us to see how this stream of power is at work in the systems of continuous monitoring and surveillance. Thirty years after Deleuze's ground-breaking essay, we need to expand his ideas of control by looking at how today's ideas of justice (and its links to terrorism, national security and civil unrest for instance) are running parallel to (and matter for) the network of (facial recognition) cameras, the systems of geolocation on our mobile phones, the social media applications by means of which we document our lives as we are on the move, and perhaps, even more significantly, in the way everyone has become integrated into the systems of power, as they using/misusing their phone apps and geolocation devices, their Facebook and Instagram posts, to install systems of control. As with DNA research, it is often thanks to all Others (your friends and followers) that facial recognition systems and other devices, making use of biometric information, work so efficiently. Over the past decade or so, a whole new system of punishment is being realized today, a system which is capable of turning society as a whole into a panopticon, a *panopticon inverted* it seems, in which you find yourself in the centre, and you are surrounded by an infinity of potential eyes.

The eyes can be found not just outside of our bodies but have become an integral part of it. Just briefly touching upon the changing ideas of health and the way control urges us into a system of continuous treatment, Paul M. Preciado (2020) gives us some examples of how elaborate biotechnological management, over the past decades, has become part of our everyday practices:

> In the domain of sexuality, the pharmacological modification of consciousness and behavior, the mass consumption of antidepressants and anxiolytics, and the globalization of the contraceptive pill, as well as antiretroviral therapies, preventative AIDS therapies, and Viagra, are some of the indicators of biotechnological management, which in turn synergizes with new modes of semio-technical management that have arisen with the surveillance state and the global expansion of the network into every facet of life.

It doesn't call for a lot of imagination to see how the strategies of isolation as enforced by the state in times of corona perpetuate this idea of biotechnological management.

Perhaps it is good to single out the three ways in which contemporary control, and its system of biotechnological management, is changing society radically:

1. The panopticon inverted – is no longer in need of the systems of confinement

When Deleuze tells us that the language of disciplinary societies is analogue, whereas the language of societies of control is digital, it is important to stress that the digital is not necessarily limited to what computers can do. The digital is a revolution in communication because it always starts from the simplest systems of calculations which allow information to flow from object A to object B, and so on. In the end, the digital is able to create a discourse that may very well appear to us through images and words in the protocols, the anti-virus software and the online security systems (active and passive) that accompany us in our daily (digital) life and are materialized in smart phones and data centres. Yet they control us, in both instances, in radically different ways compared to the disciplinary system of power.

2. The panopticon inverted – is no longer in need of the human (language)

The images and words that are now constructed by the protocols of our phones and computers *are fake*, as D. N. Rodowick[9] put it; their protocols are 'fake reality', meaning that these machines do not communicate using the words and the images they use when facing us. The disturbing fact of digital communication is that the communication that matters happens between the protocols of machine language; in the sending, receiving, storing and processing chains of zeroes and ones. Through a system of translation, some of these communications could somehow be made accessible to us (if this is needed) but in the end the information exchange that is elementary to them takes place elsewhere; it happens between the machines, not between computers and humans. Actually, this increasingly happens on the machine's terms, which means, for instance, that these exchanges, crucial to the global economy, are increasingly taking place at a speed incomprehensible to human understanding. As Mark B. N. Hansen puts it:[10]

> twenty-first century media directly mediate the causal infrastructure of worldly sensibility. Whatever impact they have on human experience specifically is a part of this larger mediation: by mediating worldly sensibility, twenty-first-century media simultaneously modulate human sensibility, as it were, beneath the senses.

Phenomenologically, this shift from analogue to digital communication, based as it is on what Mark B. N. Hansen calls a 'calculative ontology of prediction'[11] comes with 'distinct modifications in the structure of experience' (idem). The materialism that I am exploring here recognizes the consequences of this new ontology in the presence of all (that) matters. Going back to the disciplinary system, we could conclude (with Foucault) that the court houses, schools, hospitals and barracks so essential to it matter because *their form practised their function* (the lecture hall for instance practices the idea of the modern university, placing the professor – 'he who knows' – on a stage opposed to the students – 'they who want to know' – in the auditorium). The material part of the digital discourse, however, may appear very present as it involves the smart phones you held in your hand only five minutes ago. The matters concerned with digital discourse, however, in their effort to afford all forms of future images and words have smoothened their appearance in every way in the past two decades. Very much in contrast to the telephones as we once knew them, whose form invited the ear, the mouth and the hand to touch them, today's smart phones have evolved into black rectangles ready to accommodate whatever new imagery or word will arrive, and whichever part of the (human) body is willing to touch them. The object itself doesn't speak but holds its secret inside (with its reflecting screen and the impossibility to 'get in'); every phone is said to hold at least twenty-five rare earth materials.

3. The panopticon inverted – is no longer in need of the city

The digital today is able to connect everything to everything, which means that, increasingly, its flows string together very different objects (organic, inorganic, semiotic), gathering them into big datacentres, where all data is made fully compatible, before departing again. These huge black boxes (seemingly designed after our mobile phones) allow for all sorts of data traffic, and pollute our landscapes often in hidden places (creating nodes far away from the city centres). Using more energy than an entire village (and this will rapidly increase) these datacentres are in no way comparable to the buildings that knotted together the particular forms of power that characterized the disciplinary society. Located in the centres of our cities, disciplinary buildings (even the prison in its nineteenth-century appearance) were built to impress, lured the outside in and projected the inside out. Found in squares and bigger boulevards, these buildings spun the web of the nineteenth-century city that still dominates the cities in Europe and in many of its former colonies, and thus contributed in many ways to how we give form to city life. The prisons and the court houses gave us all an idea of justice and, together with police stations perhaps, organized (also materially) the idea of right and wrong. Perhaps the designs of these buildings even gave the city (not walled anymore to keep out the villains) a sense of safety. Just as its schools, universities and public libraries gave it a sense of intelligence. Like webs, like a nerve system, they gave sense to the city.

The inverted panopticon still depends on capitalism, but in a different way

In his *Postscript*, Deleuze already notices that nineteenth-century capitalism was concentrative, directed towards production, and proprietorial ([1990] 1995, 180). This means, for instance, that its labour was organized in enclosed spaces like factory halls which were designed for maximizing production, and these factories employed many and were owned by the few. Indeed, humans (workers) were part of the design, which once again reminds us of the fact that humanism (Cartesian and Kantian) was never designed for the 99 per cent. High-rise offices replaced the factories in the twentieth century, while at the same time, these offices seemed to mimic, in their appearance, the sites of confinement proper to the disciplinary system. In many ways, these phallic skyscrapers all hope to become a new landmark for our inner cities. Similar to the court houses, the universities and so on, the office buildings are intended to make the city, give it its entrepreneurial feel. In other words, from Battery Park, to the City, to La Défense to the Admiralty, these high-rise office buildings still practice a disciplinary power.

Yet, because they still depend upon a disciplinary system of power, high-rise office buildings are, ultimately, finished. Buildings like these played a key role in what now seems to have been a transition phase between the sites of confinement of disciplinary system and the free-floating forms of control that serve the societies of control. But they will no longer play a significant role in the times to come. Over the past twenty years, we have already seen that in all major centres of capitalism around the world, the office buildings are more and more being deserted. Even before the corona crisis hit us, it was clear that offices would be seen as an outcome of what Marshall McLuhan[12] calls 'the Horseless Carriage Syndrome', referring to the first cars that indeed looked like horseless carriages, as we were all still searching for what this new form of motor-based transportation would actually look like (how its form would follow its function). Offices still mimic factory halls, they aim to be concentrative, directed towards production, and they act in a proprietorial way, whereas the kind of capitalism these offices actually practice works very differently.

Today's capitalism, as Deleuze already foresaw, is no longer aimed at production (which takes place elsewhere). It is a capitalism of products; it buys activities, and it sells services, it is aimed at sales and markets.[13] Deleuze adds to this that we all know that markets are interested in control. And taking control, as we saw happening in our economies over the past few decades, has nothing to do with property anymore. The businesses that dominate our era, from Amazon to Uber to Booking.com, are not interested in ownership but only in controlling their markets. Therefore, there is no need for these firms to be concentrative. If the corona crisis has taught us anything, it is that for most employees today there is very little need to actually 'go to the office'. Work can be done from anywhere, at any time. And probably, it *has* to be done from anywhere and at any time, because the never-ending flows of capitalism require constant management and administration.

This is key to contemporary capitalism; to find a way to control the flows that matter and keep things in flow. This means finding ways to manipulate the 'rotations of the wheel' (control comes from 'contra' meaning 'against' and 'rota' meaning 'wheel'). Manipulating can be simply translated as speeding up and slowing down; you speed up and slow down the flows of information, the flows of money and the flows of people. Being in the position to manipulate these flows, the algorithms that realize these flows, and the benefits that accrue to them, the ones in charge (the Big Tech companies and social media firms today) are the ones in control. Near the end of his *Postscript*, Deleuze, reminded of Guattari, gives us a brief speculation on what this could mean:[14]

> Félix Guattari has imagined a town where anyone can leave their flat, their street, their neighbourhood, using their [. . .] electronic card that opens this or that barrier; but the card may also be rejected on a particular day, or between certain times of the day; it doesn't depend on the barrier but on the computer that is making sure that everyone is in a permissible place, and effecting a universal modulation.

Guattari's visionary dystopia may have been at work before, but it is surely the case that, since the corona crisis dominated international politics in early 2020, its forms of control have become increasingly dominant. The simplest virus, chased after by the most complex governments, caused 80 per cent of the world to go into lockdown, and most economies, a year after its initial spread, are still not willing or able to open up. Given the global impact of this, we know that our lives in the end will start up in different modus. There comes a day when we, all of a sudden, like Georg Samsa, wake up from troubled dreams, in a space that seemed familiar, but that we now experience completely differently. We will collectively wake up to a city not held together anymore by the disciplinary powers that were responsible for locking us up in our houses for the past year. We wake up to a city that perhaps, like the body of Knausgård's father, as the lockdown started, was immediately overtaken by many other forms of life, powers that had been there all along but that now, because the urban sphere (or whatever we want to call it) has died, were no longer obstructed by the unity it once was.

Guattari's aforementioned electronic card is the SIM card that always accompanies us in our mobile phone, which, contrary to what it claims to do (to serve you, the consumer, with the ability to call others, to message others and to get information on the outside world) is actually a device built for sending a continuous flow of data to the outside world, *serving everyone but you, with the requested information.* The SIM card is key to the inverted panopticon. During this corona crisis, every state, forced to act quickly and to take unprecedented measures, seems to have embraced the existing, and yet to be developed, technologies of control.

All over the world, governments (mostly independently of one another, in compliance with local laws, regional economic ties and public demand) started developing corona apps that were supposed to collect information on our whereabouts and our activities, and many also urged restaurants to set up a table reservation system using QR codes, and demanded shops stop accepting cash money and shift to electronic currencies instead – two well-known examples of how governmentality had changed. Of course, there are still all sorts of organizations guarding people's privacy that aim to prevent all of these data flows coming together. But, increasingly, companies, universities and governments find ways to combine some of these flows, which allows them to identify all sorts of patterns in consumer behaviour. Paul M. Preciado[15] said: 'The most important thing we learned from Foucault is that the living (therefore mortal) body is the central object of all politics.' This has surely not changed in the era of the digital as it reveals itself to us now, after the corona virus hit us. After the lockdown, after the city.

Of course, some of the flows that hit us are very familiar to us, as they have existed for a long time (think of digital payment systems), but their importance has accelerated dramatically during lockdown, in such a way that they now seem to have changed things permanently. As we lived in fear, trapped in our houses, glued to our computers and phones, the cities were no longer dominated by the concentrative circles that pushed us to its centres, its economy was no longer centred around production hubs, and its streets, its parks and other public spaces were no longer owned by its people. Instead, the unseen flows of data, and the devices that connect them, have firmly taken a grip on the economy, on the social and on the psychological. Shops in the city have been overtaken by webshops, and the transportation centres outside of the city connect to them to our houses. Public events are taking place online, leaving the streets empty, making the realm of the virtual the space where one is to express oneself, where capitalism triumphs and where social segregation takes place. It shows us that it is not just capitalism which has changed its form; the city, as a whole, is no longer concentrative, directed towards production and property.

But let us keep in mind that the death of the city has taken us by surprise, the way death always seems to come from nowhere, even when it concerns the terminally ill. The warnings had been there for very long, but as it happens with everything we love, very few of us could have dreamed that one day in the very near future, the city we once lived in would disappear overnight, would not matter anymore, would be overtaken by the data flows of states and the big corporations that were among us before, but found their victory in the pandemic. Also, so many specialists had already been warning us that it was only a matter of time before another big pandemic (after the Spanish flu from 1918) would hit us. And let us not focus only on the influenza pandemics that have actually been rather 'common' since the late nineteenth century (from the Russian flu, to the Hongkong flu to the Mexican flu). The pandemic has always been with us and its history is strongly entangled with the rise and fall of the greatest civilizations throughout time.

To Rome, again

We already mentioned the *Pax Mongolica*, which fell apart because of the plague. The Roman Empire, as we know it, arose because of it. This can be read in how great historians of the Roman Empire, such as Livy (64/59 BC–AD 12/17) and Dionysius of Hallicarnasus (*c.*60 BC – after 7 BC) talk of the pestilence of 463 BCE. Their fascinating (and somewhat contradictory) accounts didn't just tell us about the horror, about destruction caused by the Black Death. Almost as a prequel to Albert Camus's novel *La peste* (*The Plague*), they discussed the everyday matters that happened to the city under siege. Livy noticed the role of the *Lectisternium*, the council of gods and senators, where, in hard times, praying and policy making went hand in hand (especially during an event like a massive outbreak). It is easy to see that in our times, the scientists (virologists, epidemiologists) who have replaced the gods today were directly called on to speak the truth. Of course, scientists, like the gods, were in dispute, which, once again, was immensely useful for the senators/the politicians keen on designing their own plan.

Then, a tragedy unfolded. The people were blinded by the wisdom of their gods, the politicians were blinded by their newly acquainted powers to suppress and control, while both were suffering greatly under the plague. In that chaos, the Aequians and the Volscians, two tribes drifting from the hills around Rome, joined forces and decided to attack the Roman hegemony. First roaming the rich villages and the smaller cities in the provinces surrounding the capital, they proceeded to attack the weakened and fragile Rome. Both its consuls had already died from the plague and the senate was half its size, its wealth was as good as gone even before the pillaging and attacks started. Like Genghis Kahn, the Aequians and the Volscians did not recognize the city. And so, they had no intention to 'take it' and occupy it as a whole, to become its new rulers. Rome did not matter anymore; they took what they could. But as they left, they gave it a new life, a life impossible before when the city was still intact.

Modern history books hardly mention the Aequians and the Volscians. Archaeologists only attributed a few texts and objects to them. After the pestilence, after they attacked the city and plundered it rigorously, Rome, as we all know, found a new life, a different life. Could we say that this rebirth of Rome, started its 'eternal' life? Was this rebirth the moment we saw the true Western city arise? The city always aimed at controlling the land that surrounded it, that created the countryside, to fulfil its own needs. Rome was a city full of *hatred*, as Serres puts it,[16] that had to occupy the land of so many people (including the Aequians and the Volscians), that had to spread its tentacles across the Mediterranean and destroy Carthage. The new Rome, in the third and the second centuries BC, by including the nomadic tribes, invented the sedentary state, as we know it: a Rome that was always at war with those inside and outside its empire and that developed its economy as a continuation of war by other means and gave us imperialism and economic slavery. The *Pax Romana*, contrary to the *Pax Mongolica*, became the blueprint of what a state, as an extension of the city, would look like.

Michel Serres stresses the importance of the *Lectisternium*. That moment where the gods and the senators join forces and celebrate, where everyone would join in the copious meal, when all doors would open, when all strangers were invited in. Its probable Greek origin, Θεοξένια (*theoxenia*) marked a similar feast at a moment of despair (note that *xenos* in Greek not only means outsider or stranger but also guest). But the history of the *Lectisternia* in Rome is strongly connected to the plague. The history books, even as early as the writings of Livy and Dionysius, are in search of continuity, which means that their narratives start from the city and the state, from eternal Rome. They write about its institutions, its administrative body and the way this extended territory had to persevere in being. Their 'idea' of the city is always that of Rome after the plague. Is it because of this history, that we, city dwellers, do not understand the Aequians and the Volscians, and only write about eternal Rome? Is it because of that, that the *Pax Mongolica*, as it established such an important connection throughout the Eurasian continent as said, is still considered an oddity?

In a moment of despair, once again, we seem to be blinded by the divine sciences, while our senators are blinded by their power. Still living in Rome, no one seems to recognize that the *xenos* (the strangers, the guests) could very well have reinvented the city already, realizing the new forms of dominance. As the modern city draws its last breath, new flows of power quickly overtake the key institutions so vital for the city as we knew it.

Focused on roads and on movement, rather than on the sites that mattered so much for the state and the city, there is no reason why these new forms of control would be in need of the monumental buildings and the city centre as we know it today. Can we say that the Society of Control, also, *does not recognize* the city? Deleuze already noted that within this new system of domination, space would be organized through computers deciding whether everyone was in a permissible place. Surely the QR codes, the different corona apps, the way in which public transportation has been functioning in large parts of the world (only running for 'essential use', for the nurses and the doctors to get to their hospital, for the cleaners and police personnel necessary for society to keep functioning), give the state all the opportunities it needs to practice this universal modulation, to create more and more opportunities to monitor all of its subjects in their movement and to reorganize this new society of control according to the speeds it is allowed to move.

Closing remarks

At the end of his little book *How Contagion Works*,[17] the Italian author Paolo Giordano, an early witness of what he refers to as the horrors of the biggest health crisis of our times, reminds us of Psalm 90, the only Psalm attributed to Moses, the Psalm that talks of coming of age. It reminds us to count our days, in the hope that wisdom fulfils our hearts. Giordano reminds us of this 'timely' piece of writing to stress that we also value these times, that we don't consider them simply a boring intermezzo, and simply wait for 'the normal' to return. Yet, in the end, his reading of these lines, not unexpectedly, is profoundly Christian; he hopes all our suffering hasn't been for nothing and that in the end a new, even better 'normality' awaits us.

In the Judaic tradition it makes more sense to read this psalm as an announcement that the end is near.

When I returned to the column where the advertisement for the theatre show 'that didn't happen' (with which I opened this chapter) was located a few months later, still under lockdown, a new advertisement was to be seen at the column. It said (in Dutch); 'No more concerts', and added to this, with a hashtag, #daskut, which is the slang equivalent of 'that sucks'. In January, almost one year later, it said 'Rotown loves you', which is slang for 'Rotterdam loves you'.

It sounds like a permanent goodbye.

Notes

1 Karl Ove Knausgård, *My Struggle, Book 1* (2009; New York: Farrar, Strauss, Giroux books, 2012), 3.

2 Gilles Deleuze and Félix Guattari, *A Thousand Plateaus: Capitalism and Schizophrenia* (1980; Minneapolis: University of Minnesota Press, 1987), 354.

3 Michel Serres, *Thumbelina, The Culture and Technology of Millenials* (2012; London: Rowman and Littlefield International, 2015).

4 Herbert Marshall McLuhan and Quentin Fiore, *The Medium is the Massage, an Inventory of Effects* (New York: Bantam books, 1967).

5 Serres, *Thumbelina*, 2.

6 Gilles Deleuze, *Negotiations* (1990; New York: Columbia University Press, 1995).

7 Michel Foucault, *Ethics: Subjectivity and Truth. Essential Works of Michel Foucault, 1954-1984. Vol. 1* (New York: New Press, 1997), 82.

8 See also Deleuze and Guattari, *A Thousand Plateaus*, x).

9 D. N. Rodowick, *The Virtual Life of Film* (Cambridge, MA: Harvard University Press, 2007).

10 Mark B. N. Hansen, *Feed Forward: On the Future of 21st Century Media* (Chicago and London: University of Chicago Press, 2015), 52.

11 Ibid., 186.

12 McLuhan, *The Medium is the Massage*.

13 Deleuze, *Negotiations*, 181.

14 Ibid., 181–2.

15 Paul M. Preciado, 'Learning from the Virus', *Artforum*. May/June 2020.

16 Michel Serres, *Rome, the First Book of Foundations*, (1983; London: Bloomsbury, 2015) 5.

17 Paolo Giordano, [2020] 2020, *How Contagion Works; Science, Awareness and Community in Times of Global Crisis*. Orion Publishing co. London.

Part III

Art

8

Is human to posthuman as Earth is to post-earth?

Notes on terraforming and (trans)forming

Amanda du Preez

In an article published in 1972, Sherry Ortner asks, 'Is female to male as nature is to culture?'[1] She concludes that women are indeed universally constructed as being associated with that which most cultures devalue, namely nature. The over-identification of women with nature creates a 'vicious circle', Ortner notes, because 'various aspects of woman's situation (physical, social, psychological) lead to her being seen as "closer to nature," while the view of her as closer to nature is embodied in institutional forms that regenerate her situation'.[2] This cycle perpetuates itself since a 'different cultural view can grow only out of a different social actuality', while 'a different social actuality can grow only out of a different cultural view'.[3] I want to follow Ortner's suggestion loosely by aiming to show that, similarly, human and Earth are usually intertwined, and as a result mostly negatively viewed, in favour of (trans)formed posthuman and terraformed post-earth aspirations.

The suggested route of tackling the issue is through a visual hermeneutical analysis of selected images and imaginations portraying our relationship with Earth and Mars as post-earth. The image with its roots in the imagination is a provocative barometer of human aspirations. Furthermore, the image has a propensity for surviving and manifesting in different formats and platforms.

I will plot the case along the axis of the following aesthetic categories, namely form and formlessness, while simultaneously dialoguing these categories with concepts of human and posthuman, Earth and post-earth. The assumption is that much of the debate and discourse on human and posthuman develops along the understanding of form and the formless. Basically, humans have a form while posthumans aspire to a state of formlessness. In the same vein, Earth is understood as a planet about to disintegrate in form, while that which is beyond Earth or post-earth is a plunge into the unknown, the void and the formless. However, I will show that most dreams of posthumanism and post-earth visions are situated within a particular form and place. Thus, dreams of formlessness always already participate in form, just as form, similarly, is always already susceptible to formlessness.

Why would I relate Mars, or post-earth, and even outer space expeditions as being an adventure into formlessness? Perhaps because the formless has deep resonance with the sublime. What would settlement on Mars be but sublime? It would definitely be sublime to move beyond the known form of Earth, and subsequently a bold step into posthumanism, leaving the human form behind. My choice to equate Mars with post-earth is strategic, for not only does Mars currently seem the most popular choice for exoplanetary relocation, but it also appears to consume our imaginations amid the Covid-19 pandemic with renewed interest in the form of cinema, television series and video games.

I

Mars had a good year in 2020, but Earth, not so much. That is if the avalanche of publicity, news, energy, investments and funding spent on planning our relocation to Mars, are any indication. Not only did Mars become very visible in our evening skies during October 2020, due to its opposing position to the sun, but in the summer (Northern hemisphere) three robotic spacecraft, respectively from NASA, China and the United Arab Emirates were launched to Mars. It is estimated that by early 2021 these operations will 'deliver two orbiters, a lander, and two rovers to Mars, joining the six orbiters, one lander, and one rover that already operate there'.[4] As life on Earth became just another notch more difficult in 2020 with the crippling Covid-19 pandemic, the plans for 'Go Mars' became incrementally more attractive. In fact, it is probably not an over-interpretation to state that the pandemic has provided the opportune scope for the pro-Mars movement to push their agenda. In lieu of over-population, the climate crisis, rising unemployment and poverty due to the Covid-19 fall out, the prospects of emigrating to an uncontaminated planet are very attractively packaged.

However, the recent enthusiasm for the Mars project is not a new endeavour, since NASA has established a Mars Exploration Programme (MEP) since 1994 and Elon Musk founded the Space Exploration Technologies Corporation or SpaceX already in 2002. The MEP has the following four strategies: first to 'follow the water', then to 'explore habitability' and 'seek signs of life', and finally to 'prepare for human exploration'.[5] The current strategy is to seek for signs of life. The MEP website optimistically states: 'Even if Mars is devoid of past or present life, however, there's still much excitement on the horizon. We ourselves might become the "life on Mars" should humans choose to travel there one day. Meanwhile, we still have a lot to learn about this amazing planet and its extreme environments.'[6]

Despite NASA's optimism and endeavours, the real impetus and enthusiasm come from non-governmental projects such as Mars One (2011–19) and The Mars Generation.[7] These projects are geared towards the youth, with, for example, the founder of The Mars Generation, Abigail Harrison, or 'Astronaut Abby', promoting Mars as 'cool' and encouraging her audience 'to dream big and reach for the stars'.[8] Harrison (born in 1997) aims to inspire a young generation to become involved in STEM/STEAM subjects through their Space Camp programmes. By training Student Space Ambassadors, it is hoped that a generation 'defined' by Mars are created. 'Exploration is ingrained in our DNA', exclaims a young participant in *The Mars Generation* (Michael Barnett, 2017) documentary film. 'We have to get off this planet and land on Mars', professes another.

Currently, we have no hard evidence of any signs of life on Mars (except for the possible biosignatures of extinct micro-organisms), and neither do we have confirmation of sustainable water resources on Mars. However, we do have confirmation that Mars has a harsh and extreme climate, yet it seems as if there is an ever-increasing drive to explore and even relocate to the Red Planet. If recent academic debates are an indication of the state of the discussions and arguments, at least two recent journal themes were dedicated to the topic: *Futures* published 'Human Colonization of Other Worlds', in June 2019, and *Theology and Science* explored the matter also in June 2019 under the rubric of 'To Mars, the Milky Way and Beyond: Science, Theology and Ethics Look at Space Exploration'.[9] Fervent proponents for and against the Mars expedition are published with an urgency professed by titles such as 'Why We Earthlings Should Colonise Mars!' and 'An Obligation to Colonise Outer Space'.[10]

The reasons presented for colonizing outer space, and Mars specifically, are the promise of abundant resources to be found elsewhere, the insatiable drive of humankind for exploration and the potential for human growth. Also, that life on Earth is predicted to become harsher and more extreme due to the climate crisis. As we await the sixth mass extinction, the logic is to leave one planet behind, due to its increasing extreme environment, for another even harsher climate. I find this an interesting argument to unpack, namely why terraforming Mars (post-earth) and (trans)forming humans (posthuman), have become so urgent and high on the priority list. In effect, we are prepared to find solutions for settling in the harsher Martian environment. Still, we are not ready; it seems to involve spending the same energy to find solutions for staying on Earth (terrasaving).[11] This is a perplexing situation that is worth exploring.

If one can choose between an overheating Earth ridden by pandemics and the apparently stable and uncontaminated Mars, it is perhaps sensible to select Mars. Often in contemporary debates of the climate crisis, we see images depicting Earth on fire – literally becoming an uninhabitable planet.[12] Global warming's flames envelop the Mother planet turning it into an icon of disaster. In this image-making, Earth is composed as an alien planet, it is turned into a hostile entity, and even an 'unthinkable world'.[13] No longer our home or 'the world-for-us' but turning into a sublime 'world-without-us'.[14] The theoretical physicist Michio Kaku exclaims that 'the Earth is not a safe place', during an interview that forms part of *The Mars Generation* documentary. Earth has become 'A different planet. It needs a new name', McKibben suggests, namely 'Eaarth',[15] because it is predicted that the planet has been altered beyond recognition.

Placed together, 'Earth on fire' and Mars (Figures 8.1a and b), it is easy to judge Mars as an earth that has already burned out and beyond any plagues. It appears as if the accident or extinction event has already happened on Mars, for it is a dry, scorched and barren reddish (hellish?) planet. The flames have already exterminated all forms of life that could possibly be harmful to humans. Identifying Mars as 'dead' is not a new insight, as Robert Markley classifies Mars as a 'dying' or recently dead planet.[16] Markley plots how our scientific and cultural constructions and understandings of Mars merge with Earth: 'Mars has served as a screen on which we have projected our hopes for the future and our fears of ecological devastation on Earth.'[17] Accordingly, Mars's fate as a 'dying planet' has become a prediction of Earth's future.

Thus, if we interpret the two images together, Mars may be an alien planet that has hosted extinct life, but since Earth is, in any case, becoming strange, we can read Mars as a post-apocalyptic and post-pandemic earth. One can even imagine Mars as a planet that is uncontaminated and hygienically cleansed of viruses, almost a clean slate. Currently, as rumours spread of a third infestation of the Covid-19 before the vaccinations can reach the majority of the population, at least in South Africa from where I am writing, a Covid-free planet seems enticing. Given this evidence, perhaps one cannot be blamed for investing instead in and

Figure 8.1a and b Comparative images of Earth on fire (top) and Mars (below). Credits: (a): Burning Globe Earth (west hemisphere), by Boris Ryaposov. (b) 1.2: Valles Marineris: The Grand Canyon of Mars, Image Credit: NASA. Source: Adobe Stock: https://stock.adobe.com/45170848?as_campaign=TinEye&as_content=tineye_match &epi1=45170848&tduid=5100c1364b9b57105cafe9023578b81d&as_channel=affil iate&as_campclass=redirect&as_source=arvato.

terraforming a planet that has already been through the extinction event, rather than lingering on a planet that is diseased and about to disintegrate.

II

What is Mars like? What does it look like? More importantly, how is Mars imagined? Mars has always played a prominent role in human visions and dreams of outer space, whether it was viewed as a host for invasive Martians as portrayed in H. G. Wells's *The War of the Worlds* (1897), or a site for human resettlement as in Kim Stanley Robinson's *Red Mars* (1992). The image or idea of Mars changed over time, mostly depending on earthly politics, scientific discoveries and artistic speculations:

> Because Mars is not only a natural phenomenon but a sign, a symbol, and a power, the work of poets and fiction-makers – and of repudiated and superseded scientists and even of cranks and charlatans – is also essential to our understanding of the meaning of Mars. [. . .] Mars is part of our cultural history, a repository of human desire, a reflection of our aspirations, confusions, and anxieties.[18]

What becomes clear from our encounters with Mars is that our ideas are informed by both fact and fiction, perhaps in equal measure. The growing suspicion from the early twentieth century onwards that Mars is the breeding ground for ominous extraterrestrials has been informed by Italian astronomer Giovanni Schiaparelli's (1877) channels theory.[19] Since then, for all our prodding and plotting, no life has yet been found. This meant that, subsequently, our ideas had to change to allow for the lack of scientific evidence of any life on Mars. Although, it does appear as if the fear of Martians remains alive, as a recent article debunks the no life theory by imploring, 'Are aliens hiding in plain sight?'[20] The argument is that if you do not know what you are looking for, or what it looks like, how can you find it?

We have been allowed a new embedded non-human gaze of the red, arid Mars landscape by NASA rovers *Curiosity* (operative since 2012) and *Opportunity* (operative in 2019). The Martian surface is often compared to Earth structures such as 'the Atacama Desert in Chile (where it is very dry with similar rocks), Arizona (which has basaltic volcanism on eroded, stratified rock sequences), and Hawaii (made up of large basaltic shield volcanoes like Olympus Mons on Mars)' (Figures 8.2 and 8.3).[21] Mars is one immense wilderness with icy nitrogen caps:

Figure 8.2 Chile's the Atacama Desert is the driest place on Earth and therefore often compared to Mars's rugged, arid terrain. 20 April 2017. Credit: NASA/JPL-Caltec.

Figure 8.3 Panoramic view from 'Rocknest' position of curiosity Mars rover, October–November 2012. Credit: NASA/JPL-Caltech/Malin Space Science Systems: https://www.nasa.gov/multimedia/guidelines/index.html; https://www.jpl.nasa.gov/jpl-image-use-policy; and https://www.msss.com/policies/index.html.

Mars is no place for the faint-hearted. Arid, rocky, cold and apparently lifeless, the Red Planet offers few hospitalities. Fans of extreme sports can rejoice, however, for the Red Planet will challenge even the hardiest souls among us. Home to the largest volcano in the solar system, the deepest canyon and crazy weather and temperature patterns, Mars looms as the ultimate lonely planet destination.[22]

It is fascinating to note that in keeping with the promotion of Mars as an extreme adventurer's dream destination, in filmic renditions of outer space and futuristic scenes analogous inhospitable desert locations on Earth are selected. *Mad Max: Fury Road* (George Miller, 2015) was filmed in the Namib Desert and parts of *The Martian* (Ridley Scott, 2015) were filmed in the Wadi Rum sandstone valley in Jordan. Like Earth's deserts, Mars is also known for its sandstorms. However, in the case of Mars, these dust storms are global and occur once every three Martian years,[23] lasting for months on end and debilitating any activity.[24] How life will survive these electric sandstorms is still an open question. In the recent *National Geographic* docudrama series *Mars* (Ron Howard, 2016–18), the estimated devastation of a dust storm lasting for two months are realistically depicted, with fatal consequences for many life forms within the newly established colony.

Other consequences of the dust storms is that Mars's 'face' changes due to shifting sand formations: 'The Martian winds blow on, continuing to produce a phantasmagoria of changes that fascinate telescopic observers on Earth. What we are seeing are the ever-shifting shapes caused by wind and dust.'[25]

Thus, a shapeshifting entity with changing 'faces' as the storms blow, Mars probably requires a facelift to make it more enticing for human consumption. Suppose the crudeness of scarred Mars fails to ignite human imaginations. In that case, it is possible to create simulated images via AI to look at Mars with Earth eyes, 'Provok[ing] a contemporary nostalgia and stimulate poetic imagination'.[26] The result is *Terra Mars* (2019) an artistic rendition of Mars with the aid of AI deep learning and high-definition data of both planets. The artistic project undertakes to transpose Earth's terrains and colours onto Mars, in other words, to morph Mars into Earth. It is Mars as Earth, almost Mars in drag. *Terra Mars* is not Earth, yet, because it looks similar we imagine it as earth-like. As the artist, Weili Shi incorporates 'AI [as] the new imagination',[27] the two planets are playfully remixed into a new entity:

Some may be interested in relating this imaginary version to the astronomical facts of the Red Planet. Some may consider it as a preview of a possible outcome of human's terraforming efforts. Some may just appreciate the sheer beauty of a planet that resembles our own.[28]

III

For all its ingenuity, the re-imagination of Mars as *Terra Mars* does not change the harsh environment, and what we are left with, after all, is a lifeless desert. From the outset, I realize that defining the desert landscape simplistically as lifeless, and even as formless, is a gross misrepresentation of what it truly is and what it contains. The desert, at least the earthly version, is a complex ecosystem with abundant life. It is therefore not devoid of life, as desert dwellers like the Bedouin and the Tuareg attest. The desert is understood as a balanced place in the desert cultures – a 'balance between species, between the environment and its inhabitants, between inner and outer selves'.[29] Although one of the most extreme environments on the planet, it is a finely tuned ecosystem. The number of human inhabitants is few, and mostly the desert poses a challenge to human existence that must be carefully tallied and negotiated.

According to most cultural interpretations, the desert is a mythical landscape.[30] To be wandering in the desert is to be thrown back onto oneself, to be challenged and blessed by the gods, or so the myths and legends tell us. In the desert, the traveller is confronted by a landscape that is deceptively bare, without remarkable signposts and habitually abstract in layout. The desolate terrain mainly consists of a horizontal axis stretching as far as the eye can see against the vertical sky dominated by the circling sun.

For this reason, Walid Hamarneh reads the landscape as rhizomatic in structure, stretching between desert and oases as part of an Eastern 'eco-spatial figure'.[31] The desert stands in contrast to the Western imagination of the landscape that is more centred around the forest and fields, thus more arborescent. In her book *West of Everything*, Jane Tompkins juxtaposes how differently the human figure appears in the desert and the forest:

> When a man walks or rides into a forest, he is lost among the trees, can't see ahead, doesn't know what might be lurking there. The forest surrounds him, obscures him with shadows, confuses itself with him by its vertical composition and competitive detail. But when a horseman appears on the desert plain, he dominates it instantly, his view extends as far as the eye can see, and enemies are exposed to his gaze. The desert flatters the human figure by making it seem dominant and unique, dark against the light, vertical against horizontal, solid against plane, detail against blankness.[32]

Tompkins emphasizes the striking horizontality of the desert vista contrasted against the human figure standing upright. For me, one of the most iconic images

Figure 8.4 Famous desert scene by the well from *Lawrence of Arabia* (David Lean, 1962). Credit: Columbia Pictures.

Figure 8.5 Scene from *The Martian* (Ridley Scott, 2015). Credit: 20th Century Fox.

illustrating this point is the well-known scene in David Lean's *Lawrence of Arabia* (1962) (Figure 8.4). The cinematic choreography applied to the scene conjures a lonely rider from the mirages steadily moving towards the well, framed by two figures. This trope is fruitfully used later in cinematic explorations of other desert scenes or, rather, of Martian landscapes, as restaged in *The Martian* (Ridley Scott, 2015) (Figure 8.5) and *Approaching the Unknown* (Mark Elijah Rosenberg, 2016).

It was, in fact, T. E. Lawrence (1888–1935), the real 'Lawrence of Arabia' that described his fascination with the desert in his autobiography as:

The *abstraction* of the desert landscape cleansed me, and rendered my mind vacant with its superfluous greatness: a greatness achieved not by the addition of thought to its emptiness, but by its subtraction. In the weakness of earth's life was mirrored the strength of heaven, so vast, so beautiful, so strong. (My emphasis)[33]

Thus, a place of reckoning; a confrontation. It is also a place where distractions are vanquished. For this reason, the desert is associated with 'clarity, revelation and purity'[34] and creates a space for 'desert asceticism'[35] where mystics and prophets encountered enlightenment. It is a vast, nearly abstract landscape, overseen by the obliteration sun that has to be passed through towards the Promised Land. J. E. Cirlot notes in *A Dictionary of Symbols*:

This confirms the specific symbolism of the desert as the most propitious place for divine revelation [. . .]. This is because the desert, in so far as it is in a way a *negative landscape*, is the realm of *abstraction* located outside the sphere of existence and susceptible only to things transcendent. Furthermore, the desert is the domain of the sun, not as the creator of energy upon earth but as the pure, celestial radiance, blinding in its manifestation [. . .] burning drought is the climate par excellence of pure, ascetic spirituality – of the consuming of the body for the salvation of the soul. (My emphasis)[36]

Foreboding in its nakedness and relentless in its vastness, terms used such as 'abstraction' and 'negative landscape' open the interpretation of the desert to the aesthetic category of the sublime. Whereas the 'negative landscape' makes an apparent reference to the Kantian formulation of 'negative pleasure', as reason takes delight in its superiority in the face of an external threat. At the same time, abstraction evoked by notions of vastness, unboundedness and formlessness also echoes the sublime. Furthermore, when Donald Goergen muses: 'The desert is a call to surrender; it is also the offer of delight. The awful becomes the awe-full',[37] the awful and awe-inspiring are an obvious invocation of the sublime. In its vastness the desert is not only sublime, for physical and spiritual survival is definitely hanging in the balance, but it is also formless in its outstretched horizons. Our preference for formless landscapes, such as the desert, is to evoke sublime encounters with our species, with ourselves and the planet(s).

IV

The formless, as a concept, has a long and rich history. It is associated with chimerical monsters, the unnameable, the unrepresentable, an undefinable unease, the Freudian repressed, the alien and also notably the abject. That which is formless is without clear or definite shape or structure. It can manifest in either a surplus of form or as a lack of form. It is the nihil of form, both unlimited and limitless.

The formless has been theorized by the high priest of modernism, Immanuel Kant, in his intricate theory of the sublime. For Kant, the sublime corresponds most often with '*das Unform*' – the formless. After Kant, in the early twentieth century the idea of the formless (*L'informe*) was picked up by Bataille's bandit of contra-Surrealism and pushed further to the extreme as an anti-aesthetic operation or drive. In the Bataillian sense, the formless becomes an agent of desublimation and destabilization. In the case of the Kantian formless it corresponds with modernism's attempt to construct a rational idea onto reality, and in Bataille's case the door is opened to the postmodern mining of the formless as vastly unrepresentable and refusing all form.

For the discussion here it is important to make some precursory remarks about the formless as it operates in both the modernist and postmodernist sense. The first observation is that in the Kantian sense the formless is not considered as a category that belongs to nature, but it is a category of the mind. At first this may sound contra-intuitive, for is the sublime not brought on by overwhelming, thus formless manifestations in nature? Not so, if we follow Kant strictly in this regard, for he makes it clear that it is not the object (nature) that is sublime in itself, but the response caused in the subject:

> [W]e express ourselves on the whole incorrectly if we call some object of nature sublime, although we can quite correctly call very many of them beautiful [. . .]. We can say no more than that the object serves for *the presentation of a sublimity that can be found in the mind*; for what is properly sublime cannot be contained in any sensible form. [. . .]. Thus the wide ocean, enraged by storms, cannot be called sublime. (My emphasis)[38]

The distinction is important if we want to grasp the workings of the modernist rational mind in the construction of the formless. Upon encountering overwhelming and awesome phenomena in nature it is a battle between the imagination and the mind that ensues. Accordingly, it can be suggested that the

> sublime is found in an object whose form is so difficult or impossible for our power of imagination to render as a perceptual unity that it eventually prompts in us the idea of limitlessness (*Unbegrenztheit*). Therefore, formlessness is in fact the indirect effect or impression of the object on the mind of the subject.[39]

It is thus the modern subject that has access to the concept of formlessness via rationality, and it is through the rational mind that he can master the cosmos by ascertaining what has form and what does not. In the case of formless planets, it is then also up to the modern subject to inject meaning and form into and onto the unformed terrain. The sublime is thus an experience geared toward the realization of human freedom and a vindication of the autonomy of human rationality over sensible nature.

The postmodern trajectory of the formless works against mastery and meaning-making by emphasizing the impossibility of any form to be final and actualized. It is, rather, the limitless potential and possibility of the formless that stimulates the postmodern discourse. Lyotard's interpretation and revision of the Kantian sublime may be helpful in this regard, when he states that the postmodern sublime 'puts forward the unpresentable in presentation itself [. . .] that which searches for new presentations, not in order to enjoy them but in order to impart a stronger sense of the unpresentable'.[40]

If one were to apply this refusal of form or the unrepresentable to imagining Mars, the indefinite nature of the video game, where planetary destinies are limitless, is a prime instance. In the *Minecraft* (2011–) video game, for instance, it is possible to terraform and create custom made environments. Similarly, in the *Spore* (2008) game, players have the option to not only terraform environments, but also to 'unterraform' by using tools such as the 'Volcano Tool', 'CO2 Pump' and the 'Genesis Device'. With the mere selection from a display menu an inhabitable planet is turned into paradise:

> Terraforming an unhospitable planet consists in editing out the planetary scenes that do not add up to Earth-like conditions, thus leaving an infinite number of extraterrestrial sequences to a darkest night of possibility.[41]

Mars is considered formless and can therefore undergo limitless terraforming so that it can be formed to become habitable or suitable for Earth life forms. Because Mars is considered as the nihil of form, it can be shaped and sculpted into form, a habitat, perhaps even a home.

V

If a planet is then found to be lifeless, and subsequently formless, it is argued that we have the moral obligation to terraform such a planet. As James Schwartz proposes, precisely because 'the candidate planet is lifeless', it can be argued that it is morally permissible to proceed with Mars's terraforming. If Mars is lifeless, we will become the life on Mars as NASA's MEP enthusiastically predicts. It is not only our lives that Mars will come to witness but also our deaths. As Captain Stanaforth, in the film *Approaching the Unknown* (2016), proclaims upon landing on Mars: 'Nothing has ever lived here. Nothing has even died here. Maybe I'll live forever'.

In most terraforming debates, Earth is treated as the mere cradle for human development that needs to be discarded to fulfil our destiny of colonizing the universe.[42] The obvious implications of an infant species growing up to expand its horizons and spread its wings are clear. As are the similarities between colonization and terraforming, which both aim to remake one world into another. The arguments in favour of terraforming are compounded because there are no known planets or satellites in the Solar System, allowing humans to live there without the protection of spacecraft or spacesuits. Mars is no different, but it has several advantages. One of the most important reasons, despite the earlier similarities with Earth, is that the Martian day has a mean period of twenty-four hours and thirty-nine minutes. Adapting to the Martian day is deemed more comfortable for earthlings. Several other reasons are also offered which are not discussed here, among them the thesis that knowledge of Mars will incite knowledge of Earth. In other words, we will understand Earth better when we terraform Mars.

Terraforming participates in both the imagination and memory,[43] indicating that it is positioned between fiction and fact, connecting geological time and history to human representation.[44] It should not come as a surprise that the term was first used in a science-fiction story by Jack Williamson in 1942.[45] Williamson also coined a closely related term, namely genetic engineering, which corresponds to the human body's transformation as terraforming corresponds to world-making. Since the original fictional reference, terraforming has been utilized in scientific exploration, but it has remained widely applied in science fiction, film, television and gaming plots as previously mentioned.

We may well speculate as to why terraforming is the specific response in our time, or inquire what socio-political realities have caused or conjured terraforming as a legitimate reaction? For Chris Pak, clearly 'narratives of terraforming and geoengineering are, at their core, narratives about the Anthropocene'.[46] Both as myth and science, terraforming generates debates and responses to the anthropogenic climate crisis. Terraforming and geoengineering go hand in hand to design 'techno-utopian solutions'[47] in response to the climate crisis. It is a form of eco-modernism that appeals to human technological prowess to better the future, but is at worst 'a mode of trying on and testing out the power of images on defining a relation to the world'.[48] Planet-hacking is to imagine the world as different while not being certain 'under what conditions does an image, a surface, or a volume become a territory?'[49] In other words, how does the image of the new planet take shape? What form does it take in reality? If it is imaginable, is it then also necessarily liveable? Can it signify as (a) home?

It is essential to inquire about the possibility of the newly terraformed planet to act as, and to become, (a) home. Is terraforming not precisely an attempt to provide a solution to homelessness? The term explains the apparent link with '*terra*', '*Terra Mater*', '*tersa tellus*' and *Erde* or *Earth*. Even if we plot the terrae on Mars, Terra Cimmeria, Tempe Terra, Xanthe Terra and Terra Sirenum, it is done analogous to Earth. Our earthly frame informs the form that Mars takes in our imaginations. Here Vincent Bruyere's insights are particularly illuminating:

> For the speculative existence of terraformed worlds is always already informed by a cultural memory of *oikos* – the inhabited world, the world one longs to return to [. . .] what is terraforming if not a prosthetic memory of *oikos* – that is, a mode of curating prospects of continuity in the present that disposes of them like end credits.[50]

VI

Terraforming also calls for the (trans)formation of humans to survive in the new context. Terranauts will have to become Marsonauts. Part of the (trans) formation will be on a physical level, no doubt to survive in 1 per cent oxygen and minimal atmosphere and low gravity. The other directive is to bioengineer and reprogramme humans to become more ethical and virtuous in their dealings with the environment. Learning from our mistakes with Planet 1.0, we will create some type of (trans)formative starter pack for how to behave and respectfully deal with an entirely new and virginal Planet 2.0.

(Trans)forming humans into multi-planetary species requires radical modifications both physically and psychologically. Indeed, as Ted Peters observes: 'To become a Martian is to become a posthuman,' with the proviso that posthuman 'refers to a successor species to the current human.'[51] The idea of altering and reconstructing the human body for extraterrestrial environments and space travel came first, however, in science fiction. James Blish introduced the idea in 1952 to adapt humans through a process which he terms 'pantropy'.[52] Blish's speculations about altering the human body involve ideas about 'polypoidy, or increasing the number of cell chromosomes' by means of a 'panatrope' device.[53] What Blish is describing is a form of genetic engineering to create mutations called 'Altered Men'. According to Blish's storyline, the 'Altered Men' become fugitives who can no longer return to Earth, very similar to the fledgling replicants in *Blade Runner* (Ridley Scott, 1982). However, in an ironic twist it is only the 'Altered Men' or 'Altarians' who can survive on planet Earth after the extinction event has occurred.[54] The problem of humans who have been altered for deep space travel and planetary colonization, and their relation to unaltered earthlings, still remains unanswered in current research. It remains an open question whether the (trans)formation of humans will not lead 'to the creation of, a space-based sub species?'[55] Even of greater concern, and here Blish's science-fiction story already anticipated the present ethical consideration, is the 'extent to which these modifications would make it prohibitive for the pioneers to return to Earth, if they should so desire'.[56] The posthuman debate over what constitutes a human being is already pre-empted here by decades in Blish's introduction to how to make humans survive on other planets:

> The panatropes make adaptations, not gods. They take human germ-cells- in this case, our own [. . .] and modify them toward creatures who can live in any reasonable environment. The result will be manlike and intelligent. It usually shows the donor's personality pattern, too.[57]

After the fictive speculations about the possibility of becoming posthuman came scientific studies by researchers who first used the term 'cyborg', namely Manfred Clynes and Nathan Kline. It is important to note that the first time the term 'cyborg' (cybernetic and organism) was used was in the context of space exploration. Cyborgization or posthumanism, in its earliest strands, are therefore unequivocally linked to outer space explorations.

Clynes and Kline's 'Cyborgs and Space' (1960) is the first scientific study of how to alter the human body for outer space travel and extraterrestrial environments. They propose that space travel 'invites man to take an active part in his own biological evolution'.[58] They opt to tackle the problem through the (trans)formation of the human biology. In other words, they thought it best to adapt the human physique and psychology to space instead of considering terraforming as an option. Thus, instead of making the exoplanet ready for human existence, Clynes and Kline argued that changing or bioengineering the human body is a far better solution. Some of the 'psycho-physiological' options that Clynes and Kline suggest require cyborg dynamics are wakefulness; radiation effects; metabolic problems and hypothermic controls; oxygenation and carbon dioxide removal; fluid intake and output; enzyme systems; vestibular function; cardiovascular control; and muscular maintenance in low gravity.[59]

NASA has since decided not to opt for the full cyborg option as proposed by Clynes and Kline, but rather to invest more in the terraforming adventure. Preventative astro-medicines and technologies are researched and utilized to mitigate the dangers of space travel, but, in the contest between bioengineering and geoengineering, it does seem as if the terraforming option became more feasible and profitable in the long run. It is interesting to note that if one compares the list of cyborg alterations necessary as listed and discussed by Clynes and Kline in 1960, they correspond significantly with Mark Shelhammer's suggestions of human enhancement published in 2020.[60] Almost sixty years onward and the human form has not (trans)formed notably into the cyborg.

When we refer to the human form, which is admittedly a highly contested and fluid concept, it does seem as if astro-biologists and space psychologists not only struggle with the biology but also with the psychology of astronauts and future Martians. The physical alterations required do not necessarily alter the human psyches. One of the greatest ethical challenges that is under discussion is the 'fear of interplanetary sin transfer',[61] meaning that human misdeeds on Earth may be perpetuated on Mars. One of the options speculatively put forward is 'gene editing' which may be able to instil different behaviour 'by deleting sin genes and replace them with virtue genes'.[62] Naturally, this is an over-deterministic view of genes and their role in who and what we are or how we are formed. Our posthuman (trans)formation for Mars hangs accordingly in the balance, with many ethical and moral questions plaguing the endeavour of which the mixture between form and formlessness plays a significant part.

VII

In the premise put forward by my probing title, the dynamics and relations between the concept of human and posthuman do seem to favour the posthuman over the human. The human form is seen as not only debilitating to extraterrestrial explorations, but also as morally corrupt and clinging to a non-existent exceptionality. Susceptibility to diseases and unknown viral strains is just one of the many physical flaws that need to be bioengineered for future survival. The posthuman is constructed as the formless and virus-free solution to the human problem. In the same vein, Earth is viewed as a spaceship running out of resources, infested with diseases and, therefore, it is logically better to trade this failing vehicle for another more viable terrain, or post-earth. Mars has been selected as the next destination, one that is decontaminated, cleansed and sanitized from invasive and deadly viruses and diseases. To make earth-centric arguments amid the Covid-19 pandemic may appear outdated to space missionaries such as Musk and Bezos, for whom the human-question is clearly one of consumer comfort mixed with techno-Gnosticism. Terraforming our new 'home' to fit our needs seem evident. In fact, the proposal that Earth and human are made for each other or belong to one another, or find a home in each other, is displaced and dislodged by the Faustian spirit. If Hannah Arendt's premise is correct, that Earth is the only planet made for, or rather gifted to us, where we are born free to breathe, is there any way of thinking and terrasaving the human differently?

Notes

1 Sherry Ortner, 'Is Female to Male as Nature Is to Culture?', *Feminist Studies* 1, no. 2 (Autumn 1972): 5–31.

2 Ibid., 28.

3 Ibid.

4 Emily Lakdawalla, 'Three Missions Head for Mars', *Sky & Telescope*, 22 June 2020.

5 Nasa Mars Exploration Programme (MEP) website: https://mars.nasa.gov/

6 Nasa Mars Exploration Programme (MEP).

7 See the Mars One website: http://www.mars-one.com/ and The Mars Generation website: https://www.themarsgeneration.org/ for mission statements and updates. Although Mars One does seem like a failed project since funding was depleted in 2018.

8 Harrison's book entitled *Dream BIG! How to REACH for Your STARS* is published in January 2021.

9 The respective journal volumes of *Futures* and *Theology and Science* are available here: https://www.sciencedirect.com/journal/futures/vol/110/suppl/C, https://www.tandfonline.com/toc/rtas20/17/3?nav=tocList

10 See in this regard Robert Zubrin's 'Why We Earthlings Should Colonize Mars!', *Theology and Science* 17, no. 3 (2019): 305–16, and Gonzalo Munevar's 'An Obligation to Colonize Outer Space', *Futures* 110 (2019): 38–40.

11 See John Hart's 'Terraforming Mars and Marsforming Terra: Discovery Doctrine in Space' (2019) wherein he suggests that human consider 'terra*saving*' the Earth before they attempt 'terra*forming*' another planet.

12 See David Wallace-Wells's *The Uninhabitable Earth: Life After Warming* (2019) for instance, which introduces readers to chapters such as 'Heat Death' and 'Unbreathable Air'.

13 Eugene Thacker, *In the Dust of This Planet* (Hants: Zero Books, 2011), 1.

14 Thacker, *In the Dust*, 4–5.

15 Bill McKibben, *Eaarth: Making a Life on a Tough New Planet* (New York: St. Martin's, 2010), 2–3. See also in this regard George Monbiot's *Heat: How to Stop the Planet from Burning* (Cambridge, MA: South End P, 2009).

16 Robert Markley, *Dying Planet: Mars in Science and Imagination* (Durham and London: Duke University Press, 2005).

17 Robert Markley, *Dying Planet*, 2.

18 Robert Crossley, *Imagining Mars: A Literary History* (Middletown, CT: Wesleyan University Press, 2011), 7.

19 Apparently, it is due to the mistranslation of Schiaparelli's *canali* for the streaky marking on Mars's surface from the neutral 'canals' into 'channels'. This indicated to the popular imagination that life did indeed exist on Mars that created channels.

20 Phillip Ball, 'Are Aliens Hiding in Plain Sight?', *The Observer*, 5 September 2020. https://www.theguardian.com/science/2020/sep/05/are-aliens-hiding-in-plain-sight

21 'The Red Planet', Nasa Mars Exploration Programme (MEP).

22 Ibid.

23 Bill Sheehan, 'The Changing Face of Mars', *Sky and Telescope*, October 2020, 55.

24 Lisa Grossman, 'Mars Dust Storm Danger', *Science News*, 4 and 18 July 2020, 24. In fact, the NASA rover *Opportunity* became dysfunctional after such a dust storm.

25 Bill Sheehan, 'The Changing Face', 55.

26 Weili Shi, 'Terra Mars: When Earth Shines on Mars through AI's Imagination', *Leonardo* 52, no. 4 (2019): 357.

27 Shi, 'Terra Mars', 361.

28 Ibid., 361.

29 Weisberg, Meg Furniss. 'Spiritual Symbolism in the Sahara: Ibrahim Al-Koni's Nazīf Al-Ḥajar', *Research in African Literatures* 46, Fall, no. 3 (2015): 62.

30 See in this regard Walid Hamarneh, 'Welcome to the Desert of Not-Thinking', *Canadian Review of Comparative Literature* 41, no. 1 (2014): 86–98; Christopher Kelly, 'The Myth of the Desert in Western Monasticism: Eucherius of Lyon's in Praise of the Desert', *Cistercian Studies Quarterly* 46, no. 2 (2011): 129–41; Patricia Cox Miller, 'Desert Asceticism and "the Body from Nowhere"', *Journal of Early Christian Studies* 2, no. 2 (1994): 137–53; Mildred Mortimer, 'The Desert in Algerian Fiction', *L'Esprit Créateur* 26, no. 1 (1986): 60–9; and Meg Furniss Weisberg, Meg Furniss. "Spiritual Symbolism in the Sahara: Ibrahim Al-Koni's Nazīf Al-Ḥajar', *Research in African Literatures* 46, Fall, no. 3 (2015): 46–67.

31 Walid Hamarneh, 'Welcome to the Desert of Not-Thinking', *Canadian Review of Comparative Literature* 41, no. 1 (March 2014): 87.

32 Jane Tompkins, *West of Everything: The Inner Life of Westerns* (New York: Oxford University Press, 1993), 74.

33 T. E. Lawrence, *The Seven Pillars of Wisdom* (London: Penguin, 2000; The Oxford Text, 1926), 524.

34 Dedopulos, 'Symbolism', 2013.

35 For a discussion on fourth and fifth centuries desert ascetics, see Patricia Cox Miller. 'Desert Asceticism and "the Body from Nowhere"', *Journal of Early Christian Studies* 2, no. 2 (1994): 137–53. https://doi.org/10.1353/earl.0.0107.

36 Juan Eduardo Cirlot, *A Dictionary of Symbols*, trans. Jack Sage (Mineola, New York: Dover Publications, 2002), [Desert].

37 Donald Goergen, 'Current Trends: The Desert as Reality and Symbol', *Spirituality Today* 34, no. 1 (March 1982): 71.

38 Immanuel Kant, (§23, 5:245).

39 Uygar Abaci, 'Kant's Justified Dismissal of Artistic Sublimity', *The Journal of Aesthetics and Art Criticism* 66, no. 3 (July 2008): 238.

40 Jean-Francois Lyotard, *The Postmodern Condition. A Report on Knowledge* (Chicago: University of Minnesota Press, 1984), 81.

41 Bruyere, 'Terraformings', 45.

42 Gerry Canavan and Kim Stanley Robinson. 'Afterword: Still, I'm reluctant to Call This Pessimism', in *Green Planets: Ecology and Science Fiction*, ed. Gerry Canavan and Kim Stanley Robinson (Middletown, CT: Wesleyan University Press, 2014), 254.

43 Vincent Bruyere, 'Terraformings', *Imaginations* 10, no. 1 (2019: 40.

44 Bruyere, 'Terraformings', 40.

45 Insert story's name.

46 Chris Pak, 'Terraforming and Geoengineering in *Luna: New Moon*, *2312*, and *Aurora*', *Science Fiction Studies* 45 (2018): 500.

47 Pak, 'Terraforming and Geoengineering', 500.

48 Bruyere, 'Terraformings', 48.

49 Ibid., 50.

50 Ibid., 60.

51 Ted Peters, 'Evolving from Earthlings into Martians?' in *Human Enhancements for Space Missions. Lunar, Martian, and Future Missions to the Outer Planets,* ed. Konrad Szocik (Cham, Switzerland: Springer, 2020), 240.

52 David Ketterer, 'Pantropy, Polyploidy, and Tectogenesis in the Fiction of James Blish and Norman L. Knight', *Science Fiction Studies* 10, Science Fiction in the Nineteenth Century, no. 2 (1983): 199.

53 Ketterer, 'Pantropy', 199.

54 As Ketterer notes 'By a nice irony, the "human beings" cannot live on Earth in its present condition; only the seal-like Adapted Men, the Altarians, can do that', 202.

55 Mark Shelhamer, 'Human Enhancements: New Eyes and Ears for Mars', in *Human Enhancements for Space Missions. Lunar, Martian, and Future Missions to the Outer Planets,* ed. Konrad Szocik (Cham, Switzerland: Springer 2020), 102.

56 Ibid.

57 James Blish, 'Surface Tension', *Galaxy Science Fiction* 4, no.5 (August 1952): 8.

58 Manfred E. Clynes and Nathan S. Kline, 'Cyborgs and Space', *Astronautics* (1960): 26.

59 Ibid., 74–6.

60 Shelhamer, 'Human Enhancements', 95–6.

61 Ted Peters, 'Evolving from Earthlings', 242.

62 Ibid., 244.

9

Quarantine in waiting

Plant clocks and the asynchronies of viral time

Ada Smailbegović

Quarantine Interlude I: Foxgloves

Reading time as it moves along their stems, along the long spires of the plants with hanging bells. It is June. Knowing this without knowing as if woken up from a dream at the lower echelons of the stems the purple mouths are opening. The insides speckled with dots of darker purple at depths dispersed into lunar crescent lines within the white and pooling at the opening into smears of colour, indistinct dots. At the curling tops of the stems the buds still tightly shut and green.

Another puncture in time in this quarantine dream, now in bloom on mid stem, the ones below having shut and begun to dry, the forest itself less luminous, lush behind them in the summer heat than in the green of June's arrival. Keeping a measure of time of the summer's folding and unfolding until at the end, late August moving into September, awakened yet again, now almost without colour, only a few visitations of pink bloom at the tips of the long stems gone to seed.

The foxglove, Digitalis pupurea, folksglove, or fairyglove – whose speckles and freckles are the marks of elves' fingers, is also called dead man's fingers. It contains the poison Digitalis, first used by a Dr. Withering in the 18th century to cure heart disease. [. . .] The 'glove' comes from the Anglo-Saxon for a string of bells, 'gleow'.[1] *'Over time, folk myths obscured the literal origins of the name, insinuating that foxes wore the flowers on their paws to silence their movements as they stealthily hunted their prey. The woody hillsides where the foxes made their dens were often covered with the toxic flowers.'*[2] *Also known as 'witch's glove' in reference to the toxicity of the plant.*

Snail cinema

In *On the Movements and Habits of Climbing Plants*, Charles Darwin writes: 'When the shoot of a Hop (*Humulus Lupulus*) rises from the ground, the two or three first-formed internodes are straight and remain stationary; but the next-formed, whilst very young, may be seen to bend to one side and to travel slowly round towards all points of the compass, moving, like the hands of a watch, with the sun.'[3] In this passage, Darwin is attempting to painstakingly observe and study the movements of plants, in this case the movements of what he calls 'spirally twining plants' as they twist and turn in response to light and often wind themselves around some kind of a support-structure. On a level that transacts across figurative-material realms, Darwin is also at work, I would like to suggest, on constructing a plant clock. In other words, while the metaphor of a watch face with its revolving arms is helping him describe the searching movements of the plant's young, soft tendrils as they respond to light, the plant's movement soon also becomes a measure of time or it becomes a measure of waiting. By making seven discrete observations of climbing plants, Darwin ascertains that it takes on average two hours and eight minutes for each revolution of the plant stem to occur. What interests me here is not simply the idiosyncrasy of this as a curious fact about climbing plants but the counterpoint of the human experience of having to submit to time on non-human terms, and in particular the terms offered by a plant. In this way the duration of the plant's motion becomes a measure of human time, highlighting precisely the vast difference in how the two organisms experience temporality.

Perhaps there is something in this counterpoint of temporal relation that reveals the asynchronies of rhythms that constitute different organisms and, thus, faced with the perceptual alterity of another species' rhythm, in some sense it makes evident the contingency and particularity of the perceiver's own rhythmic constitution. As such, the act of waiting can be understood as the temporal frame in which this asynchrony and alterity of rhythms comes into the perceptual space of sensation. This understanding of what is revealed in the act of waiting is vividly illustrated by a scene that unfolds in Gilles Deleuze's *Bergsonism*, a text in which he offers a kind of primer to the philosophy of one of the most important thinkers about questions of temporality, Henri Bergson:

> Take a lump of sugar: It has a spatial configuration. But if we approach it from
> that angle, all we will ever grasp are differences in degree between that sugar and
> any other thing. But it also has a duration, a rhythm of duration, a way of being

in time that is at least partially revealed in the process of its dissolving, and that shows how this sugar differs in kind not only from other things, but first and foremost from itself.'[4]

Not only does this example point to Bergson's sense that all entities are rhythmic, not hard-edged and strictly spatially delineated, but what I would call instead *soft entities*, in other words loosely bundled compositions of different rhythms of time that allow for the unfolding of the material world, revealing a kind of crumbling vulnerability within even the texturally *hard* materials of cement or stone; but, from another dimension, this scene illustrates how waiting reveals the rhythmic difference between the sugar lump and the person waiting for it to dissolve. It reveals 'that my own duration, such as I live it in the impatience of waiting, for example, serves to reveal other durations that beat to other rhythms, that differ in kind from mine'.[5]

The period of time since the onset of the Covid-19 pandemic in March of 2020 until the present time of this writing in January 2021 has been a time not only of great devastation and death, with over 2 million dead worldwide and nearly 400,000 dead in the United States alone, but it has also been a great, unintended experiment in waiting, one in which the non-human rhythms of the virus, its speed of transmission and incubation, have set the *temporal tone* for many of the patterns of human existence. Perhaps in the most basic sense this is evident in the timeframe of the fourteen-day quarantine period, in which a human would-be patient who may have been exposed to the virus waits for the symptoms of infection to reveal themselves. Within this period of quarantine, then, it is the non-human rhythm of the virus as it meets the rhythms of the human immune system that brings into relief questions of both human mortality and finitude, but also the experiential dimension of the offset rhythm of time that manifests as waiting. Such rhythms of waiting revealed by the non-human temporal rhythms of the virus are also there in what to the human observer appear as temporal gaps between exposure events and the moment when a surge in the number of infected is detected, as well as in the initial invisibility of the virus' devastating effects on human life that are due to the interval of time, often of several weeks, between the onset of disease and the moment it kills the most vulnerable patients. We have become all too familiar with discerning such patterns of waiting in the numbers. And even the term 'quarantine' has colloquially lost the specificity of its medical meaning, coming to stretch into the blurry temporal zone of the totality of the present, one in which we are still waiting, waiting for the numbers to go down and the lockdowns to be partially or fully lifted, waiting for warm weather that could allow for socially distant encounters outdoors to take place, and now waiting for the distribution of the vaccine to become more ubiquitous. Although, with the emergence of mutations leading to new variants of the virus, it is becoming increasingly uncertain whether even the availability of the vaccine will lead us to a kind of clean-cut telos of an endpoint to the current period of time in the entanglements of human and non-human histories.

Without wanting to minimize the tragedy of the current moment of the pandemic, I am interested in the sense of waiting that appears in quarantine and how it is structured through and reveals a kind of asynchrony between human rhythms and the temporal rhythms of the non-human world. Rather than seeing the pandemic as an isolated or surprising event, I would like to place it within a whole nexus of events, among them, perhaps most significantly, climate change, in which pressures imposed by anthropogenic activity have had devastating effects on various ecosystems. Such effects often appear in fact as a form of asynchrony between organisms which had hitherto been synced up to encounter one another within the framework of evolutionary time. As a way of considering these imbricated, multilayered relationships between rhythms of human and non-human time, I turn to a text from a relatively recent, but also very distinct, historical moment when humans have had to contend with the temporalities of a virus – the moment of the HIV/AIDS epidemic that had particularly devastating effects in the 1980s and the 1990s before widespread treatment with antiretroviral drugs reduced the mortality caused by the disease. I want to be cautious here and remain cognizant of the many differences that characterize these two very different illnesses and these two very different historical moments, while at the same time suggesting that being forced to operate within the constraints of viral time opens up the wider question of how human beings encounter the ecological rhythms of non-human time.

Perhaps my inclination to juxtapose these two historical moments is driven not by any kind of desire to posit a false equivalence between them, but by a specific literary object that I would argue has the capacity to speak precisely to how a moment in human history that is shaped by an encounter with a virus can be understood in the context of other ecological rhythms that are being transformed by anthropogenic activity, and how this can have the effect of seeing it not as an isolated event but as an element in the overall pattern of environmental change. The text in question is Derek Jarman's *Modern Nature*, a journal that he kept in 1989 and 1990 after receiving an HIV diagnosis and turning to gardening at his cottage in Dungeness as a way of finding solace in this period of illness while simultaneously filming his film *The Garden*. And yet, to simply understand the creation of the garden as a process of finding comfort in the bucolic aspects of some essentialized idea of nature is to miss Jarman's repeated references to the effects of global warming on his surroundings and the seasonal rhythms of the plants that he is growing. The landscape of the garden, too, is situated near the Dungeness nuclear power station, which remains an ominous presence in the book, ever-threatening to lead to an accident that could unleash the devastation of radioactivity onto the region. In the midst of these wider ecological frames for understanding rhythms of change and the questions of human finitude that are brought out by navigating a time of illness, the vegetative temporality of the plants that Jarman is planting in the garden, I argue, begins to act as a series of strange plant clocks. These plant clocks, with their variegated temporal rhythms, allow for the possibility of accounting for the ecological complexity of human and non-human entanglements that constitute the present of a particular ecological moment without foreclosing it into an apocalyptic teleology.

In *Staying with the Trouble: Making Kin in the Chthulocene*, Donna Haraway develops a kind of ethics of time that is encapsulated in her articulation of what it means to 'stay with the trouble' in the current moment of anthropogenically driven ecological transformation: 'We – all of us on Terra – live in disturbing times, mixed up times, troubling and turbid times. [...] [S]taying with the trouble requires learning to be truly present, not as a vanishing pivot between awful or edenic pasts and apocalyptic or salvic futures, but as mortal critters entwined in myriad unfinished configurations of places, times, matters, meanings.'[6] As a counter to naming the current geological period the Anthropocene, a way of signalling that human effects on the planet have reached the scale that had hitherto largely been reserved for geological processes occurring over vast spans of time, Haraway turns instead to the term 'Chthulocene' in order to attempt to decentre the human at a moment when human effects on a multitude of other organisms have become all too centralized. Breaking up the term into its 'two Greek roots (*khthôn* and *kainos*)' Haraway offers to centre the agency of the 'chtonic ones' as simultaneously biological and mythological beings who could offer an alternative, less anthropocentrically configured vision for the ecological present: 'I imagine the chthonic ones as replete with tentacles, feelers, digits, cords, whiptails, spider legs, and very unruly hair. Chtonic ones romp in multicritter humus but have no truck with sky-gazing Homo.'[7] The second part of the term 'Chthulocene', the one signalled by the Greek root *Kainos*, speaks perhaps more clearly to the questions of temporality that I am discussing here:

Kainos means now, a time of beginnings, a time for ongoing, for freshness. [. . .] There is nothing in times of beginnings that insists on wiping out what has come before, or, indeed, wiping out what comes after. *Kainos* can be full of inheritances, of remembering, and full of comings, of nurturing what might still be. I hear *kainos* in the sense of thick, ongoing presence, with hyphae infusing all sorts of temporalities and materialities.[8]

In focusing on the variegated rhythms of non-human time, this chapter seeks to articulate a method for attending to change as it permeates the materialities of non-human worlds often in ways that are accelerated by human activity, but which may nevertheless constitute what Rob Nixon refers to as 'slow violence'. Such rhythms may in fact, even in their accelerated forms, fall below the threshold of what can be easily perceived by the human sensorium and, as such, I am seeking here, by sifting through Jarman's gradual accretion of observations of plant rhythms in *Modern Nature*, for a kind of aesthetics of attention that has the potential to bring into perceptibility such imperceptible or nearly imperceptible ecological compositions of rhythm, ones that are simultaneously patterned and also denatured and rendered asynchronous through human impact on the Earth.

This problematic of how to perceive and account for change as it occurs for another organism, when its rhythms may not always be discernible within the perceptual limitations of one's own sensorium, becomes particularly crucial at a moment when rhythmic patterns of different organisms are being transformed as an effect of the rise in temperature associated with anthropogenic climate change. Such temporal rhythms can be directly affected by temperature, so that processes such as 'larval hatching times' being accelerated 'can cause cascade-like changes in entire ecosystems, when these larvae act as food for other animals'.[9] Conversely, if such insect larvae depend on a particular plant for nourishment, the soft, succulent leaves of this plant may not appear in time to meet the needs of the hungry larvae that have hatched. In turn, '[m]any species of insectivorous birds feed their chicks with caterpillars, and [hence] for them it is important to hatch their chicks at the time that the peak in food requirements matches the caterpillar peak'.[10] Consider, for instance, the case of the ecosystem of a deciduous oak forests in which caterpillars prefer to feed on very young leaves, so that their 'eggs normally hatch around the time of budburst' and then these caterpillars, in turn acting as a prey species for various foraging bird species, such as blue tits and pied flycatchers, which in turn act as prey for the sparrowhawks.[11] In a paper published in the *Journal of Animal Ecology*, Christian Both and colleagues have shown that asynchronies develop in these temporal patterns that have arisen during the long durations of evolutionary time most likely as a result of climate change, so that while caterpillars appear at their peak earlier in the season, the birds that feed on them do not advance the hatching of their eggs in time and thus the interval in which their food needs are the greatest no longer coincides with the greatest abundance of their prey. While this study examined one particular ecosystem, in more general terms, one of the effects of climate change can be understood as a great falling out of sync of the many parts of a complex ecological symphony that had tied a multiplicity of species into the webs of entangled relations.

Such aesthetics of attention to the rhythms of change that are rippling through the materiality of non-human worlds without foreclosing their ongoingness into a chronological linearity that traverses the arc between a sense of nature as origin, as an essentialized fixity, and the apocalyptic point of no return, requires what I am calling, in the spirit of Haraway's tentacular, chthonic ones, *snail cinema*. In *A Foray into the Worlds of Animals and Humans*, the ethologist Jakob von Uexküll writes about what constitutes a moment for different species as 'the shortest segment of time in which the world exhibits no changes'.[12] This differs for different organisms so that 'a human moment lasts one-eighteenth of a second', for instance, while 'in the snail's environment, a stick that moves back and forth four or more times a second' is perceived by the snail as being at rest.[13] This means that 'the perception time of the snail takes place at a speed of between three or four moments a second. This has as a consequence that all processes of motion take place much more quickly in the snail's environment than they do in our own. [But the] snail's own movements do not seem slower to it than ours do to us.'[14] One could think of this as a kind of snail animation or snail cinema, in that if one were making a 'snail film', one would have to pay attention to how many frames a second to play in order for the stick to appear as a moving object. As such, the very edges of the stick as an object within the snail universe are constituted in relation to time. In the poem 'Snails', which appears in *The Nature of the Universe (Le Parti Pris des Choses)*, Francis Ponge models a form of *snail cinema*, for instance, by drawing on repetition and the rhythmic patterning of poetic language, to recreate what appears to the human observer as the very gradual movement of the snail through its world. 'Nothing is so handsome as this forward motion, this snail's pace, so slow, so sure, so discrete,' Ponge writes, recreating in the patterning of the repeated phrases beginning with 'so', a sense of a gradually stretching line of the snail's glistening trail or what he calls its 'silvery wake'.[15]

In positing *snail cinema* as a kind of method for writing from within quarantine, and drawing inspiration from the way in which the temporality of the virus and human finitude in Jarman's account in *Modern Nature* is never an isolated and entirely anthropocentric temporality, but one that is interstitial within and interwoven with other rhythms of ecological time that are being reconfigured as a result of the human impact on the climate and the energy cycles of the Earth, I create an interleaved texture in this chapter through a series of descriptions of plants and their rhythms of time written during periods of quarantine that have composed this past year of the Covid-19 pandemic. As such, this writing seeks to move analytically through Jarman's text as much as it also seeks to develop a practice or an aesthetics of attention that is forged in the rhythms of non-human time that open as counterpoints to one's own human rhythms in the unfolding spaces of this waiting.

Quarantine Interlude II: Birch Trees

What is uncovered appears beneath what passed. This newness gleaming in the sunlight, its silvery strips beneath the rivulets of more hardened matter at the time's unfolding edge. What is unwound and strips off, a kind of dusty particulate not unlike snow.

And yet seen from the water, they are gleaming, each one. A kind of thought's brightness, its shimmer discerned in the passing of woods one returns to the birch tree meditation to find the line to the trees, a line of necessity and transformation. So that what is at depth is newer than what is at the surface. This form of time that is multiple, a silver and on occasion pink beneath the paper outside.

Plant clocks

Writing about a garden from his childhood, his grandmother's garden, Jarman considers the duration of spring flowers as a kind of shimmer, signalling their relative ephemerality, the short window of their duration in comparison to the durations that shape a human life: 'These spring flowers are my first memory, startling discoveries; they shimmered briefly before dying, dividing the enchantment into days and months, like the gong that summoned us to lunch, breaking up my solitude.'[16] It is the appearance of flowers in his account, perhaps both in their individual particularity of a single blossom and in the waves of different species blooming at different moments within a season, that come to punctuate the intervals of human temporality, much like a gong that may break the intervals of a human day into specific habits or occasions. The flowers may act here much as Bergson's sugar cube does within the suspended interval of waiting or solitude to point to a distinction between human and floral rhythms and hence perhaps to defamiliarize the human rhythms from what may be more usual devices for measuring the intervals and chronologies of time, such as those offered by the even increments of a mechanical clock. And yet, I would argue that plants in Jarman's text assume the role of 'strange clocks', allowing for a kind of relief from countable or measured time, which draws the human figure ever closer to the telos or the edge of finitude; rather, these strange *plant clocks* open up the possibilities of time folding into cyclical patterns of seasonal reoccurrence, alternate intervals of duration, and a creation of what Haraway may refer to as the thick presence of *Kainos*, which 'can be full of inheritances, of rememberings' and the indeterminacies of what 'might still be' coming.[17] Such ripplings of remembering are evident here, in this example, even simply in the way that a childhood garden appears in memory within the texture of the present garden that Jarman is constructing in Dungeness in the late 1980s and the early 1990s.

I want to linger here for a moment on the concept of a shimmer as one way in which Jarman formulates the temporal edges of a particular moment, but also on its evanescence or ephemerality. Often the descriptions of the landscape of Dungeness are punctuated by the changes in light and the manner in which the colours of the plants are infused by such changes in ambient conditions:

> The rain and fine warm weather have quickened the landscape – brought the saturated spring colours early. The dead of winter is passed. Today Dungeness glowed under a pewter sky – shimmering emeralds, arsenic, sap, sage and verdigris greens washed bright, moss in little islands set off against pink pebbles, glowing yellow banks of gorse, the deep russet of dead bracken, and pale ochre of reeds in clumps set against the willow spinney – a deep burgundy, with silvery catkins and fans of ochre yellow stamens fringed with the slightest hint of lime green of newly burst leaves. This symphony of colour I have seen in no other landscape.[18]

The transformations in colour that are catalogued here are causally entangled in an irresolvable sense between the seasonal changes that are bringing new colours into the tissues of the plants and suffusing the 'newly burst leaves' with 'hint[s] of lime green', for instance, and the manner in which the ambient qualities of the 'pewter sky' themselves are producing a kind of glow in the colouration of the vegetation. In a sense the nature of the plant entities themselves is inseparable from the conditions of their perception. In parallel with this, it is the juxtaposition of entities with one another that leads the whole landscape to function not as a listing of individual plants or geological features, but as what Jarman calls a 'symphony of color'.[19] For instance, moss which appears 'in little islands' is rendered vivid not just by its own intrinsic colour but by the contrasting background of 'pink pebbles'.[20] As such, I would like to suggest that Jarman is interested in rhythmic units of ecological composition that are framed by temporal rather than spatialized edges, and which form pools of time or duration. Such pooling of time, in turn, disrupts the chronological pull of time towards a particular kind of telos. His use of the word 'quicken' at the opening of this passage carries the double meaning of both signalling that an entity is enlivened, stimulated and made to shine or burn more brightly, and also as a designation of a rhythm of time that is speeding up. In connecting these two meanings, the term 'quicken' illustrates how an alteration in a series of material qualities, such as a faint flush of colour entering a landscape or ambient light causing elements of the landscape to shimmer, signals a change in rhythms of the material world and hence a shift in its temporal composition.

Often the events that occur in the landscape are interwoven with the actions that Jarman is performing himself, producing a kind of narrative continuity in which the non-human world offers a rhythmic counterpoint to human time: 'At nine-thirty the sun sets behind Lydd church; The night stock scents the air. At ten I switch the lantern on; a bright pink moth shimmers on the pale blue wall. I quickly turn the pages of my book: Small Elephant Hawk.'[21] Here the punctuating beat of mechanical clock time sets up the staging for the events that ensue: the sun sets at nine-thirty and the lights are turned on at ten. And yet, it is the appearance of the phenomena of the night, the scent of the air, the appearance of the Small Elephant Hawk moth that become other punctuating beats of time interspersed among the beats of the clock and ones that ultimately behave differently from its regular time intervals by creating durations or intervals in which time pools and its denizens shimmer in an ephemeral duration, like a bright pink moth on a pale blue wall. Such moments are durational in much the same way as the moment of waiting for a sugar cube to dissolve, in that they defamiliarize human rhythms and undo their telos; and yet the phenomenology here is more one of lingering, rather than of waiting.

Perhaps the *shimmer* of such moments is most evident when they are counterposed to the appearance of actual clocks in the text. There are the clocks of childhood. First 'Grandfather's black marble clock in the shape of a temple, ticking away', which seems to indicate a kind of progression of countable time.[22] And, second, the more zoomorphic clock that is gifted to Jarman by his parents on their return from a ski trip: 'On their return they crept into my room in the dead of night and silently fixed a Swiss clock on the wall at the foot of my bed – a gruff little owl whose eyes moved in time to the tick.'[23] While this second clock assumes the shape of an animal, its zoomporphism is really a disguise for a more mechanomorphic understanding of time, one that guides the movement of the eyes of the owl to follow the beat of regularized, countable intervals. Perhaps the most striking appearance of an actual clock occurs when Jarman is faced with an attack of toxoplasmosis which takes away the clarity of his sight. Lying in a hospital bed he is unable to fill the hours with activities such as reading, and instead watches the blurry face of a clock:

> No books to read, no newspapers. So, what did I think about during the long hours? I watched the clock. On the first day its face was a fuzzy halo, the digits telescoped and dis-appeared. On the second day I could see the red second hand move in a jumble of black. On the third day I paused, looked and looked again and read the time. On the fourth day I could read the numbers round the dial – people appeared out of the gloom, some younger, others older; their outlines filled in like pieces of a fancy jigsaw.[24]

This scene operates in several different ways, the most striking one of which is perhaps the focalization of temporality through a figure of a clock during a time when the effects of illness, caused by the ways in which Jarman's HIV-positive status leaves him vulnerable to other infections, reach a crisis point. The clock intrudes here to produce a sense of countable time: days are numbered and pass into their incremental hours. And yet, perhaps this kind of a reading flattens the sense that, at this moment of intense illness, time has also disappeared or slipped away; it has become blurry or obscured, and one must wait for the anchor of its reappearance in the analogue image of the face of a clock. In fact, it is often in moments of physical illness and discomfort that time becomes confused, with Jarman proclaiming that he is 'suffering from a confusion in time', at times even forgetting 'whether it was today or yesterday' that something occurred.[25]

The reappearance of a clock in the space of visibility, as Jarman's vision slowly returns, indicates a stepping out of such spaces of temporal confusion, and at the same time it signals a sense of countable or mechanized time that is so often effectively resisted in the text through the appearance of what I am calling 'plant clocks'. The mechanical clock time here maps much more clearly onto what Jarman on another occasion refers to as 'monotheistic time', 'time with beginning and end, literal time, monotheist time, for which you are unfailingly charged'.[26] Such time, with its singular chronology and rhythm, threatens to take over at moments when the experience of illness assumes a kind of teleological directionality towards death. These are often the moments when Jarman encounters the fear and prejudice that others have towards his HIV-positive status, fear that leads them to foreclose the window of the present moment towards the telos of death, as in a moment when he is 'stopped by a painted middle-aged lady who said, "I'm glad you're not dead Derek, the papers say you are terribly ill".'[27] At another moment, reflecting on how he is seen as a result of being publicly open about his HIV-positive status, Jarman states: 'What is certain is [that] strangers I meet in the street all look on me as "dead". I have to underline the fact that I'm OK; but doing this doesn't convince them.'[28] The time of the garden, in contrast, resists this teleology towards death, opening up different, non-linear, polyrhythmic versions of time: 'The gardener digs in another time', Jarman asserts, 'without past or future, beginning or end. A time that does not cleave the day with rush hours, lunch breaks, the last bus home. As you walk in the garden you pass into this time.'[29] Even in times of intense illness, in the hospital bed, Jarman seeks this form of garden temporality, 'planting the garden in [. . .] [his] mind, sowing fennel and calendula'.[30] At such moments of illness, away from the literal garden, its temporality nevertheless appears in various guises, for instance a moment when Jarman's friend Tilda arrives and 'spray[s] [. . .] [him] with her Bluebell perfume'.[31] Such moments open up a duration, what I have been calling a kind of pooling or shimmering of time, which allows for a lingering within such intervals of temporal suspension. Another such moment, evocative of the ambient, shimmering effects of sunlight on the symphony of the garden's mercurial colours, occurs when, in the middle of a CT scan, 'a fire alarm [. . .] [goes] off as the scan [. . .] [comes] to an end', and Jarman is 'rushed up some stairs and onto the street, where someone' brings him a chair.[32] Another window of time opens within this interruption of the expected narrative chronology: 'We sat for ten minutes in beautiful sunlight. It was a false alarm.'[33] Within this interval of time, the experience of the body is transformed from being the object of a diagnostic apparatus to one of pleasure and suspension in an interval of luminosity.

Even more explicitly, the desire to enter the temporality of the garden is often counterposed to the teleology of death, with Jarman proclaiming, 'I do not wish to die . . . yet. I would love to see my garden through several summers' or, on one occasion when he is released from hospital after a bout of illness, he states, 'I'll see the summer flowers at Dungeness, the poppies and the tree lupin.'[34] As such, the garden often becomes a site of an opening of a new cycle of time, a site of renewal. At one point in the text, a denizen of the garden, a bee, offers almost a kind of allegory for such possibilities of renewal, which veers away from death:

> Richard told me a trapped bee had flown up and down his window. In the morning it was curled up nearly dead on the sill. He put some water near it. It did not move. Then a large glob of honey. Its long proboscis unfurled and in ten minutes the honey disappeared. The bee grew glossy, bright black, its eyes twinkled; and suddenly it took off like an arrow into the sunlight. Back home to my garden.[35]

This anecdote of the bee serves as a kind of allegory of Jarman's own pattern of recovery, one that takes him from a lengthy stay in the hospital back to Dungeness where he hopes to continue working on his garden. In this way, the bee's revivification with the help of a 'glob of honey' and the sense of its 'gloss', shine or glow, as well as its departure into a space of sunlight, comes to echo the manner in which intervals of brightness infuse the landscape with the intensified colours of plants, but also the ways in which Jarman's body recovers time and again, through its cycles of nightly sweats, from the various complications of HIV. There is a refusal here of the teleologies of linear time or a form of temporality that is driven towards an endpoint or death and an embrace of the patterns of time that arise in the garden, ones that often dwell within cycles of seasonal return, promising both renewal and carrying the traces of remembrance of earlier seasons: 'I counted well over 50 buds on the daffodils I planted last year. None are open yet, but if this warm weather continues they should be out within the week. These are an early variety. The King Alfred's I put in early last September are hardly breaking through the ground.'[36] The daffodils here carry complex foldings of seasonal time, bearing in their spindly bodies both the remembrance of their planting the previous year, and carrying a nascent sense of emergence, of the not quite yet, as they are suspended in this moment of description as buds, before blossoming.

Even in noting multiple varieties of daffodils, with distinct seasonal patterns, Jarman is multiplying temporalities, creating in his garden a more variegated sense of time's composition. Much of *Modern Nature* reads as such variegation of temporal rhythms, often enacted through lists of the temporal patterns of the blossoming of different flower species: 'Last night a walk at sundown along the beach: opium poppy, scabious, sea pea, white clover, restharrow, wild carrot, woody nightshade, evening primrose, mustard, mayweed, chamomile, mallow, alkanet, daisy, larkspur, wild pansy, snapdragon, sowthistle, tufted vetch, hare's-foot, herb Robert, hop trefoil, sun spurge – all in flower.'[37] These lists of all of the flowers observed within a certain interval lead the mind, through the language of description, to imagine a sense of patterned variation, a multiplicity of floral rhythms coming into synchronous, coincident time. I am reminded of similar lists of flowers in Marianne Moore's poem 'An Octopus': 'Larkspur, blue pincushions, blue peas, and lupin; / white flowers with white, and red with red; / the blue ones 'growing close together / so that patches of them look like blue water in the distance'.[38] Through the patterning of colours these lines create a figure for what I have been conceptualizing in this section on 'plant clocks' as a kind of pooling of time. Within Moore's metaphor the singular flowers come to lose their distinctness as the blue flowers are pressed in tight proximity with other blue flowers, forming the impression of pooling patches of water in the landscape. While Moore is writing about the visual patterning of flowers through colour, so that the formal juxtaposition of the names of flowers in the poem generates a parallel to the kind of pooling of colour that she is describing, I would like to draw on this image from 'An Octopus' as a metaphor for what I am calling the 'pooling' of time in Jarman's *Modern Nature*. In other words, the flowers in Jarman's work do not act in their singularity, but form instead rhythmically structured ecological compositions, modes of framing ecological time into synchronous patterns enacted formally in the text through the lists in which each sequential element punctuates, and ultimately adds to and reciprocally composes, the pool of time with its own rhythm.

And yet, such synchronicities of ecological rhythms are subject to the effects of anthropogenically induced global warming, a concern that had been known since 'the discoveries of the Swedish scientist Svante Arrhenius in the 1890s', but, as Dipesh Chakrabarty points out in 'The Climate of History', had not led to widespread 'discussions of global warming in the public realm' until 'the late 1980s and early 1990s'.[39] It is clear that concerns about global warming are permeating Jarman's text, whose writing coincides with this particular historical moment. On numerous occasions he registers the weather on a particular day in relation to the effects of climate change, noting, for instance, '[a] brilliant sunny day, as the greenhouse effect takes hold' or observing the weather on his forty-seventh birthday, which takes place on 31 January 1989 as again bright and sunny with 'crocuses [...] blooming', 'daffodils [...] in bud [...] [and] [t]he roses [...] already breaking into leaf'.[40] It is so warm on the particular occasion of his birthday at the end of January that he finds himself 'sitting in the sun with only a pullover – something I have never done on my birthday, which has always been a cold, grey day' (6). Such manifestations of the greenhouse effect as patterns of unseasonable weather, which offset the temporal patterns of plant growth and budburst, creating the kinds of asynchronies associated with climate change that I discussed earlier, also open up wider anxieties about rising sea levels and the appearance of a hole in the ozone layer: 'Three days of a May heatwave – the greenhouse effect sets in. Dungeness is to disappear in 100 years' time beneath the waves along with its power station – which, it's said, will take 100 years to dismantle. A meteor passes close to the earth, and the ozone hole shifts over southern Australia.'[41] At such moments, longer durations, ones that complicate any sense of a singular focus on the finitude of a human life, enter into view as temporalities of ecological change threaten to disrupt the majority of ecological rhythms that currently compose a particular landscape in the present moment. The questions of energy consumption and energy flows are also brought into the foreground not only through the changes in climate caused by the burning of fossil fuels and the consequent greenhouse effect, but by the presence of the Dungeness nuclear power station, which looms in the landscape of the garden, threatening to both blow up and create a catastrophe in an immediate sense and also bringing into view the long durations of the half-lives of nuclear materials and wastes, which will linger in the landscape and wherever they eventually may be disposed for hundreds of years, in a sense dwarfing the duration of a human life.

The presence of the nuclear power station, and the threat of the long durations of radioactivity that it brings into view, are certainly one of the preoccupying forces in *Modern Nature*. The activities of daily life literally take place in the shadow of the power station: 'Picked samphire along the nuclear power station. Delicious local strawberries for tea.'[42] Images of the power station are featured in the film *The Garden* and, on at least one occasion, it becomes the subject of art, with Jarman taking out his new paints and 'blocking in three canvases of the nuclear power station across the garden at dusk'.[43] Such moments pose questions of what it means to attend aesthetically to possible effects of nuclear catastrophe, and also open up Jarman's text and my analysis here to a critique of the inadequacy of aesthetic means to in any way address such ecological problems. And yet, at the same time, *Modern Nature* persists in intermixing and creating composite temporalities in which the durations and rhythms of illness and renewal are entangled with the seasonal cycles of time and the more punctuated appearance of flowers coming into bloom, with their shimmering, ephemeral durations, but ones that nevertheless suspend or pool time and in this sense resist its teleological pull. At the same time, such temporalities of 'plant clocks' are never configured simply as essentialized nature or simply an idealized realm of renewal from which the edges of human finitude can draw in order to dissolve themselves; rather they remain intermixed with the shifting temporalities and asynchronies created by anthropogenically induced processes, such as climate change, or, as Jarman succinctly puts it, '[c]onversation throughout the day has revolved around the greenhouse effect and HIV'.[44]

In a sense, if there is one ethos of time that the text persistently returns to, it is a resistance to a kind of undoing of such composite or multiple temporalities and their homogenization and/or straightening into a linear chronology leading towards a particular end. Writing about daffodils, at one point, Jarman bemoans the disappearance of their particular temporal rhythm, which acted as a kind of seasonal 'plant clock' marking the onset of spring:

> 'Daffodils come before the swallows dare and take the winds of March with beauty'. When I read these words they are tinged with sadness, for the seasonal nature of daffodils has been destroyed by horticulturists who nowadays force them well before Christmas. One of the joys our technological civilization has lost is the excitement with which seasonal flowers and fruits were welcomed; the first daffodil, strawberry or cherry are now things of the past, along with the precious moment of their arrival. [. . .] I expect one day to see daffodils for sale in Berwick Street market in August, as plentiful as strawberries at Christmas. [. . .] But the daffodil, if only the daffodil could come with spring again, I would eat strawberries with my Christmas pudding.'[45]

This passage speaks to a sense of desire for plants to act as certain kinds of time markers or what I am referring to as 'plant clocks' in this chapter, retaining their differentiated and distinct seasonal rhythms. Such 'plant clocks' would resist what Anne-Lise François, a great contemporary thinker of flowers, poetry and ecological temporality, refers to in her essay 'Flower Fisting' as a loss of 'sensitivity to time and with it the capacity for context-specific variation' in the face of homogenizing and instrumentalizing patterns of time produced by industrial agriculture.[46] In drawing on such 'plant clocks' to generate a more variegated sense of time, composed of multiple coincident ecological rhythms, Jarman resists the teleological pull of time towards the edges of human finitude created by the HIV epidemic, and dwells instead within the shimmering pools of temporal duration, which, at least temporarily, exist outside of the sequential, chronological flow of monotheistic time. While the current moment of the Covid-19 pandemic, and its accompanying patterns of quarantine and waiting, are in many ways distinct from the historical moment of the late 1980s and the early 1990s documented in *Modern Nature*, there is an invitation in Jarman's text to not isolate the temporalities imposed by the virus as an agent of disease from the temporalities of anthropogenically induced and accelerating processes of ecological transformation, such as climate change. Moreover there is an invitation to develop a set of practices of attention within the space of waiting that I have been referring to here as *snail cinema* – ones that hold a possibility of discernment of variegated rhythms of time that are relevant for the composite ecologies of human and non-human organisms; or, as Jarman describes, such practices of temporality and attention that unfold in the counterpoints of human and non-human time: 'In that precious time I would stand and watch the garden grow, something imperceptible to my friends. There, in my dreaming, petals would open and close, a rose suddenly fall apart scattering itself across the path, or a tulip lose a single petal, its perfection shattered forever.'[47]

Quarantine Interlude III: Douglas Firs/ Blackberries/Wildfire Smoke

In late August the wildfire smoke travels up the west coast, on what is a sunny day no luminosity, no shimmer of light on the plants or the sea, the mountains near but invisible in their looming shapes, only an oval of brightness in the sky indicating the position of the sun. The lineaments of smoke passing across its surface into fine lines as in front of a lamp drawing a projection.

A closing of soot in the throat, along the path blackberries, some still in bloom, with flowers not quite white, but tinged pink, a telltale sign of late summer. The fruits hold multiple times on a single branch, some still a bright green and almost as hard as wood and some turning from maroon to dark purple in spots to the nearly black, some gnarled by the beaks of birds dripping streaks of inner juice on the hot pavement.

Somewhere through the smoke the scent of warmed fig leaves or as one approaches the three tall firs along the dusty yellowed grass, the thin sounds of birds on the air and in between the fingers, counting the low arcs of flight towards the trees. Their branches, even in the still, dead smoky air, still in movement changing the arrangement, the rearrangement of visible shapes. Their unstillness.

Notes

1   Derek Jarman, *Modern Nature* (Minneapolis: University of Minnesota Press, 2009), 81.

2   'Digitalis', *Wikipedia*. https://en.wikipedia.org/wiki/Digitalis Accessed: 5 February 2021.

3 Charles Darwin, *On the Movements and Habits of Climbing Plants* (Cambridge: Cambridge University Press, 2009), 2.

4 Gilles Deleuze, *Bergsonism*, trans. Hugh Tomlinson and Barbara Habberjam (New York: Zone Books, 1991), 31.

5 Ibid., 32.

6 Donna J. Haraway, *Staying with the Trouble: Making Kin in the Chthulocene* (Durham and London: Duke University Press, 2016), 1.

7 Ibid., 2.

8 Ibid.

9 Jan Zalasiewicz, Mark Williams, Will Steffen, and Paul Crutzen, 'The New World of the Anthropocene', *Environmental Science and Technology* 44 (2010): 2228–31, 22–9.

10 Christian Both, Margriet Van Asch, Rob G. Bijlsma, Arnold B. Van Den Burg, and Marcel E. Visser, 'Climate change and unequal phenological changes across four tropic levels: constraints or adaptations?' *Journal of Animal Ecology* 78, no. 1 (January 2009): 73–83, 74.

11 Ibid., 75.

12 Jakob von. Uexküll, *A Foray into the Worlds of Animals and Humans*, trans. Joseph D. ONeil (Minneapolis: University of Minnesota Press, 2010), 52.

13 Ibid., 52, 72.

14 Ibid., 72.

15 Francis Ponge, *The Nature of Things* (*Le Parti Pris des Choses*), trans. Lee Fahnestock. (New York: Red Dust, 1995), 23.

16 Jarman, *Modern Nature*, 7.

17 Haraway, *Staying with the Trouble*, 2.

18 Jarman, *Modern Nature*, 31.

19 Ibid.

20 Ibid.

21 Ibid., 18.

22 Ibid., 258.

23 Ibid., 29.

24 Ibid., 304.

25 Ibid., 270–1.

26 Ibid., 30.

27 Ibid., 220.

28 Ibid., 232.

29 Ibid., 30.

30 Ibid., 258.

31 Ibid., 225.

32 Ibid., 271.

33 Ibid.

34 Ibid., 294.

35 Ibid., 278–9.

36 Ibid., 12.

37 Ibid., 301.

38 Marianne Moore, *Observations*, ed. Linda Leavell (New York: Farrar, Straus and Giroux, 2016), 89.

39 Dipesh Chakrabarty, 'The Climate of History: Four Thesis.' *Critical Inquiry* 35 (Winter 2009): 197–222, 198–9.

40 Jarman, *Modern Nature*, 5–6.

41 Ibid., 74.

42 Ibid., 296.

43 Ibid., 225.

44 Ibid., 289.

45 Ibid., 12–13.

46 Anne-Lee François, 'Flower Fisting.' *Postmodern Culture* 22, no. 1 (September 2011): no pg.

47 Jarman, *Modern Nature*, 7.

10

Thinking and/over/in the pandemic

From *contact points* towards *contact zones* potentially reconciling us with the ultramicroscopic sub-layers of life

Martin Grünfeld

Introduction

The SARS-CoV-2 contaminates bodies potentially leading to dry cough, fever, respiratory problems and death. However, the virus not only affects organisms infected by it. As Alain Badiou observes: 'it seems that the challenge of the epidemic is dissipating the intrinsic activity of Reason.'[1] Not only has Covid-19 infected bodies around the globe, it has also infected our thinking. This ultramicroscopic agent oscillating between life and death inflicts our lives and infects our thoughts. Precisely, this transference of the virus from infecting bodies of millions of people to the minds of billions interests me. Even when we are trying to isolate ourselves from the virus by staying home, or perhaps especially when we withdraw from our everyday life, our minds are infected, and yet we seem to be unable to reconcile ourselves with the loss of autonomy and control that Covid-19 ushers in. In this chapter, I seek to explore how the virus affects our lives and thoughts, and if we can find a possible way towards reconciliation with this ultramicroscopic sub-layer of life.

In the following two sections of the chapter focusing on a *viral imposition* and our imbalanced *pre(dis)positional responses*, I begin by exploring the turbulent forces of the pandemic putting our thinking under stress. In the pandemic situation, we simply do not know how to position ourselves. Our habits are disrupted and yet we continuously return to the known to find comfort and safety.

I begin this chapter by specifically exploring how the invisible ultramicroscopic virus becomes entangled with our everyday practices and experiences, when even the simplest task such as opening a door potentially turns into a fearful encounter with the more-than-human virus. Yet this potential encounter also marks a moment of connectedness and an opportunity for us to think and act beyond the habitual. After this opening discussion of the viral imposition, I turn to the philosophical debate following the lockdown of Northern Italy in search of a way to think the current situation. However, what I find particularly interesting in this debate is the prepositional imbalances of thought fluctuating between declaring the end of the world (Žižek) and resorting to the known, perceiving of Covid-19 as a regular flu (Agamben). Such thought figures of the pandemic are characterized by a surprising clarity and attempts to regain control of the situation with reference to the known (previous work and scientific authorities). Despite the viral imposition, the thinkers manage to move from their habitual predispositions to prepositional imbalances, leaving the ultramicroscopic virus so forcefully contacting us unthought.

In the final two sections, I discuss how we can reconcile ourselves with the more-than-human sub-layers of life so powerfully affecting our lives and infecting our thoughts at this moment. First, by discussing art, especially focusing on Tagny Duff's daring proposition to perceive viruses as evolutionary companions, I discuss the difficulty of establishing contact with the more-than-human. Duff shows us two different paths, one in the form of a speculative dialogue and the other as material encounters of companionship. While the format of writing remains a much too anthropocentric tool, I find a real potential for reconciliation in the strange encounters with the viruses Duff makes possible in her *Cryobook Archives*, which turns into an unusual site for companionship with viruses. Second, setting off from this idea of strange material encounters with viruses that goes beyond their usual articulations as coughing and fever, I consider the museum as a potential contact zone with the more-than-human. While the spread of Covid-19 has led to closed museums and galleries across the globe, perhaps such places can become sites for reconciliation providing orderly and safe, yet utterly strange, material encounters. This leads to my final speculative questioning: How can museums respond to this overtaking and embrace the entrance of the outside? I suggest a perhaps strange juxtaposition: the posthuman museum as more than an oxymoron, namely as a host of living assemblages possibly enabling us to reconcile ourselves with the sub-layers of life.

A viral imposition: The doorknob as a contact point with the more-than-human

Shortly after the lockdown of Copenhagen in 2019 due to the increasing spread of Covid-19, I experienced a rupture in my everyday dealings and thoughts. I had not been infected by the virus, yet my actions and thoughts had become uncertain, disturbed, interrupted and affected by a *viral imposition*. Habitual processes and practices I took for granted in my everyday life, such as touching, talking and breathing, had been hijacked by questions of risk, exposure and infection. By the mere possibility of its presence, the invisible ultramicroscopic virus becomes entangled with practices and experiences; our sense of autonomy, prediction and control overthrown by the de-familiarizing power of the viral imposition placing upon us burdens and requirements: an imposition of a sub-layer of life usually hidden but now present among us, with powers to affect and infect us and close down entire societies. In a pandemic situation, even the simplest task such as opening a door invokes elements of fear and paranoia about what kind of uncanny presence may be sticking to our hands.

We used to be able to move effortlessly through walls thanks to the marvellous invention of doors. As Jim Johnson (or Bruno Latour) remarks, 'walls are a nice invention, but if there were no holes in them, there would be no way to get in or out', yet if you just make holes in the walls anything can get in or out.[2] The invention of the hole-walls we call doors depends on a crucial technology – the hinge. The hinged door selects what gets in and out.[3] Yet there is a problem with doors: 'Visitors push them to get in or pull on them to get out (or vice versa), but then the door remains open.'[4] This problem leads the hybrid author Johnson to salute hydraulic door-closers for their ability to slowly and reliably close doors.[5] While Johnson heralds the hinge, surprisingly they seem to forget another crucial part of the door making it possible to open and close it – the doorknob. While some doors are automated (e.g. in supermarkets), others are manual, and the doorknob is a crucial part of a manual door. Yet in the pandemic situation, precisely the doorknob poses a new problem for our everyday dealings. Instead of merely functioning as a selective barrier between inside and outside, it becomes a contact point – a passageway between body and virus. When we fumble trying to get in or out, using sleeves, elbows or other means, we encounter a breakdown in our daily life entering and leaving buildings: a transformation of the door from passage to contact point.

Perhaps Martin Heidegger's distinction between *readiness-to-hand* and *present-at-hand* can help us understand this breakdown.[6] In his tool-analysis, Heidegger argues that, ontologically speaking, use is a fundamental mode of engagement in our everyday dealings in the world. As Hubert Dreyfus explains: 'we do not usually encounter (use, talk about, deal with) "mere things" but rather we use the things at hand to get something done'.[7] This is what characterizes tools – they are ready-to-hand. Yet tools work their magic without entering our awareness; they are notably invisible.[8] What this entails is that tools withdraw from view unless they are broken. As Dreyfus also points out: 'if the doorknob sticks, we find ourselves deliberately *trying* to turn the doorknob, *desiring* that it turn, *expecting* the door to open'.[9] Broken tools are disturbing because their withdrawal is annulled – they become hauntingly present-at-hand. Although the doorknob has become present-at-hand in the pandemic situation, it remains, however, fully functional, contributing to the attainment of some end (making it possible to open and close the door while selecting who can enter and leave) and having this function can explain its existence.[10] The doorknob is neither sticking nor too loose and apparently needs no fixing. Yet, following Graham Harman's rereading of Heidegger's tool-analysis, the doorknob is in a certain generalized sense broken, because any being encountered is broken.[11] According to Harman, 'the phenomenon of broken tools' can be 'extended far beyond the scope of failed hammers, since every entity can be defined by its reversal from sheer execution into a sort of tangible aura'.[12] In this sense, the doorknob is broken not because it is failing to fulfil its function as opener and closer, but because it has become present-at-hand. Doorknobs are supposed to remain unnoticed, invisible. This is the 'function or action of the tool, its toolbeing, is absolutely invisible-even if the hammer never leaves my sight'.[13] The breakdown becomes a process of rupture.[14] A rupture that calls upon us to find new ways of coping that restore the doorknob to its silent existence as ready-for-hand; ways of coping that point us in direction of a rupture not merely of our everyday engagement with doorknobs but our relationship to the sub-layers of life.

Instead of merely a tool for opening and closing doors enabling us to move effortlessly through walls, the doorknob has also become a point of passage for the virus to move from the outside and into our bodies. This, however, is not a case of trans-functionalization – the doorknob is not functioning in a radically different way.[15] As Bruno Latour points out, society depends on many associations between actors including microbes, which we have known since Louis Pasteur.[16] The doorknob has always carried out this multi-scalar function as a point of passage between inside and outside. Today, however, the situation is different:

not only has the doorknob become a potential contact point with the new virus in town, imposing a risk of infection, but it has also become a point of reflection on the contact between virus and our exposed bodies. This multi-dimensional contact point emphasizes our permeable bodies and connectedness in the world. The increasing spread and mortality rates have called upon us to find new ways of coping with this hidden passage between the outside and our exposed bodies. We gradually get used to handling doorknobs (and other everyday actions) in new ways such as increased cleaning practices, using elbows to open doors and push buttons or perhaps investing in a plastic door opener. Yet I wonder if, rather than just restoring our everyday practices to the realm of invisible readiness-to-hand, we should stay with the initial rupture and scrutinize the viral imposition on our everyday actions and thoughts. As Dreyfus, for example, points out: once 'ongoing activity is held up, new modes of encountering emerge and new ways of being encountered are revealed'.[17] Perhaps we could reframe the viral imposition as a (deadly) opportunity for philosophy to engage with the sub-layers of life?

Maybe the viral imposition could even provide a passageway to the outside of philosophy described by Quentin Meillassoux as the *great outdoors*: 'that outside which was not relative to us, and which was given as indifferent to its own givenness to be what it is [. . .]'.[18] What Meillassoux means by this is that philosophy since Kant has been thinking in correlations between subject and object, excluding an outside bigger than ourselves. A great outdoors not delimited to a nature separate from society but inherently part of our everyday dealings and thinking. Today we are called upon to think beyond our everyday dealings by the viral imposition, causing nature to re-enter our lives. Within this moment we experience our connectedness to the world and our vulnerability. The doorknob, more than merely a selective aid providing passage between inside and outside, accentuates the opportunity of our current situation to think and act beyond the habitual. With the viral imposition, the door is no longer just an entrance point between outside and inside – a mere passage to pass through – but instead an uncertain contact point between people, pathogens and thinking.

Pre(dis)positions: Oscillating thought figures of a pandemic

If we dare to take on the challenge to see the viral imposition as an opportunity to bring our thinking beyond the habitual, how is thinking in the pandemic situation touched by and touching the viral imposition? Scientists, epidemiologists and health personnel, insistently and admirably fight to predict, control and contain the pandemic to keep us safe and healthy. Yet the current pandemic situation affects us personally and existentially beyond questions of health and safety. In this situation, we need more than scientific authorities, yet such authorities also provide a constant yet uncertain ground for our thinking. This is particularly evident in a philosophical debate Giorgio Agamben sparked with his response to the political measures taken in Italy to prevent the spread of the virus. A debate marked by an oscillation between *over-* and *under-*thinking the situation. In the following, I focus on responses from three key figures (Agamben, Badiou, Žižek), but I must emphasize that my discussion is not revisionary – my aim is not to judge whether their claims are factually correct, nor am I taking sides in the debate. Rather, I am interested in their responses as figures of fluctuating thoughts: a thinking out of balance struggling to find its ground within a prepositional schism between *over- and under-thinking* the situation.

After the lockdown of Northern Italy, Giorgio Agamben published a response on *Quodlibet* questioning the epidemic situation and the political motives behind the lockdown. Agamben refers to such measures as 'frenetic, irrational and entirely unfounded'.[19] In Agamben's view, the press is spreading panic and political authorities are taking unfounded emergency measures that will affect the daily life in entire regions in Italy. In his critique of political authorities, Agamben refers to another authority – the National Research Council (CNR) – which at that point in time stated that there is no epidemic in Italy and that Covid-19 only causes mild to moderate symptoms in most cases.[20] While Agamben begins his critique by questioning why the state and media do everything they can to spread fear, he moves swiftly from a hypothetical argument to a sure footed critique: 'The disproportionate reaction to what according to the CNR is something not too different from the normal flus that affect us every year is quite blatant.'[21] For Agamben, the state misuses the Covid-19 outbreak to legitimize a state of exception with serious limitations on the daily life and free movement of its citizens. Although Agamben's concern is the daily life of citizens, the everyday remains in the backdrop as something we can and should rehabilitate in his familiar critique of the political measures. In this rehabilitation, the virus has no role to play, but is diminished as something known with reference to the regular flu. The virus remains an absolute outside of Agamben's thinking – a thought figure fluctuating between over-thinking the political measures taken to prevent the viral spread and under-thinking the threat of the virus.

Almost a month after Agamben sparked the debate, Badiou responds calmly and reasonably: 'From the start, I thought that the current situation, characterised by a viral pandemic, was not particularly exceptional.'[22] For

Badiou, the naming of the virus becomes a crucial marker defining the situation – its true name reveals that it is a sequel rather than the emergence of something radically new. On 11 February 2020, the *International Committee on Taxonomy of Viruses* announced the official name for the virus as SARS-CoV-2.[23] For some scientists, however, the name of the virus does not matter, while other scientists worry that the use of a well-known name may confuse the public and impede efforts to control the spread.[24] Based on a remarkable trust in scientific naming practices, Badiou finds comfort in the familiar and reaches the conclusion that there is nothing exceptional about the virus. While markedly different from Agamben's hard-hitting critique of political misuse of power, Badiou in his response similarly draws on scientific authorities and resorts to the known. His main target in the text is over-thinking in various guises: 'I am reading and hearing too many things, including in my immediate circles, that disconcert me both by the confusion they manifest and by their utter inadequacy to the – ultimately simple – situation in which we find ourselves.'[25] Badiou's response to the pandemic situation is mainly to critique fellow intellectuals for over-thinking the situation and to bring some simple ideas he happily classifies as Cartesian.[26] Cartesian, however, without even the slightest trace of the famous doubt, Badiou's streamlined reasoning maintains control of the allegedly simple situation. A simple situation that in Badiou's view does not call for 'the constitution of a new way of thinking'.[27] This is under-thinking par excellence: a thinking presupposing control and prediction, in which the situation does not call upon us other responses than isolation and patience. The virus remains an absolute outside from which our thinking can isolate itself.

Roughly 100 days after the outbreak of Covid-19 in Wuhan, (perhaps) the fastest thinker on the planet, Slavoj Žižek, published his book *Pandemic!* With a clarity shining almost as bright as Badiou's Cartesian reasoning, Žižek draws the exact opposite conclusion: this is the end of the world as we know it! After opening his book with two (almost too) habitual references to Hegel, making us feel safe, Žižek catches us off guard with the prophetic announcement: 'The only thing that is clear is that the virus will shatter the very foundations of our lives, causing not only an immense amount of suffering but also economic havoc conceivably worse than the Great Recession. There is no return to the normal.'[28] Already in February, Žižek compared the disruptive powers of the virus to the *Five Point Palm Exploding Heart Technique*, which provides a 'Kill Bill'-esque blow to global capitalism.[29] This stands in direct opposition to Badiou's downplaying of the political efficiency of epidemics.[30] If Badiou is under-thinking the situation, Žižek over-thinks the consequences its potential consequences.

While Badiou orients himself towards the past (previous epidemics and formerly known viruses), Žižek focuses on the future and the possibility of the growth of a new communism – a communism he vaguely describes as 'some kind of global organization that can control and regulate the economy, as well as limit the sovereignty of nation-states when needed'.[31] Yet this new communism is also largely a familiar reiteration of Žižek's previous attempts to proselytize a new form of communism.[32] For Žižek, the pandemic forces us to confront the normality of the normal and the possibility of a better future.[33] A better future is, however, not a self-given outcome. Rather, Žižek's unbalanced thinking oscillates between optimism and pessimism, clarity and uncertainty, the known and unknown, control and limits, dreams and nightmares.

In a pandemic situation, there is nothing surprising about the fact that we resort to well-worn paths to provide us with safety – what is really frightening is what we don't know, as Sergio Benvenuto points out.[34] The thought figures scrutinized here seem to create an illusion of mastery and control by following habitual thought figures (e.g. Žižek resorting to the usual suspects Hegel, Marx and Lacan or Agamben describing a state of exception).[35] Yet what I find particularly puzzling is how these turbulent thoughts can be expressed with such certainty. Only in Žižek's response, do we get a sense of the viral imposition affecting not only our bodies but thoughts, dreams and nightmares. But even in isolation, thinking is infected and caught out of balance. Out of balance it clings to whatever seems solid, often embodied by health and scientific authorities. Science alone, however, cannot support our thinking the present moment. Rather, we must reconcile ourselves with a sub-layer of life, which has been and will always be here, as Žižek also suggests.[36] Despite their intentions to either calmly downplay the situation or revolutionarily aspire towards a better future, Agamben, Badiou and Žižek altogether move from habitual predispositions to imbalanced prepositions without including the more-than-human outdoors so forcefully contacting us.

A daring proposition: The virus as a work of art and an evolutionary companion

The viral imposition has defamiliarized our lives, leaving us within propositional imbalances in our struggle to isolate ourselves from the sub-layer of life so powerfully infecting our thoughts and affecting our bodies. Perhaps it would be tempting to view the viral spread of Covid-19 and its defamiliarizing effects as (akin to) a work of art. At least, since Victor Shklovsky, art has been associated with a power to make strange. Shklovsky defines the purpose of art as the overcoming of 'the deadening effects of habit by representing familiar things in unfamiliar ways' as David Lodge explains.[37] In other words, through the effect of estrangement, art may help us recover the sensation of life beyond habit. The pandemic situation has precisely brought us beyond habit – it has created an opening for us to recover what our habits hide, but also created a possibility of reconciliation with the hidden sub-layers of life usually (and still) invisibly co-present on the planet. And yet claiming that the viral spread of Covid-19 resembles art may sound all too familiar. Recall Karlheinz Stockhausen's famous description of the deadly attacks on 9/11 as the greatest work of art imaginable. This provocative utterance certainly made a stir, but as Richard Schechner argues, the statement must be understood in the context of the history of avant-garde art and the call for a destruction of existing aesthetic, social and political systems.[38] However, as Schechner points out, Stockhausen is also expressing his desire for art to occupy a significant position in the world.[39] In that sense, 9/11 was more powerful than art, because as Schechner argues, 'terrorism, at the scale of 9/11, works like art more on the states of mind and feeling than physical destruction.'[40] At the time of writing, 85.2 million people worldwide have been confirmed infected by Covid-19 and 1.8 million people deceased from infection.[41] These numbers are unfathomable. Yet the viral spread of Covid-19 also works akin to art albeit on a global scale affecting the minds of billions of people.

However, there is (at least) one important difference between perceiving 9/11 and the Covid-19 pandemic as akin to art. This difference is emphasized in Stockhausen's description of the sheer work put into the execution of the 9/11 attack: terrorists rehearsing for ten years, preparing fanatically and willing to die for their cause. In contrast, the work leading to the global spread of the pandemic cannot be linked to one or more human actors directly involved in its realization (although we keep searching for that mysterious patient zero). This is important because we often associate art with (human) artists creating works. However, we must bear in mind that in the development of post-digital artistic work in the late 1990s biological agency was employed in performative ways, marking a shift from human actions to non-human agency.[42] Yet in contrast to Covid-19, biological agency is still 'employed' by somebody in post-digital art (usually an artist, a lab technician or researcher). Meanwhile, the viral spread can (at least) be linked to a market in Wuhan, possibly bats, business travellers and global air travel, ski resorts in Austria and Italy, choir singers and religious gatherings and allegedly doorknobs. While such diverse contact points globalize the viral spread, and can quite literally lead to the end (causing infection and death), such contact points can only be the beginning of our attempt towards reconciliation with the sub-layers of life.

What I want to do here is not to engage in the question of the limits of art and the ethical implications involved in grandiose and potentially repulsive statements such as claiming the Covid-19 pandemic as art. Rather, I wish to stay within unfamiliar terrain and consider how to relate to this absolute Other of the pandemic in ways that move beyond our initial sense of a viral imposition burdening our lives and leading to prepositional imbalances of thought and isolation. But how? Perhaps what Ian Bogost has called *alien phenomenology* could be a fitting guide: alien phenomenology is a speculative approach to reality aiming at the wackiness of things and amplifying the black noise of objects:[43] a black noise of something more – an exotic world of incomprehensible objects. To amplify the black noise of objects, 'one must proceed like the carnival barker rather than the scholar: through educated guesswork'.[44] Guesswork characterized by analogical speculations developing as a 'benighted meandering in an exotic world of utterly incomprehensible objects'[45] and questioning what it is like to be a thing. Precisely through speculation and educated guesswork, the artist Tagny Duff in her recent essay 'Speaking with Viruses' brings us closer to an imagined point of contact with the viral perspective.

In her essay, Duff insists on speaking with viruses, instead of writing about them, countering our tendencies to anthropomorphize viruses as vicious evil aliens and the like.[46] This move already brings us beyond our initial sense of a viral imposition. Her essay develops as a dialogue between a human infected by a virus and a choir of viruses, which marks a transgression beyond the familiar articulation of viruses through bodily responses such as coughing and sweating: What develops in the dialogue is a strange juxtaposition of unlikely conversation partners, bringing us well beyond known responses to viral infections. Gradually the dialogue develops from the questioning of how we can better understand the invisible microcosmic world towards perceiving viruses as companions on our evolutionary journey.[47] With this reformulation of viruses as evolutionary companions, rather than hostile enemies, our tendencies to isolate our thoughts and see the virus as an impostor are challenged by the bigger picture of coexistence on the planet. As the viral choir expresses it: 'Our lives are entangled with yours. Evolution of the planet depends on it.'[48] The dialogue develops as a form of reconciliation with our evolutionary companions and the development of a common understanding of cohabitation dependent on our abilities to move beyond our tendencies towards human exceptionalism. Yet the reconciliation remains unfulfilled, haunted by the question of survival. Beneath the momentary optimistic vision of cohabitation lies pessimism and fear – a fluctuation of thought not unlike the prepositional schism I explored in the previous section.

While the dialogue develops as a speculative conversation, a question continuously reappears: How can we find a way to speak together beyond our bodily reactions to infections, hostile anthropomorphic projections and delimitation of viruses as study objects in science? This questioning also gestures towards a meta-level of her essay, namely the mode of contact Duff establishes with the viruses through written form. Although Duff emphasizes that we must move beyond human exceptionalism and our anthropomorphic tendencies to perceive viruses as vicious enemies, giving voice to viruses in the form of a dialogue and perceiving them as companions is also an anthropomorphizing act. However, as Bogost observes, 'we are destined to offer anthropomorphic metaphors.'[49] Indeed, anthropomorphizing gestures such as the divinization of nature can work against anthropocentrism, as Jane Bennett points out.[50] But despite the inevitable, indeed potentially productive anthropomorphism without anthropocentrism characteristic of Duff's dialogue, she risks limiting the viral perspective, when the viruses are conformed into speaking a clearly understandable semi-academic English. As expressed by Bogost, there is a danger that writing creates a myopic view of other forms of being that populate the world.[51] Consequently, our job is to get our hands dirty and practice ontology, rather than preach it.[52] This, however, is precisely what Duff has been working on for years, creating speculative encounters with viruses: for example, in her work the *Cryobook Archives* featuring a series of handmade books made from human and pig tissue, HaCat cells and synthetic Lentivirus.[53] In 2015, the *Cryobook Archives* were exhibited as part of a nicely furnished living room library at *Espace Multimédia Gantner*. Playing on the duality of the meaning of Living Room Library, the site became an unusual place for companionship, inviting visitors to sit and read and enabling them to perceive viruses otherwise – as more than just enemies.[54] This unusual place constitutes the possibility of a strange material encounter with the ultramicroscopic layer of life and a potential opening towards reconciliation.

Juxtapositions: The posthuman museum as a potential *contact zone* with the sub-layers of life

Perhaps Duff's *Cryobook Archives* can help us engage with the virus beyond our senses of viral impositions and inclinations to isolate ourselves from the violent ultramicroscopic alien, instead of awkward and fearful possible exchanges linked to *contact points*, creating a *contact zone* for strange material encounters. *Contact zone* appears here in an extended sense of the concept originally proposed by Mary Louise Pratt and applied to the context of museums by James Clifford to argue for museums as places of contentious and collaborative interactions.[55] For Clifford, the notion of contact zone invokes the spatial and temporal copresence of subjects previously separated historically and geographically but whose trajectories now intersect.[56] Originally the concept addressed the question of power relations in colonial encounters. However, as Clifford notes, the notion of contact zone can be extended to include cultural relations within the same state, region or even city and attends to not only geographic and historical differences but also social differences.[57] Here I extend the concept even further to include the biological differences so nicely intersecting in the encounter with Duff's cryobooks. By creating a contact zone with the more-than-human, Duff enabled visitors and viruses to co-exist without infection, thereby creating an extended sense of 'us' including the microscopic world.

The museum, as Clifford also stresses, is a useful place for gathering and valuing an us.[58] Yet as Paul Rabinow wrote well before the pandemic: 'The challenge is to turn a collection of separate entities, however distinctive, into a dynamic site for experiencing and reflecting on our history, our future and our uneasy and unsure mutual connectedness.'[59] Rabinow emphasizes that we need to think through the 'our' of our history, future and potential connectedness but notice the humble uncertainty of the 'unsure' connectedness. Today we experience a global connectedness: Our bodies have become hyper-connected or *trans-corporeal* to borrow a concept from Stacy Alaimo.[60] As Levi Bryant stresses, 'Trans-corporeality teaches us of a world where things that seem to be over there and thus apart from us intermesh with us in ways that significantly impact our local manifestations and becomings.'[61] If we take Rabinow's challenge seriously and attempt to turn the museum into a dynamic site for experiencing and reflecting not only on our history but also on the future and our uneasy mutual connectedness, we must include the absolute Other that connects us today – Covid-19. To do this, we must consider the fundamentally strange juxtaposition *the posthuman museum*.

Yet the museum is usually anthropocentric and species restrictive: we are the monarchs ruling in the land of beings. As Simon Knell describes it, the museum is working as a cultural guardian with a long-term duty to preserve and present the patrimony of a nation, culture or community.[62] Our imaginary of the modern museum inscribes it within a temporal ideology as an institution connecting the past to the future. As Jean-Paul Martinon points out, the future is turned into an outcome of a grand narrative of progress – a narrative that replicates a Hegelian understanding of time, where history is seen as the march of humanity towards freedom and the future as a necessary accomplishment of this march.[63] However, in a certain sense the museum has always been posthuman. Not only in the exhibitions and public spaces but also in our controlled storage facilities, a more-than-human presence has been lurking in the shadows – heritage eaters challenging our sense of control and power. This realization resonates with Cary Wolfe's argument that instead of conceiving of posthumanism as being the *post* of humanism, we need to think of it as coming both *before* and *after*. *Before* because it names the embodiment and embeddedness of the human in a biological and technological world.[64] In that sense, we have always been posthuman as Katherine Hayles also points out.[65] And *after* because the posthuman names a historical moment in which the decentring of the human is increasingly impossible to ignore.[66] This may sound troubling, but as Wolfe stresses it does not necessarily point towards the apocalyptic or the anti-human.[67] Although the decentring dethrones us as the monarchs ruling in the kingdom of being(s), we must remember the *before*, which entails that even though it felt like we were the true rulers of the world, it has always already been more-than-human affecting and infecting us. But, although we have always been posthuman, the intensification of the decentring of the human within a more-than-human (biological and technological) world is a defining trait of our historical context accentuated by the global spread of Covid-19.[68]

Still, the museum would be an awkward host of biological processes. At the museum, the lives of objects are defined by former context and use, while literal present-day life processes are suppressed.[69] This is a *politics of death* – a politics demarcating the boundaries between the life and death of objects. A politics blessing objects with value and defining the traces that will live on culturally and become part of our history. A politics determining what we can and cannot do with objects: how we preserve, exhibit and perceive them. The politics of death inserts a sensible order within which certain aspects of our culture and history become visible, while others remain invisible and obscure. Within this logic, we the humans occupy the central position of control as the doers: collecting, preserving objects, documenting, interpreting and exhibiting. Yet these measures of control also separate us from the objects. As Clémentine Deliss argues in her recent book, museums are inherently biased against the body, regulating the range of visitors' motions and delimiting their experiences to a disembodied opticality.[70] As Deliss suggests, the viral crisis and the fear of zoonotic contamination may lead to a more restricted access to objects such as human and animal remains.[71] I think we can broaden this worry and project that the fear of contamination may lead to even more sterile and optically distanced experiences for visitors.

Yet, precisely as that weird place in-between life and death at the intersections of past, present and future, the museum might be capable of creating contact zones with the more-than-human, enabling visitors to engage in strange material encounters through juxtapositions across temporal and spatial scales. But can the museum embrace this historical momentum and move beyond its anthropocentric roots and perhaps find a path towards reconciliation with the sub-layers of life? In a short text on posthuman-museum practices, Fiona Cameron suggests that in a more-than-human world, museums are ideally placed to promote posthuman theories and practices of life through curatorial practice.[72] Yet, as Cameron points out, our concepts of objects as well as modes of collecting, ordering and exhibiting are mainly understood in terms of human subject/object relations based on human-centred interpretations and selection criteria. For Cameron, this calls for an ontological refashioning that aims at re-working the humanisms, going beyond the usual stories we tell, to include production details, geographical locations, materials, environment and other actants. Just as Duff creates the possibility of experiencing companionship through strange material encounters, we should do more than changing our descriptive categories and the narratives we craft. An ontological refashioning entails more: it calls for a rethinking of the temporal resistance to change inherent in the museum and the objects we choose to collect and exhibit based on logics of preservation suppressing life processes.[73] Indeed, in her recent book *Curated Decay*, Caitlin DeSilvey encourages us 'to think about what could be gained if we were to care for the past without pickling it'.[74]

Instead of marking a dystopian end of the museum, the uncanny juxtaposition of the posthuman museum might usher in the beginning of a redistribution of the sensible order inherently tied to the institution since the Enlightenment and create the possibility of developing new contact zones with the more-than-human. A redistribution that challenges anthropocentrism and invites us to embrace a status as humble agents in the living assemblages that make up the museum (and world). A site where we no longer perceive of ourselves as the monarchs ruling in the kingdom of beings but attempt to move beyond human exceptionalism and transform the museum to become a host of living assemblages. A site where we are no longer prepositionally distanced (over and above) what we perceive as microbial impostors or heritage eaters, but deeply engaged with the more-than-human sub-layers of life. A posthuman museum – perhaps?

Notes

1 Alain Badiou, 'On the Epidemic Situation', accessed 5 May 2020, https://www.ver sobooks.com/blogs/4608-on-the-epidemic-situation.

2 Jim Johnson, 'Mixing Humans and Nonhumans Together: The Sociology of a Door-Closer', *Social Problems* 35, no. 3 (1988): 298 and 304. Note that the text is written by Bruno Latour, who uses the pseudonym Jim Johnson to mark a distinction between the author-in-the-text and the author-in-the-flesh. The point behind using the pseudonym was that American sociologists are not willing to read things referring to specific times and places that are not American. Here I will play along and designate the author as Johnson.

3 Johnson, 'Mixing Humans and Nonhumans Together: The Sociology of a Door-Closer', 299.

4 Ibid., 300.

5 Ibid., 302.

6 Martin Heidegger, *Sein Und Zeit* (Tübingen: Max Niemeyer Verlag, 2001).

7 Hubert L. Dreyfus, *Being-in-the-World: A Commentary on Heidegger's Being and Time, Division I* (Cambridge, MA, London: MIT Press, 1991), 62.

8 Graham Harman, *Tool-Being: Heidegger and the Metaphyics of Objects* (Chicago: Open Court, 2002), 16, 19.

9 Dreyfus, *Being-in-the-World*, 70.

10 William C. Wimsatt, 'Teleology and the Logical Structure of Function Statements', *Studies in the History and Philosophy of Science, A* 3, no. 1 (1972): 6.

11 Harman, *Tool-being*, 44.

12 Ibid., 48.

13 Ibid., 19.

14 Ibid., 47.

15 Slavoj Žižek, *PANDEMIC! Covid-19 Shakes the World* (Cambridge: Polity Press, 2020), 114.

16 Bruno Latour, 'Is This a Dress Rehearsal?', accessed 6 August, 2020, https://critinq. wordpress.com/2020/03/26/is-this-a-dress-rehearsal/.

17 Dreyfus, *Being-in-the-World*, 70.

18 Quentin Meillassoux, *After Finitude* (London: Bloomsbury, 2014, cop 2008), 7.

19 Giorgio Agamben, 'The Invention of an Epidemic', reprinted in Michel Foucault et al., 'Coronavirus and Philosophers', accessed June 5, 2020, https://www.journal-psychoanalysis.eu/coronavirus-and-philosophers/.

20 Ibid.

21 Ibid.

22 Badiou, 'On the Epidemic Situation'.

23 'Coronavirus: The First Three Months as It Happened', Nature Publishing Group, accessed 30 July 2020, https://www.nature.com/articles/d41586-020-00154-w.

24 Ibid.

25 Badiou, 'On the Epidemic Situation'.

26 Ibid.

27 Ibid.

28 Žižek, *PANDEMIC!*, 3.

29 Slavoj Žižek, 'Coronavirus Is a "Kill Bill"-Esque Blow to Capitalism and Could Lead to Reinvention of Communism', accessed July 30, 2020, https://www.rt.com/op-ed/481831-coronavirus-kill-bill-capitalism-communism/.

30 Badiou, 'On the Epidemic Situation'.

31 Žižek, *PANDEMIC!*, 44–5.

32 David J. Gunkel, 'Deconstructing the Panic of Pandemic: A Critical Review of Slavoj Žižek's Pandemic! COVID-19 Shakes the World', *International Journal of Žižek Studies* 14, no. 2 (2020): 4.

33 Gunkel, 'Deconstructing the Panic of Pandemic', 6.

34 Sergio Benvenuto, 'Welcome to Seclusion'. Reprinted in Foucault et al., 'Coronavirus and philosophers'.

35 What I mean by habitual thinking here can perhaps best be described with reference to Heidegger, who in his introduction to metaphysics argues that man 'is always thrown back on the paths that he himself has laid out: he becomes mired in his paths, caught in the beaten track' (Martin Heidegger, *An Introduction to Metaphysics* (New Haven, CT; London: Yale University Press, 1968), 157). An honest meta-reflection: this is not the first time I refer to this image of habitual thinking as wandering along the same paths.

36 Slavoj Žižek, 'Monitor and Punish? Yes, Please!', accessed 5 May 2020, https://thephilosophicalsalon.com/monitor-and-punish-yes-please/.

37 David Lodge, *The Art of Fiction* (New York: Penguin, 1992), 53.

38 Richard Schechner, '9/11 as Avant-Garde Art?', *PMLA* 124, no. 5 (2009): 1820.

39 Schechner, '9/11 as Avant-Garde Art?', 1826.

40 Schechner, '9/11 as Avant-Garde Art?', 1828.

41 Johns Hopkins University, national public health agencies. Last updated 4 January 2021, 10:06 GMT.

42 Jens Hauser and Lucie Strecker, 'On Microperformativity', *Performance Research* 25, no.3 (2020): 4, https://doi.org/10.1080/13528165.2020.1807739.

43 Ian Bogost, *Alien Phenomenology, Or, What It's Like to Be a Thing*, Posthumanities 20 (Minneapolis: University of Minnesota Press, 2012), 35.

44 Ibid., 31.

45 Ibid., 34.

46 Hauser and Strecker, 'On Microperformativity', 3.

47 Tagny Duff, 'Speaking with Viruses', *Performance Research* 25, no. 3 (2020): 165, https://doi.org/10.1080/13528165.2020.1807743.

48 Ibid., 165.

49 Bogost, *Alien phenomenology, Or, What it's Like to Be a Thing*, 65.

50 Jane Bennett, *Vibrant Matter: A Political Ecology of Things*, A John Hope Franklin Center book (Durham: Duke University Press, 2010), 120.

51 Adam Bencard, 'Exhibitions as Philosophical Carpentry: On Object-Oriented Exhibition-Making', in *Exhibitions as Research: Experimental Methods in Museums*, ed. Peter Bjerregaard, Routledge Research in Museum Studies (London: Routledge, 2019).

52 Bogost, *Alien phenomenology, Or, What it's Like to Be a Thing*, 91–2.

53 Tagny Duff, 'Cryobook Archives', accessed November 5, 2020, http://tagnyduff.com/projects-current/cryobook-archives/.

54 Jens Hauser, 'SO3. Art, Biologie, (Al)Chimie: Guide De L'exposition', 2015, 7.

55 Philipp Schorch, 'Contact Zones, Third Spaces, and the Act of Interpretation', *Museum & Society* 11, no. 1 (2013): 68.

56 James Clifford, *Routes: Travel, and Translation in the Late Twentieth Century* (Harvard University Press, 1997), 192.

57 Ibid., 204.

58 Ibid., 218.

59 Paul Rabinow, 'A Contemporary Museum', in *Object Atlas: Fieldwork in the Museum*, ed. Clémentine Deliss (Frankfurt am Main: Weltkulturen Museum, 2011), 7.

60 Stacy Alaimo, *Bodily Natures: Science, Environment, and the Material Self* (Bloomington: Indiana University Press, 2010), 2.

61 Levi R. Bryant, *Onto-Cartography: An Ontology of Machines and Media* (Edinburgh: Edinburgh University Press, 2014), 49.

62 Simon Knell, 'Introduction: The Context of Collections Care', in *Care of Collections*, ed. Simon Knell (London: Routledge, 1994), 2.

63 Jean-Paul Martinon, 'Museums, Plasticity, Temporality', *Museum Management and Curatorship* 21, no. 2 (2006): 158, https://doi.org/10.1080/09647770600702102.

64 Cary Wolfe, *What Is Posthumanism?* (Minneapolis, Minn.: University of Minnesota Press, 2010), xv–xvi.

65 N. Katherine Hayles, *How We Became Posthuman: Virtual Bodies in Cybernetics, Literature, and Informatics* (Chicago: The University of Chicago Press, 2008), 291.

66 Wolfe, *What Is Posthumanism?*, xv–xvi.

67 Hayles, *How We Became Posthuman*, 291.

68   See also Robert Pepperell, *The Posthuman Condition: Consciousness Beyond the Brain* (Bristol: Intellect, 2003).

69   See Martin Grünfeld, 'Culturing Impermanence at the Museum', in Impermanence: Exploring Continuous Change across Cultures, ed. C. D. Warner, T. Otto and H. Geismar (UCL Press, forthcoming).

70   Clémentine Deliss, *The Metabolic Museum* (Berlin: Hatje Cantz, 2020), 15.

71   Ibid., 98.

72   Rosi Braidotti and Maria Hlavajova, eds., *Posthuman Glossary*, Bloomsbury collections (London: Bloomsbury Academic, 2018), 349.

73   See Grünfeld, 'Culturing Impermanence at the museum' for more on this.

74   Caitlin DeSilvey, *Curated Decay* (Minneapolis: University of Minnesota Press, 2017), 188.

11

Viral agencies and curating worldly life differently in museum spaces

Fiona Cameron

Introduction

The Covid-19 pandemic was a shock but hardly a surprise. Despite predictions of emerging potentially catastrophic viral agents and a strong history of such occurrences, we were unprepared. In discussing the H5N1 avian influenza strain in Indonesia, viral ethnographer Celia Lowe observes, 'microbes are made significant in given contexts, and the material properties play an iterative role in shaping the milieu in which they come to exist.'[1] Covid-19 is a significant curatorial agent co-making a new milieu with us borne out of previous forms. Coronaviruses exist in the background as silent life forms in our bodies and are made significant when their contagion spills over and threatens human populations, their health, their interests or has the capacity to violently kill.

Covid-19 and its intent to replicate and its ability to suddenly disorganize and rearrange, to take control and take life, operates in more-than-human sympoietic relations. It inserts itself and infects not just our bodies but the complex ecologies of life itself, social and political systems, economies, the material circumstances of life as a radical, rhizomaticcuratorial agent. What is emerging are dense more-than-viral eco-curating processes and domains of influencing in becoming.[2]

Covid-19 and its eco-curating processes have shaken world political systems and global capitalism to the core, leading to the collapse of whole industries and job losses, destabilizing health systems and killing millions. This viral agent has highlighted socio-economic disparities, brought underlaying racist ideologies to the fore and driven an upsurge in domestic violence in lockdown. Aircraft sit on tarmacs. Cars remain stationary. The virus, and its drive to replicate, is reorganizing museum spaces leading to closures, pushing some into administration, changing attendance patterns through physical distancing and replacing face-to-face and tactile activities with digital engagement.

Museums portray themselves as vulnerable victims of the pandemic. However, I contend that museums are complicit in the creation and spread of this new viral kin, because they have in many instances promulgated thoughts and acts of dis-embeddedness, hubris and un-mindedness in respect to the non-human world which we embody and upon which we depend. Here the porosity, vulnerability, and the symbiotic nature of our own bodies, is highlighted where the sovereign individual is no longer tenable. Museums therefore also become radical viral inhabitations and potential spreading venues and events.

In this chapter I conduct an ecologizing experimentation of planetary worlding in the context of Covid-19.[3] Drawing inspiration from multispecies research, the work of Eben Kirksey, Stefan, Helmreich, Celia Lowe, Donna Haraway and ecological more-than-human thinking, new types of profoundly intimate communities and eco-curating processes are made visible in museum spaces. Curatorial practice, museum space, exhibitions, collections, audiences, curators and all manner of non-human stakeholders emerge as trans-corporeal entities in multiple material, biological, energetic, cultured and discursive co-constitutive enmeshments knitted together at a molecular level, genetically, chemically, elementally, energetically but also virally.[4] Further to this, the Anthropocene in the current pandemic becomes the Virosphere,[5] an unimaginatively vast and potent agent shaping political, economic and social forces outside human capacities of control, and with the potential to become a new topic for museum engagement, social, political and agential reform.

Viral inhabitations and digital transformations

A recent survey of European museums by NEMO, the Network of European Museum Organisations, shows that the majority of museums worldwide are closed, leading to a dramatic drop in income especially for larger institutions in tourist destinations.[6] The findings show that more than 60 per cent of museums have increased their online presence through social media, exhibiting a renewed focus on digital cultural heritage as digital representations of collections are producing more virtual tours, online exhibitions, podcasts, talks on zoom, Google handouts, live content and game creation and increased online visits.[7] Greater attention has been directed to crisis awareness, including the formulation of pandemic emergency plans for both the public and internal work processes, and more flexible work methods in the museums in general.

Similarly, the findings of UNESCO's global survey shows that out of an estimated 95,000 museums around the world, around 90 per cent of institutions have been affected by temporary closures.[8] In order to continue their work and activities many institutions are bolstering their existing strategies through online engagement, drawing on previous digitized content, digitizing current exhibitions and events, exploring the potential of ICT tools and social media in new ways to communicate with their audiences.[9] Hastings Contemporary in the United Kingdom, for example, has taken advantage of its closed spaces to promote museum tours with telepresence robots to overcome barriers of isolation and targeted to people in lockdown and those with disabilities.[10] The Getty Museum has made its online collection available for use in Nintendo's Animal Crossing, New Horizons video game, allowing users to transform their homes into world class art galleries, fill their island with art or create their own custom patterns.[11]

The UNESCO report indicates that many museum institutions have devised new ways of maintaining contact with their audiences and generating alternative financial resources, using the digital environment through virtual visits and the use of social networks. As elsewhere in the world, Russian museum professionals, as Anna Guboglo[12] explains, have adopted multifarious digital strategies from virtual museum tours, social media activities, artistic video and photo installations, online lectures, children's interactive and educational sessions, and posts relating to the quarantine experience. Other institutions are expanding their social service activities to support community mental health and well-being in combination with digital methods. The Garage Museum of Contemporary Art in Moscow launched the 'Everything Will Be Good' campaign, providing lunches for elderly people, medical personnel, volunteers and immigrants.[13] Other museums are addressing the needs of their communities by donating masks and gloves to hospitals and increasing digital services to engage and comfort people staying at home.[14] The Catalyst Science Centre and its MindLab project provided telephone support and mentoring for vulnerable young people.[15] Fundamentally institutions are rethinking their operations and social roles in terms of accelerating digital transformation – a new normal for museum practice and operation in order to increase their accessibility and maintain relevance.

Digital transformation, however, highlights inequities, especially between genders, in regard to access to digital tools and technologies. The UNESCO report recommends that the way forward is the implementation of a more balanced digital policy, focusing on the digitization of collections, an up-to-date inventory of collections, minimum IT infrastructure, sufficiently stable internet access and adequate staff skills.

The digital solution in museums, like many other sectors, is a direct response to social distancing, in which communal and creative programming seeks to create proximity and intimacy with their collections through higher quality digitizations, for example, to bring together those who are not geographically proximate in an effort to create museum experiences of a different kind.

In a recent *Museum and Society* special issue, museum scholarship explores the pandemic as a social, psychological, economic and cultural phenomenon.[16] But, most importantly, this scholarship aims to promote a discussion about and a critique of the digital solution, and in doing so seeks to complicate the relations between virtual and physical experiences in the museum realm. Media scholars Areti Galani and Jenny Kidd[17] explain how the epidemic has 'forced a de-prioritization of touch and physicality' as individuals have been forced to isolate or socially distance themselves, as institutions shift to digital formats. In doing so, they focus on the integration of digital and material collections as combining hybrid materialities, and at the same time highlight the inadequacy of digital engagement in such situations. Similarly, museum scholar Lindsay Balfour[18] addresses material and auric experiences when she discusses the pandemic in the context of the 9/11 Museum and Memorial in New York. Balfour asks how does one convey the 'enormity and gravity' of absence and death through digital media? While praising Russian museums' efforts to serve 'as models of public service and collaboration', Anna Guboglo recognizes the limits of virtual museum tours or exhibitions and argues for the importance of virtual offerings that educate, reduce isolation and decrease boredom.[19]

Structural inequality reveals itself in the pandemic and makes explicit the deep systemic oppressions, inequalities and privilege most societies were built upon.[20] Some museums are responding to identity, gender politics and racial ideologies, seeking to rectify the structural inequalities surfacing as a result of the pandemic, many of which are also historically their own: that is, through their mandate to highlight prejudice, combat racism, and engage more diverse communities often deploying the digital solution to achieve these ends. The Museum of Chinese in America (MoCA), New York, sought to combat anti-Chinese prejudice towards Asians and Asian Americans arising in light of Covid-19 cast as a Chinese flu.[21] Through their OneWorld project, the museum collected oral stories of Asian Americans making these historical resources available in schools.

The brutal killing of George Floyd by Minneapolis Police Department officer Derek Chauvin further highlighted structural barriers, institutional racism, racial injustice, isolation, frustration and high unemployment among Black communities. The Black Lives Matter movement comprises communities most at risk of Covid-19 and its consequences, and provided an opportunity to air these grievances.[22] The Orange County Regional History Center staff in Orlando, Florida, collected a face mask with anti-Trump messaging (one says 'Trump Resign'), a photo of a protester holding up a sign for July Perry who was lynched 100 years ago in the Ocoee massacre in Florida, and a postcard with victims of police brutality listed so people could chant their names together at a Black Lives Matter protest in downtown Orlando.[23] The Smithsonian National Museum of American History in Washington is building on its collection of protest art to document and bear witness for future generations. The New-York Historical Society in Manhattan has been collecting protest items related to the killing of Floyd, the subsequent protests that his death ignited and how people are responding to systematic racism across the world. The collection comprises T-shirts, political leaflets and protective eyewear worn by protesters to protect themselves from pepper spray and tear gas.[24]

Museums across the world are radically reorganizing their operations, engagement practices and prioritizing digital transformation as yet another way of seeking to remain relevant or even to survive. At the same time, institutions become co-opted into global biosecurity agendas, implementing a new normal based on risk management, containment, physical distance and the protection of the sovereign individual, while at the same time documenting structural inequalities.

In doing so, museums are narrating and shaping new realities, instituting new physical forms and spatial arrangements, producing new knowledge, using new media platforms for storytelling, gathering emotional experiences of the 'new normal', highlighting uncertainty within an institution that has traded on offering certainty, and new models of community organizing.

As cultural theorist Brett Neilson reflects, the virus does not respect boundaries and is presented as an entity outside of us, which sovereign power can control and protect us from.[25] As a result we are witnessing a hardening of borders in an attempt to externalize the virus, or to contain it within urban spaces, through the identification of hotspots, tracing design, hand washing, sanitizing and masks. What is emerging are contagion regimes that seek to protect the porous body. Accordingly, a new vision of porosity is emerging, acting against the principles of taxonomy which many natural history museums have historically promulgated. Museum institutions themselves have become sites for sovereign power through hand cleaning, through the use of tape, stencils and all manner of markings on the floors for social distancing, QR registration, mask wearing, all of which are directed to the governance and control of populations.

All these things, from digital transformation to regimes of biosecurity, sovereign power and control within museum spaces, are examples of viral curation born out of the scientific, biochemical and medical research on the mechanisms of viral spread. These mechanisms in which viral curation are enfolded, rest fundamentally on the genetic material of the virus, its RNA and radical inhabitations with their human hosts, and the presence of RNA detected using RT-PCR – the reverse-transcriptase polymerase chain reaction or serology tests for antibodies – the identification of clusters and hot spots, genomic relations between strains and contact tracing, the routes and mechanisms of transmission and, in the future, the viability of vaccines. Tracing the eco-curatorial movements of the virus is contingent on knowing more about it, through the sourcing more data about how it behaves, its mutating strains and its host. The dominant forms of viral curation rest on physical distancing and are most starkly illustrated through the radical attention given to digital technologies in museum engagement.

Viral curation is centred around safety and directed towards the organization of space, the monitoring of movement, the surveillance of surfaces and of touch, of bodily intimacy and aerial dispersal in efforts to disrupt the virus in its never-ending search for a new host. Museums become sites for biomedical bodies and polities in which the permeability of the self is highlighted and technological surveillance in respect to physical distancing is implemented.

The biological redesign of museum spaces and rhythms of museum practices and operations in the interim is informed by research conducted by scientists and clinicians in recognition that aerosols, in addition to larger droplets, can transmit the novel coronavirus. Identifying viral agency and the routes and sequences of transmission are resulting in significant changes in how communities engage in museum spaces, activities and, indeed, the future of museum work and individual job descriptions in which a focus on well-being is present. While social distancing and mask wearing in the short term has had some success in controlling transmission and enabling many museums to open their doors, the redesign of museum spaces and activities is indeed significant. This includes online ticketing, queue lines, a greater use of outdoor spaces for activities, a shift from free-flow exhibition spaces to directed routes, the reduction of wall text, a greater use of phone apps and the conversion of touch interactives to touchless.[26]

Collecting social contagion

Many museums have also put in place Covid-19-related collection policies and forged new acquisitions procedures and practices to collect contagion. These collections and their preservation act as forms of documentary evidence and include photographic archives, artefacts and oral histories, so that we might recall, and future generations might understand, this current moment in history.

The National Museums of Scotland Covid-19 collecting activities are directed to representing the impact of Covid-19 across Scotland as it unfolds, through tangible, three-dimensional objects, supported by digital and print material, and pursued and gathered up in a highly sensitive manner.[27] Examples include a face shield made by a teacher at Lochaber High School in the Highlands using a 3D printer, then finished with plastic panels and delivered to local Belford hospital by the Lochaber Mountain Rescue Team. This object, curator Sarah Laurenson explains, 'crosses several areas outlined in our plan: the impact on the National Health Service (NHS), personal protective equipment (PPE) shortages, the community response and finally, if tangentially, school closures.'[28] A pair of knitted hearts from NHS Greater Glasgow and Clyde, for example, metaphorically connect patients with the loved ones from whom they are separated.[29] This collection focuses on the vulnerable health worker, the carrier, the patient in quarantine, community mutuality, populations in lockdown, emotional responses to social isolation, the death of loved ones, the porous body and mechanisms of containment such as the mask and shield.

The Powerhouse Museum in Sydney Covid-19 collection 'captures the urgency of the time; the collaborative nature of the responses; medical treatments and research; systems of communication and technological innovation, and cultural and artistic expressions including data interpretation, and expressions of the care, fear and resilience demonstrated by people and communities.'[30] This collection's temporal framing reflects the sudden onset of the pandemic in Australia in March 2020, the first lockdown, through to everyday life with the virus.[31] Examples include 'bush billboards' created by women artists Anne Thompson, Vivian Thompson, Marissa Thompson, Nicole Rupert and Lynette Lewis working at Ernabella Arts in the Pukatja Community, APY Lands, South

Australia. In this series of works, the women collaborated to make signs in the Pitjantjara language of the Anangu community to communicate important health and well-being messages in the early stages of the pandemic in Australia. Hand-painted on repurposed car bonnets, turned upright and positioned in prominent places, these 'billboards' in Pukatja, 'Pika nyanga kura wiyaring kunyyjaku' warned locals to 'Follow these rules to help keep you safe from that virus'.[32] The impact on First Nations and diverse communities were also represented through multi-lingual public health posters made by the Northern Land Council and the Aboriginal Medical Services Alliance NT; home-based teaching material in English, Arabic, Dari and Turkish and video of online performances and social events. Other acquisitions include masks, scrubs and other personal protective equipment made by Australian fashion labels including Cue. Paste-ups and signs that appeared around cities and suburbs with messages of care and togetherness are gathered up alongside stories around the effect on retail, such as the exponential rise in online shopping including sales in lingerie and adult toys. Artistic works reflect on periods of lockdown and quarantine; design objects and photographs document the streets of Sydney during lockdown, alongside items that capture the changing nature of visual communication and the built environment in this era. Working with the Westmead Institute for Medical Research (WIMR), the Powerhouse Museum is building a biomedical collection including medical and scientific material related to the development of a Covid-19 vaccine, contact tracing research and technology, and stories from lead researchers and patients with whom they are working.[33]

Like the National Museums of Scotland collection, the Powerhouse Museum collecting initiative reflects the human-viral interface as a social response to the material properties and behaviour of Covid-19. They are collections of contagion control and design, focused on physical distancing, containment and safety, the responsible citizen, the reliable diagnosis, at risk people, carriers, infected people, infection prevention and vaccination, and an emerging regime of care. What is evident is how the perceived agency of Covid-19, and the notion of contagion control through distancing, barriers, vaccines and so forth, through a cultural lens, changed the status and image of people and society: from expressions of fear of one another because of contagion to the stigmatization of those with the disease. These collections are categorized by behaviours of the individual in lockdown, individuals as risktakers, as carers and as companions, or as Covid-19 safe individuals. For example, fashion masks and home schooling materials represent fashion conscious and conscientious culturally diverse citizens who practice social distancing as a cultural form. Behaviour, safety and the reconfiguration of space and mobility is represented by the photographs that document the streets of Sydney during lockdown. Some are motivated by, or seek to capture, the psychological, a whole range of emotions, of fear, despair, isolation and empathy, through paste-ups and signs that appeared around cities and suburbs with messages of care and togetherness. Other collections are classified according to an individual's Covid-19 status and the intimate relations they share with the virus. The biomedical collection in development at the Powerhouse Museum, for example, is configured around radical or potential inhabitations. Some individuals, therefore, become Covid-19 positive, become carriers, super spreaders or are at risk, are returned travellers in hotel quarantine, front-line workers, survivors, elderly people in ICU or daily reported mortality figures. Other collections represent medical workers who seek to prevent infection, using PPE gear, safety protocols, masks, shields, gloves and gowns.

Alongside these Covid-19 collections, a new vocabulary of visual imagery, narration and description emerges or re-emerges, historically embedded and borne out of previous pandemics or co-opted from political, medical, governmental and cultural contexts co-opted into museum spaces and activities and in collections documentation. This is not just the name coronavirus and later Covid-19, but also 'pandemic', 'contagion', 'case fatality rate', 'immunity', 'mutations', 'host', 'Covid safe', 'infection', 'mobility' and 'lockdown'. A distinctive spatial turn emerges within museum spaces, one that is made and remade in response to shifting viral temporalities and biomedical advice. Museums have historically been reoccupied with temporal markers, linear concepts of history and ways of thinking based on a progressive logic of advancement.

These Covid-19 collections are producing 'the new normal', relationally configured as spatially or structurally discrete. While an expression of viral enmeshment or indeed potential contagion, they, and the way they are interpreted, hold us apart from the non-human world. They are expressions of control: that is, controlling the rate of infection, representative of the war against the virus.

These collections and forms of thinking are enshrined as cultural heritage, which is what museums as societal and officiating institutions see as important to pass on to future generations. They could be reinterpreted otherwise as a condition in which viral inhabitations are a condition of life. Here we witness the emergence of a new type of Viroscene heritage and waste formed around a human agency of containment and control. Virospheric heritage are the masks and shields we choose to discard, the obsolete ICU machines, decommissioned aircraft, the ruins of industrial scale farming facilities becoming viro-fossils, in which the hard parts of all these things appear in the geological record recovered from the archaeological sites of the future.[34]

Complicity

The meeting of Covid-19 and people in museum spaces highlights our dysfunctional relationship with the non-human world as a series of profound failures. This is because museums sanctify modernity and its ambitions, including its destructive practices and forces. Museums are no longer safe spaces, that is, if they ever were. Covid-19 fundamentally changes the perception of ourselves and our relationship to the non-human world in which non-hierarchical and sympoietic relations are a condition of biological, cultural and political life. We are not sovereign individuals or singular organisms.

Museums as pedagogical institutions have had a fundamental role in organizing modern life and defining what world views, narratives and ways of life are sanctioned and given importance. Typically, in the West, this includes global capitalism, human hubris, nature as resource, industrialization and technological progress. These unequal structures, thoughts and acts are complicit in supporting and normalizing the livelihoods based on destructive practices that have led to the emergence of viruses.

It is well known that modernity and its organizing logics have alienated humans from the natural world in such a way that allow destructive practices to be sanctioned. Structures, thoughts and acts of un-mindedness and hubris enable viruses to emerge and spread. Furthermore, many museums have been complicit in forming multiple othering categorizations not only in terms of humans based on 'racial' differences, in which many are seen as closer to nature, but also a whole host of animate and inanimate things including plants, animals, fungi, viruses, bacteria, all of which are set apart from dominant forms of humanism.

Collections and museum exhibitions in history, natural history and technology often represent and therefore endorse the political, economic, social forces and destructive practices that increased the risk of new viruses emerging and contributing to the current pandemic. Collecting is an activity of discernment directed at deciding what is important to save for future generations. In this regard, museums decide what objects best showcase contemporary life and therefore normalize such thoughts, frames and acts.

While many biological exhibitions and collections showcase biodiverse ecosystems, museums at the same time have been complicit in enrolling their audiences in ecological relationships and thoughts that are human-centric and dis-embedded, in which they come to see themselves as commanders in relationships with non-human others and earthly processes.

The museum form is founded on Western metaphysics. The whole museum project is entirely dependent on objects, defined entities and the classification of life and inanimate things into non-interacting categories. They project a view of life as composed of distinct entities, objects and substances, with well-defined and reasonably stable boundaries, rather than as objects and entities as embedded, embodied dynamic ecological compositions.[35]

The way many museums present biological individuality is sometimes a problem. Human bodies are often presented as structurally discrete and distinct from other entities. Taxonomies, analytical categories and narratives create spatial and temporal categories between forms of life and hold animals and microbes, for example, in hubristic, relational categories with humans, rather than as kin in embodied, entangled, interdependent relationships. We are not singular organisms; indeed, we host multiple entities including billions of viruses and bacteria as part of integrated biological systems and processes.

All things are classified as living or non-living. This approach has had major implications for our understanding of biological entities such as viruses. As biological scientists John Dupré and Stephan Guttinger explain, 'viruses are often portrayed as stable distinct individuals that do not fit into a more integrated, collaborative picture of symbiosis as individuated living entities.'[36] Viruses instead should be understood as processes, rather as than individual entities, and offer an opportunity to understand the collaborative and integrated nature of the world.[37]

Most importantly, taxonomy is based on phylogeny, and as Donna Haraway explains, is a form of categorization that does not take into account that organisms come into being through complex webs of constitutive relatings.[38] While distinctions do indeed exist between species, they are not as clear cut as taxonomic categorization would suggest, nor do they exist outside their ecological situations. Furthermore, the study and presentation of animal evolution in museums generally takes prominence over other domains of life because they are visible organisms and higher up in the so-called evolutionary chain.

The basis of museum biological research is founded on the study of vertical genetic evolution over hologenomic association. Natural history collections have often been presented in taxonomic series, in showcases that seek to highlight their structural differences and similarities as a hierarchy of evolution rather than their co-constitutive relations. Curators at the Natural History Museum, London, for example, use specimens and taxonomic categories to help identify new species and understand how life on Earth evolved. Many of these collections originate from Charles Darwin's expeditions, and include his finches collected from the Galápagos Islands during the second voyage of the Beagle that informed his theory of genetic evolution.[39]

Through pedagogical activities museums promote the notion of the individual as sovereign. Importance is placed on ourselves and the genealogies of our own thoughts, actions and our moral reform, rather than on species-being as co-constitutive, or in the promotion of feelings of attunement or *worlding with* practices.

Multispecies ethnographers Eban Kirksey and Stephan Helmreich remind us of the host of organisms whose lives and deaths are dependent on humans and how organisms and their livelihoods are shaped by political, economic and social forces.[40] Modern society, Kirksey and Helmreich explain, has stigmatized certain types of non-humans and animals, such as bats, birds and even pigs as pathogens living on the margins, thereby promoting, fear, disrespect, exploitation or casting them as dangerous multispecies relations and as threats to human life, rather than respect and conviviality.[41] Many of these species have been cast as dangerous hosts of zoonotic viruses arising as a result of the industrial scale farming.[42] Viruses are seen as barely alive, even as non-living, simply because we can't see them and, while they appear alongside humans in the bios, are seen as killable rather than as symbiotic, and at times beneficial, collaborators in life. Museums have historically been complicit in promoting these categories of non-human others. Countering these narratives of fear and superstition, and the idea that bats are dirty disease carriers, the Smithsonian National Museum of Natural History has reinterpreted its 140,000 bat specimen collection as a resource to understand and protect bats, whose numbers are declining.[43]

A report published recently by the Intergovernmental Science-Policy Platform on Biodiversity and Ecosystem Services (IPBES) says that,

the same human activities that drive climate change and biodiversity loss also drive pandemic risk through their impacts on our environment. Changes in the way we use land; the expansion and intensification of agriculture; and unsustainable trade, production and consumption disrupt nature and increase contact between wildlife, livestock, pathogens and people is the path to pandemics.[44]

The collections that museums acquire oftentimes are complicit in creating these new ecological circumstances. The destruction of ecosystems and large-scale industrial farming that bring humans and non-humans together involve the exchange of microbes and exposure to new ones; but at the same time, new forms arrive through spontaneous mutations in humans. When ecosystems are destroyed, non-humans are exposed to humans at the edges of their habitat. Or, when ecosystems are destroyed, non-humans expand their territories into urban areas, increasing the likelihood of zoonotic transmissions.

Through their collections and exhibitions, museums have traditionally followed the routes and sequences of neoliberal capitalism, often supporting a global capitalist ethos through displays of wealth and privilege. All these collections and activities represent the acceleration of capitalism within museum spaces. Through collecting discarded or obsolete technology, agricultural equipment, industrial and steam machines, documented and presented as exemplars of modern progress, economic growth, industrialization, and colonialism, museums become complicit in the endorsement of structural inequity, environment destruction, climate change and the pathogen of neoliberal capitalism.

The Museum of Applied Arts and Sciences in Sydney collection comprises steam machines, transport, technology, scientific and industrial processes, and consumer products. The museum therefore is an artefact of the Industrial Revolution, a celebration of industrial progress, and of the supreme ability of humans to harness the non-human world as resources for economic growth.[45] MAAS, in short, is a celebration of modernity and its Australian accomplishment. However, in the context of the climate crisis, MAAS's collections now have other resonances: Indigenous dispossession, extraction and ecological collapse. These collections are embedded in the physical substrates of the biosphere and therefore in ecospheric problems that have profound ecological consequences.[46] For example, the Boulton and Watt steam engine is a climate machine or climatic ecological composition[47] in the sense that it is composed in relations between: the metals belonging to the geological substrates of the planet and their extraction; the combustion integral to its mechanic function; the acceleration of capitalist industrial production embedded in its design; the exploitation of the land and Indigenous dispossession; air pollution; and rising CO_2 levels. Built in 1784 in the Boulton and Watt factory in Birmingham, this engine has long been celebrated as an emblem of the 'age of steam', but as a device deeply embedded in an emerging global carbon economy. It is now as much a harbinger of climate change as it is an icon of the Industrial Revolution.[48] Indeed, 1784, as the year of the invention of the stream engine, has been proposed as the date the Anthropocene understood as a new geological epoch and the beginning of the Great Acceleration.[49] MAAS's wool collection, which includes wool samples and technology spanning the period from 1804 to 2003, documents the history of the Australia's wool industry, industrial scale wool breeding programmes, and the emergence of the Australian merino in the context of the new environmental conditions and its historical importance in the development of the national economy. However, this collection is also burdened with a destructive environmental history, the demise of habitats and biodiversity loss, in which the rise of agri-capitalism not only destroyed local ecologies, created new animal genomes embedded in the composition of the wool, but was complicit in global climate change, as emissions from agriculture account for a significant proportion of historical emissions.[50] The mining collection, and other geological samples, represent the opening up of the Australian continent to the extractive industries which have been historically pivotal in the development of the Australian economy and which have been major contributors to the country's global emissions and the destruction of ecosystems.

Machines of various types and forms are not only human inventions but, rather, are founded on engineering and culturing the non-human world through the appropriation and incorporation of animate and inanimate materials. The making of early steam machines like the Boulton and Watt, household items and cultural infrastructures such as water pipes, involve the incorporation and culturing of timber complicit in deforestation. Agricultural equipment made with metal depended on the availability of iron ore in which this history of geo-extraction is embedded in its very composition.

Viral contagion multiplies through the routes, flows and sequences of neoliberal capitalism and its mobility. The material culture of global circulation, travel and global supply chains, such as aircraft, trains and ships, represent spreading mechanisms. The *Marine Navigation* exhibition at the Deutsches Museum, according to the exhibition text, 'allowed mankind to open up the world, encouraging communications and trade'. Many of the objects on display showcased advancements in steel hulls and mechanical propulsion, all of which are the trademark of the industrial age representing the most important technological periods: sail, steam and the diesel engine.[51]

The Smithsonian Air and Space museum collection includes more than 30,000 aviation and 9,000 space objects, and is best known for its rare and historically significant aircraft and spacecraft, such as 1903 Wright Flyer, representing the beginning of flight. The Boeing Milestones of Flight Hall celebrates some of the most significant airplanes, rockets and spacecraft in history, and includes

Charles Lindbergh's solo trip across the Atlantic in his *Spirit of St. Louis*; the first American jet aircraft, the Bell XP-59A Airacomet; the Bell X-1 in which 'Chuck' Yeager first broke the mythical 'sound barrier'. These milestones, according to the Museum, 'have made our planet smaller and the universe larger'.[52]

Museum displays of the Anthropocene, such as the landmark exhibition, *Welcome to the Anthropocene: The Earth in Our Hands* (2014) at the Deutsches Museum in Munich, and the *Anthropocene* exhibition at the Museum of Tomorrow in Rio de Janeiro, focus on human-centred narratives in regard to human mastery of the planet and humanity's destructive forces. But what we are witnessing now is not human mastery but viral power. Covid-19 is now a more influential agent than humans. The Viroscene and its potential destructive forces have brought capitalism to a standstill. The human is emerging as a new object in the Viroscene, one that will no doubt serve as new exhibition content for the future.

While viruses can be recognized by cell receptors deep inside bodies, Lowe explains, 'they are not accessible to perception, proprioception, or interoception'. Viruses can only be inferred through symptoms or recognized artificially or in a transformed state through scientific investigation. They are only able to be seen under powerful microscopes.[53] This is what makes viruses different from other organisms that have a discernible presence able to be put on display. For these reasons they are given very little attention in museum space.

The pandemic disrupts existing species relations between people, museums, buildings, staff and audiences, and remakes these ontologies in new ways, therefore gesturing towards new opportunities for re-making fundamental museum forms. Museums are complicit in the spread of capitalism, on one hand, and become subjects of its failure, on the other.

Viral inhabitations

The Covid-19 virus is a new organizing force in the museum sector, that has the potential to enable us to think and live differently, but not in a normative sense. The pandemic starkly illustrates the permeability of nature and culture and, indeed, the inadequacy of taxonomic categories in reflecting life itself. Perhaps we needed a viral contagion to become more ecologically minded and empathetic species-beings.

Historically, museums comprise separate departments and promote separate domains of life based on disciplinary categories. Our lifeworlds and bodies, however, have always been profoundly more than human; deep, complex and dynamic enmeshments of socio-economic, political, cultural, technological, biological and all manner of planetary domains and forces, all of which the museum sector has failed to adequately acknowledge and represent.

New humanisms emerge and forms of human agency come to the fore in becoming viral communities, all of which are inhabitations of a distinctive kind that museums must promote. The social and the cultural as a distinct domain of life, and as a specific type of human-centred ecological thought, is therefore held open again in museums.

Here, feminist theorist Donna Haraway's use of the biological concept of sympoiesis[54] as a way of explaining multispecies enmeshments is useful for considering Covid-19 as a more-than-human embodied subject and curatorial agent in museum spaces. For Haraway, sympoiesis means 'making with'. That is, everything is co-constitutional and important for each other's survival. Nothing makes itself, nothing is really autopoietic or self-organizing: 'sympoiesis enfolds autopoiesis and generatively unfurls and extends it.'[55] Critters, therefore, as Haraway explains, 'become-with each other, compose and decompose each other, in every scale and register of time and stuff in sympoietic tangling, in ecological evolutionary developmental earthly worlding and unworlding.'[56]

We are profoundly sympoietic. We become with viruses. We are viral bodies, viral carriers and hosts creating new viruses within ourselves. As part of the human 'metagenome,' Lowe explains 'viruses inhabit every corner of our bodies, vastly outnumbering human and bacterial cells alike, and are arguably responsible for life as we know it.'[57] Multiple viral fragments come together as an entangled genealogy with other species spanning 300 million years.[58] Viruses exist invisibly within and around us.[59] We are part of the viral mix in which new viruses form within us and across us in recombination with other species.[60] It is likely that Covid-19 is not one single event, but a multiple recombination of events in which viral strands come together and mix and then become part of other events.[61] With Covid-19, multispecies shared vulnerability comes to the fore. We share H_2 receptors on the outside of our cells, for example, with cats in meshes of sympoietic becoming.

The virus is inside us and asserts itself; its intention is to survive and multiply. New humanisms arise as fundamental viral inhabitations and reposition the humanist figure in viral clouds. Our sympoietic natures rest on the similar cellular machinery we share with viruses. Covid-19 invades us as its host cell, binding with our molecular machinery, producing its progeny, and then exits the cell and invades others.[62] As literature scholar James Baumlin observes, the signs and alarms are inside us as Covid-19 takes hold and latches onto our cells, to infect, to disrupt and to shed, coursing through our organs, blood stream, respiratory system,[63] leading to cytokine storms and potential death. The idea of the sovereign individual and the human body as structurally bounded is no longer tenable. Human hubris is brought into question. The virus highlights our permeability and the porous processes in which we continue to be made and remade.

Haraway invites us to make kin with multispecies.[64] It is not a case of making kin with Covid-19, however, as the virus is already kin, with long a genealogy of familial, sympoietic relations. There is no division between us and our viral kin.

It is acknowledged that humans are embodied in elemental and chemical processes and through the exchange of DNA in evolution. As Nigel Clark explains, the historical embodiment of past experiences that inscribe the efforts and trials of other bodies and aptitudes in dealing with past environmental limitations, are stored in complex chemistry memories as a deep material force.[65] These chemical memories materialize the distribution of fat stores as a result of environmental stresses and food shortages and skin tone as a response to solar flux.[66] Similar sympoietic processes, in becoming with viral kin, both inside and outside our bodies, help us ward off other more deadly viruses and are therapeutic agents in place of antibiotics. They destroy cancer cells and hold genetic innovation as a mode of evolution. Viral kin are also deep material forces in our bodies. Viral code is inserted into DNA, in which some strains are linked to long-term memory function. Others encode proteins that move information between cells. Viruses have infected egg and sperm, inserting their genes into ours for many millennia.[67] Humans' ability to have live births is attributed to a bit of genetic code that was co-opted from ancient retroviruses that infected our ancestors more than 130 million years ago.[68] We are radical viral kin interfaces within ourselves, binding and inhabiting as practices of co-making in tighter, deeper enmeshments fundamental to our prospects of living and dying. The perceived unity of the sovereign individual is disrupted.

Haraway's interpretation of sympoietic is biological and focused on life forms. Sympoiesis, for Haraway, is synonymous with compost, a mesh of decaying organic matter and aerobic processes in becoming. Charles Darwin's theory of evolution through the exchange of DNA between species is just one sympoietic thesis. Haraway's multispecies entanglements is another. Media theorist Jussi Parikka's geomaterial thesis for digital media[69] is yet another. All these theses are examples of more-than-human co-making with, in and through different genetic, geological materials and biological processes. Haraway explains that, biologically, 'all things beget other things'.[70] The viral sympoietic thesis is, however, one of planetary worlding, a co-constitutive material enmeshment on a planetary scale, dramatically shaping an emerging milieu in which they come to exist. This confluence of viral forces and their unintended consequences is what Lowe calls 'viral clouds'.[71] The sympoietic evolutionary thesis extends to all domains across cultural, political, social, technological, economic realms of life, including earthly processes, as a complex co-making and becoming with planetary histories, through different and complex registers of interrelatedness and their enactions.[72] All things beget other things in dense, more-than-viral eco-curating processes.[73] Covid-19 curating, for example, has usurped the geopolitical in the same way that climate change has done. The global geopolitical returns to the national, to the regional, to the local as situated practices of sympoietic making with others.

We are bound into sympoietic enmeshments of becoming, not just biologically with viruses, but also through a complex of associations with, between and across global capitalism and its failures – the unravelling of economies and industries, the resurgence of nationalism and the composing of new forms of sovereignty, of border regulation, travel and its restrictions, atmospheric relations and the drop in CO_2 emissions, environmental destruction, extraction, toxic environments, deforestation, viral infection and its threats unfurling and reshaping a 'new normal' of cultural and political life and as folded and enfolding material processes. It represents viral and eco-systemic processes of sympoietic tangling and becoming with others[74] as community, and also as a deeply material process from the profound, intimate sharing of cell machinery, molecular, DNA, chemical, elemental, metal, mineral, metal, animal and plant life to complex technological and cultural infrastructures, social, political institutions, community organizing, digital transformations at multiple scales, as situated and dynamic histories of co-making and becoming of shaping and reshaping. The virus exists in co-making relations with human and animal evolution, but also as a social, political, technological development in which earthly life is curated by all manner of entities through sympoiesis. This is what I call ecological compositional design or eco-curating processes in which one action begets another and another and so forth, as a complex mesh of begetting.[75]

These viral entanglements, enfoldings, interdependences and inhabitations are much more deeply bonded and fundamental to life prospects than we could have ever imagined. More-than-viral curating through sympoietic evolution in more-than-human settings is co-making and materializing diverse economies; it has brought neoliberal capitalism to its knees, reduced greenhouse gas emissions, instituted regimes of control, co-made huge amounts of waste from PPE gear and masks to supermarket packaging. None of these events pre-exists our enmeshment with viral kin, although preconditions activate such enfoldings. These preconditions include, for example, prehistory and the emergence of coronaviruses to the emergence of neoliberal capitalism and its hubristic, extractivist, colonialist and destructive logics. The invention of aircraft and shipping routes, the development of the biological sciences, taxonomy, the viral spread of the museum form directed to resource extraction and laboratory investigation and racial ideologies, lay the foundations for viral emergence. The emergence of the modern state and the notion of borders, the advent of the steam machine and mechanical, industrial scale farming, environmental collapse, biodiversity loss, geological extraction and alchemy became tangled up with other sympoietic processes.

The war against the virus is erroneous. In debunking the myth of human hubris, feminist posthuman theorist Rosi Braidotti explains that the human subject never masters, nor possesses but, rather, inhabits, crosses and is always in community with others.[76] Indeed, how will this viral kin co-make our bodies in the long term, and what residue makers will remain? Viral kin in and with us has the potential to express what Braidotti calls an affirmative, ethical dimension as a form of new world building, and, for Haraway, as a new ethics of care and response-ability. What is emerging is a sympoietic thesis of care and empathy, new social institutions, political structures and community organizing.

We are sympoietic, we have shared material histories and have knitted together, at a molecular level, with the elements of water, fire and air, with wood, metals, minerals, chemical and viral histories and, therefore, with museum buildings, digital programmes and all manner of collections in museum spaces. Viral life forms have always inhabited museum spaces with us and in us. Viral curating is implicated in museum histories from the materials with which buildings were made, to the design and flow of spaces, to the cultural, technical and biological collections through sympoietic making, with different registers of inanimate, animate things and processes. Museum surfaces, stainless steel door handles, railings, and toilets are inhabited by viral life forms. Doors and handles made from extracted materials, iron, chromium and carbon contribute to environmental destruction and biodiversity loss, and their human culturing (design, engineering and production) into these forms using carbon intensive production methods are places for viral droplets to inhabit for seventy-two hours. Their contagion is co-made with these metals and surfaces, in which people pass and disperse droplets.

Museum staff, visitors and collections themselves live with and comprise coronaviruses. All collections comprise non-humans and their entanglements with human designs. Biological collections, as possible hosts of coronaviruses, become entangled with museum practices of collection and documentation deployed for sympoietic, rather than for taxonomic, research. The Natural History Museum in London, for example, is using its collection of frozen bats, rodents and many other host animals that embody preserved pathogens, linking them to new Covid-19 research that seeks to link disease outbreaks to pathogen hosts. Using genetic analysis, museum curators are using DNA sequences of pathogens in animals and humans to identify and track pathways of transmission.[77] Similarly, curators in the natural sciences and mammology researching bat biology, ecology, evolution and conservation at the American Natural History Museum, have established a Covid-19 research initiative identifying unrecognized host species for SARS-CoV-2, using the institution's natural history collections and related data that will help future sampling for emerging viruses.[78]

The power of viral eco-curating, in its ability to rearrange the social, the ideological and the material, is refiguring the very DNA of museum institutions, akin to what I called rhizomatic liquid museum forms.[79] These movements represent efforts to curate beyond the digital solution, sparked by instituted viral contagion in respect to museum closures, the inability to admit visitors to enclosed spaces and the way in which museums might adapt to these circumstances in recognition of the mechanisms of viral spread and its social constraints. The routes, sequences and the material properties and behaviour of the virus is scripted into museum physical forms, at the same time unfurling or decomposing the material and spatial inhabitations of physical museum buildings and leading to the development of outdoor and immersive exhibits. 'Free the Museum' seeks to challenge the museum world to rethink definitions of the museum as large physical edifices, their location, format, the type of objects on display with the intention of activating new museum models, transforming everyday places into the museum experience out in the world for reflection, healing, activism and informal learning.[80] By thinking outside building edifices, 'Free Museum' seeks to embrace the notion of ubiquitous museum practice and museology as a series of locational activations embedded in community. Retail experiences in a thrift shop are museum-ified, where QR codes are linked to stories of their original owners. Sound galleries become integrated into construction canopies around Chicago, or as pop up in a London street on the influence of Bauhaus furniture.[81]

From dis-embeddedness to sympoietic design in museums

In the recent collection, *Pandemic*, Rebecca Solnit predicts that, 'the pandemic is the end of something, a version of postwar prosperity for the global north predicated on exploitation of other regions, of other human beings and of nature itself, of a set of assumptions about our capacity to control that nature, of many orders that are about to become history'.[82] The many lockdowns, Solnit suggests, has made a lot of people question what they considered to be 'normal', 'valuable' or 'productive'.[83] We have witnessed empathy for doctors, nurses, health-care workers and waste disposal workers. People's well-being has usurped economic growth for a moment in many places. Homelessness for many essentially ended overnight due to lockdowns. The post-Covid-19 rebuild has the potential to lead to the emergence of a different kind of economy and politics. For those on the left, the crisis therefore opens up opportunities to build a more caring community, to usher in post-carbon and post-capitalist economies, and to inspire an ideological shift away from the economy to new community forms based on mutuality, generosity, empathy, inclusion and hope.[84]

Museums of all figurations have important roles to play in the Covid-19 rebuild, in not just narrating or representing new relations of viral inhabitations or changing physical structures, but also in shifting structures, thoughts, ideologies, as well as assisting in the incorporation of new forms of design for ethical re-worlding and responsibility.

The ethical dimension of a post-Covid-19 rebuild must signal the end of museum practices that promulgate the thoughts and actions that have got us into this mess. Museums have the capacity to shift these forms of thinking, hubris, exploitative mindsets, capital as aspiration, racial and gender inequalities, and practices and thoughts that promote dis-embeddness. Indeed, many museums are already doing this work, such as the Museum of Capitalism, an institution based in Oakland, California; New York City; and Boston, through its mission to educate about the ideology, history and legacy of capitalism through artefacts of capitalism, exhibitions and programmes.[85] Pedagogical work is directed to promoting justice for victims of capitalism, those who have resisted this mode of economy and those who have helped to develop alternatives in an effort to inspire future generations. We have also seen an ethical commitment to highlight and address structural inequalities and racial prejudice through connections between museum collecting and documenting the Black Lives Matter movement.

Over the last twelve years, I have been pioneering a new field of research and practice centred around the emergence of posthuman-museum practices and museologies, conducting ecologizing experimentations across domains of museum practice, from climate-change narratives to institutional forms, to collections and documentation, to digital cultural heritage and to the new museology.[86] These ecological experiments and reconfigurations have been strategic, directed towards promoting a new ethics of care that might encourage respect for various forms of animate and inanimate things; promoting multispecies flourishing and connections, intercultural relations, inclusiveness and interaction, and the return of modern societies to their rightful place as part of a larger dynamic that ultimately has the potential to support the continuation of life itself. In doing so, I sought to lever museums' expertise, knowledge, authority, trust and power to achieve this.[87] Ecological thinking is no longer the sole domain of the biological sciences. We need to embed ecological thinking across museum practice in light of instituting sympoietic thought and design agenda across all aspects of museum work.[88]

In returning to the pandemic and its representation, museums have been preoccupied with viral design in control mode, one directed to preventing viral dispersal. But, as institutions, museums have an important role to play beyond human-centred forms of biosecurity and social control, in generating different models of life.

Museums, for example, can showcase and mobilize different ways of living with contagion as a constitutive form, not in quarantine mode, but rather as contagion mutuality as a form of life. Exhibitions and programming can promote ideas and practices of multispecies flourishing, for example, or collaborations between humans and their viral kin, or showcase human destructive practices that encourage pathogenic viral emergence. They can also exhibit histories of colonialization and exploitation towards the non-human world, in which it is figured as an exploitable resource to serve human needs. Institutions, in a critical mode, can challenge capitalism as a blueprint of global and technocratic control.

Furthermore, institutions can challenge the spatial and temporal assumptions that sit behind contagion. They can make explicit that we are not taxonomic, we are not held apart; rather, everything begets everything else in sympoietic relations, understood as profoundly deep histories of humans and non-humans in relational symbiotic terms. Human agency must be recast as sympoietic, in which *making with* is linked to ecological communitarian design. In doing so, museums can refigure taxonomies as forms of relational patterning. Institutions can promote 'friendly' forms of agriculture and habitat re-wilding to support multispecies flourishing.

New genetic and information technologies could be used to make viruses visible in museum spaces, so they become a lever to help rethink new polities of confederation in a more-than-human sympoietic world.

Sympoietic thinking and ecological communitarian, or compositional design, could be instituted across domains of museum curatorial practice. New narratives have the potential to emerge based on the relational refiguration of human and viral agency and by ecologizing human hubris as something that has always been ecological. Thinking with language, text and speaking in a sympoietic way performs a distinctive sympoietic emergence in the way others respond, as tangles of speaking, as tangles of narrating and as ways of illustrating and representing tangles.

Institutions could showcase the idea of contagion seepage as one in which the past, present and future co-implicate as multiple rhizomatic histories. Narrating and documenting contagion, or sympoietic histories, for example in an expanded thesis, involves the folding and enfolding, begetting with, unfurling, decomposing and composing processes, through and across social, cultural, biological, terrestrial, planetary, economic and technological domains. Their enfoldings with viral power do not precede their relatings, but rather emerge out of previous complex sympoietic processes as mutating, and new mutant, forms through a long and deep history of enmeshment and becoming.

Co-opting embodied and embedded sympoietic exhibition, documentation and design principles enables the enaction of Haraway's 'thick presence', that offers up different spatial and also ethical relations of thinking, acting, movement and exchange in museum spaces, programmes and exhibitions for a post-Covid-19 world. Thinking with other epistemologies, such as Indigenous knowledge, about biodiversity and in narrative, in worlding formation, in forming identity and concepts of agency, provides new ways of dwelling in the world.

Notes

1   Celia Lowe, 'Viral Clouds: Becoming H5N1 in Indonesia', *Cultural Anthropology*, 25, no. 4 (2017): 625–49; Celia Lowe, 'Viral Ethnography: Metaphors for Writing Life', in *Troubling Species: Care and Belonging in a Relational World*, ed. Multispecies Editing Collective (RCC Perspectives: Transformations in Environment and Society 2017), no. 1, 92).

2   Fiona Cameron, *The Future of Digital Data, Heritage and Curation in a More-than-Human World* (Abingdon: Routledge Environmental Humanities Series, 2021); Fiona

Cameron, *Museum Practices and the Posthumanities: Curating for Earthly Habitability* (Abingdon: Routledge Environmental Humanities Series, forthcoming, 2021); Fiona Cameron, 'Theorizing Digitizations in Global Computational Infrastructures', in *The International Handbook of New Digital Practices in Galleries, Libraries, Archives, Museums and Heritage Sites*, ed. Hannah Lewi, Wally Smith, Steve Cooke and Dirk vom Lehn (Abingdon: Routledge, 2019), 55–67; Fiona Cameron, 'Posthuman Museum Practices', in *Posthuman Glossary*, ed. Rosi Braidotti and Maria Hlavajova (London: Bloomsbury Academic, 2018), 349–51; Fiona Cameron, 'Ecologizing Experimentations: A Method and Manifesto for Composing a Post-humanist Museum', in *Climate Change and Museum Futures*, ed. Fiona R. Cameron and Brett Neilson (Abingdon: Routledge Museum Research Series, 2014), 16–33; 3, no. 3 (2008): 229–43.

3 Cameron, 'Ecologizing Experimentations: A Method and Manifesto for Composing a Post-humanist Museum', 16–33.

4 Cameron, 'Ecologizing Experimentations: A Method and Manifesto for Composing a Post-humanist Museum', 16–33; Fiona Cameron, 'Theorizing Digitizations in Global Computational Infrastructures.'

5 Carl Zimmer, 'Welcome to the Virosphere', 24 March 2020. *New York Times*, https://www.nytimes.com/2020/03/24/science/viruses-coranavirus-biology.html.

6 NEMO (Network of European Museum Organisations) (2020) https://www.ne-mo .org/fileadmin/Dateien/public/NEMO_documents/NEMO_Corona_Survey_Resu lts_6_4_20.pdf, 1.

7 NEMO, 'Corona Survey Results', 2, 5.

8 Ibid., 13.

9 UNESCO 'Museums around the World in the Face of COVID-19', 2020, https:// unesdoc.unesco.org/ark:/48223/pf0000373530, 8, 14.

10 Hastings Contemporary, 'Robot Tours', 2020, https://www.hastingscontempora ry.org/exhibition/robot-tours/; Amy Levin, 'Isolation as a Collective Experience: Museums' First Responses to COVID-19', *Museum and Society* 18, no 3 (2020) 295–7 https://journals.le.ac.uk/ojs1/index.php/mas/issue/view/202.

11 Getty Animal Crossing Art Generator, 2020, https://experiments.getty.edu/ac-art -generator.

12 Anna Guboglo, 'Digital Museology Under Test: Challenges and Opportunities for Russian Museums', *Museum and Society* 18, no 3 (2020): 311–13 https://journals.le. ac.uk/ojs1/index.php/mas/issue/view/202.

13 Guboglo, 'Digital Museology Under Test: Challenges and Opportunities for Russian Museums.'

14 Guboglo, 'Digital Museology Under Test: Challenges and Opportunities for Russian Museums.'

15 Jade French, Nic Lunt, Martin Pearson, 'The MindLab Project. Local Museums Supporting Community Wellbeing Before and After UK Lockdown', *Museum and Society* 18, no 3 (2020): https://journals.le.ac.uk/ojs1/index.php/mas/issue/view/20.

16 Levin, 'Isolation as a Collective Experience : Museums' First Responses to COVID-19.'

17 Areti Galani and Jenny Kidd, 'Hybrid Material Encounters – Expanding the Continuum of Museum Materialities in the Wake of a Pandemic', *Museum and Society* 18, no 3 (2020): 298–301 https://journals.le.ac.uk/ojs1/index.php/mas/issue/view/202.

18 L. A. Balfour, 'Ground Zero Revisited – Museums and Materiality in an Age of Global Pandemic', *Museum and Society* 18, no. 3 (2020): 295–7 https://journals.le.ac.uk/ojs1/index.php/mas/issue/view/202.

19 Guboglo, 'Digital Museology Under Test: Challenges and Opportunities for Russian Museums.'

20 Marina Sitrin, ed. *Pandemic Solidarity: Mutual Aid during the Covid-19 Crisis* (London: Pluto Press), xvii.

21 Museum of Chinese in America, One World Covid 19 collection (2020) https://moca40.mocanyc.org/oneworld/.

22 Nadja Sayej, 'Their Stories Should be Told Right: How Museums are Documenting the Protests', *The Guardian*, 7 July 2020, https://www.theguardian.com/artanddesign/2020/jul/07/museums-document-black-lives-matter-protests, Tuesday, 7 July 2020.

23 Sayej, 'Their Stories Should Be Told Right: How Museums Are Documenting the Protests'.

24 Sayej, 'Their Stories Should Be Told Right: How Museums Are Documenting the Protests'.

25 Brett Neilson, Migration and Labour *Contagion Design: Labour, Economy, Habits, Data, Symposium,* 2020, https://www.westernsydney.edu.au/ics/events/contagion_design (audio recording).

26 Emma Thorne-Christy, 'Rethinking Where We Exhibit in Light of COVID-19', MuseumNext, 15 November 2020, https://www.museumnext.com/article/rethinking-where-we-exhibit-in-light-of-covid-19/.

27 Sarah Laurenson, Calum Robertson and Sophie Goggins, 'Collecting COVID-19 at National Museums Scotland', *Museum and Society* 18, no 3 (2020), 334–6 https://journals.le.ac.uk/ojs1/index.php/mas/issue/view/202.

28 Laurenson, Robertson and Goggins, 'Collecting COVID-19 at National Museums Scotland'.

29 Museum of Home, 'Stay Home Collecting Project'. 2020, https://www.museumofthehome.org.uk/explore/stay-home-collecting-project/; Tim **Deakin,** 'A New Kind of Challenge: Curating in the COVID-19 crisis', *MuseumNext*, https://www.museumnext.com/article/a-new-kind-of-challenge-curating-in-the-covid-19-crisis/.

30 Museum of Applied Arts and Sciences, Coronovirus collection https://collection.maas.museum/set/7574.

31 Ibid.

32 Ibid.

33 Ibid.

34 Cameron, *The Future of Digital Data, Heritage and Curation in a More-Than-Human World*.

35 Cameron, 'Posthuman Museum Practices'; Cameron, *The Future of Digital Data, Heritage and Curation in a More-than-Human World*; Cameron, *Museum Practices and the Posthumanities: Curating for Earthly Habitability*; Cameron, 'Theorizing Digitizations in Global Computational Infrastructures.' Cameron, 'Posthuman Museum Practices'.

36 John Dupré, and Stephan Guttinger, 'Viruses as Living Processes', *Studies in History and Philosophy of Biological and Biomedical Sciences* 59 (2016): 109.

37 Ibid.

38 Haraway, *Staying with the Trouble: Making Kin in the Chthulucene*.

39 Natural History Museum, London, 'Museum Specimens Could Help Fight the Next-Pandemic: Why Preserving Collections is Crucial to Future Scientific Discoveries', 16 December 2020, https://theconversation.com/museum-specimens-could-help-fight-the-next-pandemic-why-preserving-collections-is-crucial-to-futu re-scientific-discoveries-148293.

40 Eben Kirksey and Stephan Helmreich, 'The Emergence of Multispecies Ethnography', *Cultural Anthropology*, 25, no. 4 (2010): 545.

41 Ibid.

42 Ibid.

43 Smithsonian National Museum of Natural History, 'The Art and Science of Bats', 2020, https://www.si.edu/spotlight/bats.

44 Intergovernmental Science-Policy Platform on Biodiversity and Ecosystem Services (IPBES), https://www.ipbes.net/pandemics-media-release.

45 Fiona Cameron and Ben Dibley, 'Curating Museum Collections for Climate Change Mitigation' Australian Research Council Linkage Project, 2021–3.

46 Cameron, *Museum Practices and the Posthumanities: Curating for Earthly Survival*.

47 Cameron, *The Future of Digital Data, Heritage and Curation in a More-Than-Human World*; Cameron, 'Posthuman Museum Practices.'

48 Cameron and Dibley, 'Curating Museum Collections for Climate Change Mitigation'.

49 Paul *Crutzen* and Eugenie *Stoermer,* 'The Anthropocene', IGBP Global Change Newsletter 41 (2000): 17–18.

50 Cameron and Dibley, 'Curating Museum Collections for Climate Change Mitigation'.

51 Deutsches Museum, Marine Navigation exhibition https://www.deutsches-museum .de/en/exhibitions/transport/marine-navigation/.

52 Smithsonian National Air and Space Museum, Boeing Milestones Flight Hall, https ://airandspace.si.edu/exhibitions/boeing-milestones-flight-hall.

53 Lowe, 'Viral Ethnography: Metaphors for Writing Life', 93.

54 Haraway, *Staying with the Trouble: Making Kin in the Chthulucene*, 58.

55 Ibid.

56 Ibid., 97.

57 Lowe, 'Viral Ethnography: Metaphors for Writing Life', 93.

58 David Cyranoski, 'Profile of a Killer: The Complex Biology Powering the Coronavirus pandemic', *Nature* 581 (May 2020): 24. https://www.nature.com/articles/d41586-020-01315-7.

59 Lowe, 'Viral Ethnography: Metaphors for Writing Life', 92.

60 Lowe, 'Viral Clouds: Becoming H5N1 in Indonesia.'

61 Eben Kirksey, 'The Emergence of COVID-19: A Multispecies Story', *Anthropology New* 12, no. 1 (2020): 11–16.

62 Cyranoski, 'Profile of a Killer: The Complex Biology Powering the Coronavirus pandemic', 26.

63 James Baumlin, 'From Postmodern to Posthumanism: Theorizing Ethos in an Age of Pandemic', *Humanities* (2020): 9–46.

64 Haraway, *Staying with the Trouble: Making Kin in the Chthulucene*, 58.

65 Nigel Clark, *Inhuman Nature: Sociable Life on a Dynamic Planet*. (California, Sage, 2011), 209.

66 Ibid.

67 Lowe, 'Viral Ethnography: Metaphors for Writing Life', 93.

68 Rachel Nuwer, 'Why the World needs Viruses to Function' BBC Future, 18 June 2020, https://www.bbc.com/future/article/20200617-what-if-all-viruses-disappeared.

69 Jussi Parikka, *A Geology of Media*, (Minneapolis: University of Minnesota Press, 2015).

70 Haraway, *Staying with the Trouble: Making Kin in the Chthulucene*, 58.

71 Lowe, 'Viral Ethnography: Metaphors for Writing Life', 92.

72 Cameron, *The Future of Digital Data, Heritage and Curation in a More-Than-Human World*.

73 Ibid.

74 Cameron, Fiona. 'Theorizing More-Than-Human Collectives for Climate Change Action in Museums'.

75 Cameron, *The Future of Digital Data, Heritage and Curation in a More-than-Human World* Cameron, *Museum Practices and the Posthumanities: Curating for Earthly Habitability*; Cameron, 'Theorizing Digitizations in Global Computational Infrastructures'. Cameron, 'Posthuman Museum Practices'; Cameron, 'Ecologizing Experimentations: A Method and Manifesto for Composing a Post-humanist Museum.'

76 Rosi Braidotti, *The Posthuman* (Cambridge: Polity, 2013), 193.

77 Pamela Soltis, Joseph Cook, Richard Yanagihara, 'Museums Preserve Clues that can help Scientists Predict and Analyze Future Pandemics', 24 June 2020, The

Conversation, https://theconversation.com/museums-preserve-clues-that-can-help-scientists-predict-and-analyze-future-pandemics-141175.

78 American Museum of Natural History, 'The Science of Covid 19', https://www.amnh.org/explore/covid-19-science.

79 Cameron, 'Liquid Governmentalities, Liquid Museums and the Climate Crisis'; Cameron, 'The Liquid Museum: New Ontologies for a Climate Changed World.'

80 Emma Thorne-Christy, 'Rethinking Where We Exhibit in Light of COVID-19', 15 November, 2020, https://www.museumnext.com/article/rethinking-where-we-exhibit-in-light-of-covid-19/.

81 Free the Museum, https://www.freethemuseum.org/.

82 Marina Sitrin, ed. *Pandemic Solidarity*: Mutual Aid during the Covid-19 Crisis (London: Pluto Press, 2020).

83 Solnit, *Pandemic Solidarity* (Foreword), 178–9).

84 Neil Howard, 'A World of Care', in *Life after Covid 19: The Other Side of the Crisis*, ed. Martin Parker (Bristol, Bristol University Press, 2020), 21–30.

85 Museum of Capitalism, https://www.museumofcapitalism.org/events.

86 Cameron, *Museum Practices and the Posthumanities: Curating for Earthly Habitability*; Cameron, 'Theorizing Digitizations in Global Computational Infrastructures.'; Fiona Cameron, 'Stirring Up Trouble: Museums as Provocateurs and Change Agents in Polycentric Alliances for Climate Change Action', in *Addressing the Challenges in Communicating Climate Change Across Various Audiences*, ed. Walter Leal Filho, Bettina Lackner and Henry McGhie (New York: Springer, 2019) 647–73; Cameron, 'Posthuman Museum Practices.' Cameron, 'The Liquid Museum: New Ontologies for a Climate Changed World.' Cameron, 'Theorizing More-Than-Human Collectives for Climate Change Action in Museums'; Fiona Cameron, 'From 'Dead Things' to Immutable, Combinable Mobiles: H.D. Skinner, the Otago Museum and University and the Governance of Māori Populations', *History and Anthropology* Special Issue, 25, no. 2 (March 2014): 208–26; Fiona Cameron, 'We Are On Nature's Side? Experimental Work in Rewriting Narratives of Climate Change for Museum Exhibitions', in *Climate Change and Museum Futures*, eds. Fiona R. Cameron and Brett Neilson (Abingdon: Routledge Museum Research Series, 2014), 51–77; Cameron, 'Ecologizing Experimentations: A Method and Manifesto for Composing a Post-humanist Museum.'; Fiona Cameron, 'Climate Change, Agencies and the Museum and Science Centre Sector', *Museum Management and Curatorship* 27, no. 4 (October 2012): 317–339; Cameron, 'Liquid Governmentalities, Liquid Museums and the Climate Crisis.' Fiona Cameron, 'Object-orientated Democracies: Conceptualising Museum Collections in Networks', *Museum Management and Curatorship* 23, no. 3 (2008): 229–43.

87 Cameron, 'Ecologizing Experimentations for a Post-Humanist Museum.'

88 Cameron, 'Ecologizing Experimentations for a Post-Humanist Museum'; Cameron 'Posthuman Museum Practices'.

Index

www.ingramcontent.com/pod-product-compliance
Lightning Source LLC
Chambersburg PA
CBHW050417280326
41932CB00013BA/1900